A DICTIONARY *of* DREAM SYMBOLS

With an introduction to Dream Psychology

ERIC ACKROYD

To my wife Judith and my children
Paul, Pippa, Vicky, Tobias and Rupert

First published in the UK in 1993
by Blandford, an imprint of Cassell & Co,
Reprinted 1993, February 1994, May 1994, July 1994, October 1994, May 1995,
1997 (twice), 1999 (twice), 2000, 2001, 2007, 2009 (twice), 2011

This edition published in the UK in 2005 by Cassell Illustrated,
a division of Octopus Publishing Group Ltd
Endeavour House, 189 Shaftesbury Avenue, London WC2H 8JY

Distributed in the USA and Canada by Sterling Publishing Co. Inc.,
387 Park Avenue South, New York, NY 10016-8810

British Library Cataloguing-in-Publication Data: a catalogue record
for this book is available from the British Library

ISBN 1-84403-353-8
EAN 9781844033539

Design by: John Round Design

Printed and bound in China

CONTENTS

INTRODUCTION

Every image that comes up in a dream means something, but the same image may mean different things for different people or for the same person at different times in his or her life. The purpose of this dictionary is, therefore, to present the various possible meanings of the images that may occur in your dreams; it is up to you to select the one that seems to apply to your particular situation.

In this Introduction we look at how to work out which of the meanings given for a particular dream image – person, object, scene, spoken or written words, etc. – applies to your own external situation or inner state of mind. For the present, be assured that interpreting your dreams is not the formidable task it may at first seem; it is certainly not a job that must be handed over to some expensive specialist consultant. It is something you can do for yourself, so long as you have at least a respectful attitude towards your dreams, with a belief that they may have something valuable to say to you, and a determination to be open and honest with yourself. More often than not, the people, places, objects and events in your dreams represent parts of yourself: feelings, fears, desires, attitudes and so on. You may not be consciously aware of these, and one of the main functions of dreams is to make you aware of these hidden parts and to ask you to give them your attention. You therefore need to be willing to accept that there may be aspects of your personality that you do not know about or, more important, have not acknowledged. This is where honesty comes in: being honest with yourself means acknowledging those parts of you that, for whatever reason, you have so far preferred to ignore.

How to Interpret Your Dreams

First, here are a few simple tips for anyone embarking on the great adventure of interpreting dreams.

Recording your dreams

Get into the habit of writing down your dreams straight away. That means having pen and paper – preferably an A4 notebook – at your bedside and the determination to wake up and sit up after a dream and immediately write it down. It is a good idea to put the day and date at the top of the page before going to sleep. This is an outward expression of your serious intention to take note of your dreams; and it also means that, on waking, you can get straight down to the business of writing out your dream.

Anything that might come between the dream and the writing could obliterate or severely reduce your recollection.

Instead of writing, you could use a tape recorder – unless you have a sleeping partner whom you would rather not waken. Whichever method you use, be sure to use the present tense: not 'I was walking along the road, when a car overtook me . . .', but 'I am walking along a road; a car overtakes me . . .' Using the present tense helps you to relive the dream more vividly, with the result that you will enter more fully into the dream and therefore remember more of its detail.

If you possess a computer and know how to use it, it could be useful for your dream interpreting. Select a program that will enable you to record your dreams and to sort through them from time to time to see if there are any recurring themes. For further information see Calvin Hall's book, *The Meaning of Dreams*.

Record your dreams in as much detail as possible. Anything in a dream may be important when it comes to interpretation. What in the dream itself seems to be quite trivial or merely incidental to the main action may, in fact, turn out to be the key that unlocks the meaning of the whole dream. For example, always note the colour and shape of anything. If there is any movement, in what direction is it – right or left, clockwise or anticlockwise, towards or away from you? Is a person male or female, young or old, fair or dark, attractive or unattractive, smiling or frowning? What is he or she wearing; and what does the person say (exact words, if possible)? Is the sundial or bird-bath in the centre of the garden or off-centre? Are the plants in bloom or not, and if they are, what colour are they? What season of the year is it? How many women (or steps, or animals) are there? Is the house or other building old or new, and on which floor of the building does the action take place?

Don't worry too much if such details do not appear in your dreams. I am only saying that, if details are given in a dream, you should not omit them from your report. And having been told this, you will probably find that from now on your dreams do contain lots of detail that was either not present or not noticed in previous dreams.

Look at several dreams together

Don't think you have to work out the meaning of every dream straight away. Of course, there is no harm in jotting down what strikes you there and then as its obvious meaning. However, before finally making up your mind about the meaning of any single dream, it is best to make a record of several dreams and look at them together, to see if there is a common pattern. There may be a recurring image, or different images saying the same thing.

It may also be enlightening and practically helpful to look back every now and then over the dreams of the last year, or two or three years, or even longer. That way you may see how much or how little you have changed over that period. You will see how much you have learned from your dreams, or how much – or little – notice you have taken of them in ordering or re-ordering your daily life.

If you make a mistake in interpreting a dream, you may find that your next dream corrects your mistake. Dreams come from the unconscious, and the unconscious works intelligently and with a purpose. If you respect your unconscious and show your respect by paying attention to what it is saying to you in your dreams, your unconscious will cooperate with you and assist you towards a true understanding of its messages.

The psychological significance of dreams

A dream not only appears within the context of an ever-continuing series of dreams; it also occurs within the context of your life as a whole – your family life, your work, your love- (and hate-) life. Your dreams reflect your deepest emotional responses to your waking-life experiences. It follows, therefore, that a correct interpretation of your dreams will only be possible if they are viewed in the context of your outward life.

This obviously includes what is happening to you now, the situation you are in now, your present problems, ambitions, fears and so on. It may also include, however, the whole or any part of your past life. Your most deeply seated attitudes, hatreds, prejudices, habits, fears, guilt-feelings and pains of all kinds may stem from experiences in your early life. Wordsworth's 'The child is father of the man' is full of truth: the adult personality is largely conditioned by childhood experiences or, more precisely, by the emotional impact of those experiences on the child. And what doesn't come from childhood comes from traumatic experiences in our later life: the present state of our psyche is the result of our emotional self's reactions to the experiences and situations that life has thrown at us.

What this means is that a correct and useful interpretation of your dreams requires a full awareness and understanding of what is happening to you now and what has happened to you in the past. Is this a tall order? Yes, it is. But don't be daunted by it. Remember that the unconscious is ready to cooperate with you and, indeed, lead you. Your unconscious is a storehouse containing all the emotionally charged experiences of your life, and it may be just these decisive emotional reactions – fear, hatred, resentment, guilt and the like – that are expressing themselves in your dreams. All you need to know about yourself, past and present, is being supplied to you in your dreams. In other words, your dreams will give you all you require for understanding them and applying them appropriately and creatively in your life.

It may be true that the present condition of your psyche, and consequently the present circumstances of your life, have been shaped more by emotional reactions to events than by intelligent and objective decision-making on your part. What is equally true, however, is that you can at any time take control of your life and begin to determine your own future. Your dreams will help here. They can tell you what has been going on inside you so far, and they can also tell you what you need to do or stop doing in order to achieve greater happiness in the future. Through your dreams, your unconscious will tell you what you need. The rest is up to you, your conscious self.

Sequence in dreams

Often the part of a dream that is remembered first and therefore recorded first is the last part of the dream. In fact, the tendency is to remember and write down all the sections of a dream in reverse order. This should be borne in mind when getting down to the business of interpreting your dreams: sometimes, for instance, the last part of a dream gives a solution to a problem posed in the first part of the dream.

Simple meanings

What has been said above about the deep meaning of dreams needs to be balanced against other considerations. Not all dreams have profound psychological significance. Some are mere repetitions of the day's events. Nearly all the dreams that young children tell us about are of this kind: after a day at the seaside or at the fair a three-year-old will often relive its delights and excitements in dreams; similarly a bedtime story may retell itself in a young child's dream.

Some dreams may have straightforward physical explanations. A full bladder may cause you to have a frighteningly embarrassing dream about wetting your pants, for example.

So do not assume that every dream has a deep meaning. Not every dream will contain a life-transforming revelation – but any dream might! Even the apparently most trifling dream story may be trying to tell you something important about your life. If, for example, you told me you had dreamed of an earthquake, I would generally suppose that it was an indication either that your personal world was in danger of falling apart or at least that you were deeply – perhaps unconsciously– fearful that it might fall apart. I would therefore want to ask you about your marriage or other domestic relationships and about your work situation. However, I would also ask if you had recently been reading something or watching something on television that might have prompted that sort of dream. If you had just been reading a vivid account of an actual earthquake, your dream might have been simply going over the story – a chewing-the-cud sort of dream. On the other hand, it is likely that even dreams which take their symbols from very recent experience are using those symbols to represent something that is going on inside you.

On the whole, the truth would seem to be that if you are only trifling with your dreams, their content will tend to be trivial; if you take your dreams seriously, their content will tend to be serious and significant. If what you want from your dreams is a fuller understanding of yourself and, eventually, fuller control over your life and the attainment of your proper 'destiny', your dreams will not let you down. They will give you all you need.

The Unconscious

'The interpretation of dreams is the royal road to a knowledge of the unconscious activities of the mind? So said Sigmund Freud in his classic book, *The Interpretation of Dreams*. There can be no reasonable doubt that there is an unconscious dimension in the human psyche or mind or personality. We frequently find ourselves doing things that we did not consciously intend and that may even contradict our conscious intentions. The reasons for these actions may not be immediately apparent, but everything has a cause. If, therefore, the causes of these actions – their motives – are not conscious, they can only be unconscious.

The phenomenon of post-hypnotic suggestion gives supporting evidence for the existence of unconscious mental processes. We have all seen or heard of cases where people have been hypnotized and then told by the hypnotist that on waking they will perform a certain action (stand on their head, or take their clothes off, or whatever). On waking the people have done exactly what they were instructed to do, but when asked why they did it, they couldn't answer. Clearly, it was not their conscious mind that had motivated these actions; these actions had taken their conscious mind by surprise. The motivation for these actions was unconscious.

Dramatic examples of unconscious motivation were found by Freud in his experiences during the First World War, when he treated soldiers sent to hospital from the front line. Some of these soldiers were suffering from paralysis of an arm or leg, although no physical cause could be found. Using hypnosis, Freud discovered that, despite the genuine and sincere protestations of the patients, the cause of the paralysis was a desire to get out of a situation – the battlefront – which had filled them with fear. The desire was totally unconscious: it had not manifested itself at the conscious level of the mind.

In these cases the paralysis was a symptom, a physical sign of a mental (albeit unconscious) dis-ease. Now, Freud came to see dreams as functioning in the same way as symptoms: dreams signal some mental disturbance – a frustration, a conflict, or whatever – at the unconscious level.

Whatever other functions dreams may have, their most important function is to reveal what is going on in your unconscious mind, the unconscious depths of your self. To ignore your dreams is, therefore, to refuse the self-knowledge that is the key to true happiness, the key to inner peace and joy, the removal of the tension that is a symptom of inner conflict, the solving of your personal problems and the establishing of a more richly satisfying mode of life.

Admittedly, there are other ways of getting acquainted with your unconscious self. Hypnosis is one. Analysis with or without hypnosis is another. Both are costly, but if you can afford them and can find a reputable practitioner, by all means use them. And if you are in desperate need of help, go to a professional psychotherapist even if you can't afford to! Or go to a genuine spiritual teacher, or even to a 'spiritual' or 'psychic' healer.

Again, it is possible to get some understanding of your unconscious self by observing oddities in your external behaviour – slips of the tongue or slips of the pen, awkward or clumsy behaviour in certain situations, irrational acts such as repeatedly washing your perfectly clean hands. But even the correct interpretation of such types of behaviour (which in some cases may require more knowledge of psychology than you possess) may throw only a disappointingly partial light on the workings of your unconscious; and an incorrect interpretation, or a failure to find any convincing interpretation, may only throw you into an even deeper state of confusion.

The major and most accessible source of information about your unconscious self is undoubtedly your dreams, of which you have a constant supply. 'To sleep, perchance to dream'? No, there is no 'perchance' about it. You dream every time you sleep. You may deny this, but you can easily discover the truth of it for yourself: just go to bed each night with pen and paper ready to record your dreams, and you will very soon find that you have many more dreams than you ever 'dreamed' of.

Some people claim they never dream. What that really means is that they never recall their dreams. Some people even boast about never dreaming. They imagine that by not dreaming they enjoy deep, uninterrupted, more beneficial sleep. They are wrong on at least two counts: first, they do dream – everyone does; secondly, by not recognizing this they are forfeiting a golden opportunity to win self-knowledge and self-fulfilment.

Those who brag about never dreaming may do so because they imagine there is something neurotic about dreams. It is certainly true that one function of dreams is to inform the conscious mind of any unhealthy processes that may be at work within us. But that doesn't mean that our dreams are neurotic. Bragging about a lack of dreams is a sure sign that the person is hiding his or her fears behind a foolish bravado, preferring to remain ignorant of his or her own neurotic hang-ups. But ignorance is not bliss.

Remember that everyone – or very nearly everyone – is to some degree or other neurotic: inner conflicts, phobias, guilt-complexes are not confined to the inmates of mental hospitals. This being so, it makes sense to use any available means for getting to know about these things so as to do something about them. If a neurosis is severe you may need to consult a psychotherapist; but in most cases looking at your dreams will be enough to guide you towards fuller self-knowledge and fuller psychic health.

Bear in mind also that you don't have to be neurotic to benefit from paying attention to your dreams. There is always room for more personal development and improvement. Dreams can heal, and they can make you whole. And, psychologically speaking, healing and wholeness are one and the same thing.

Many people – especially men – are frightened of emotions; frightened of expressing them, or frightened even to acknowledge their existence. That is another reason why many people shy away from the idea of examining their dreams, which are usually emotional in their content. It is important to realize that it is only repressed emotions that are potentially dangerous, those that are excluded from consciousness and consigned to the dark cellars of the unconscious mind.

If you get acquainted with what is going on in your unconscious, you will begin to take better control of your life. You will also feel better, your life will he richer, more effectual and more satisfying, because you are now using creatively the psychic energy that was previously going to waste.

Which Meaning?

I have already said that some dreams are more meaningful than others. Some merely repeat the events of the preceding day. Others could be described as divine revelations, showing you a reality more profound, more stable and enduring, both more awesome and more blissful than anything in your day-to-day waking experience, knowledge of which may radically transform your life by changing your attitudes and values.

The vast majority of dreams come somewhere between these two extremes. Some may centre on sexuality, expressing sexual frustrations and desires. Others may have to do with problems or ambitions in your work, family problems, social ambitions; others may arise from personal psychological problems, some of them stemming from childhood, some from a later stage in your life.

The question therefore arises, how do you know which of these areas of dimensions of your life is causing – and reflecting itself in – a particular dream? A single dream image may carry several possible meanings, and which meaning is to be attached to this image in a particular dream or series of dreams may depend on which area of your life is giving trouble or undergoing some significant change or challenge. Honesty and a little common sense will usually be enough to tell you which part of your life is the most likely trouble-spot.

Let us take an example. Suppose that the sea plays a dominant role in your dream or in a series of dreams. The sea is a common symbol of the feminine. The 'feminine', however, is a wide and compendious category, and in dreams the sea may represent your actual mother; or the womb; or your own femininity (this may apply to men as well as to women); or fertility and creativity; or the potential for new life; or the unconscious mind; or that mystically experienced depth of reality where you and Nature, you and the All are one.

So how do you decide which level or area of sea symbolism applies to you? Well, by all means take every possible meaning into serious consideration, but usually you will find that there is one particular meaning that 'rings a bell' for you. Have you not yet liberated yourself from your mother, so that you have not yet established and affirmed your own individuality? Are you still attached to your mother by some mental umbilical cord, still dominated and restricted by your mother's personal image or style, or her set of values and opinions? Take a very honest and objective look at yourself (and, if appropriate, ask your partner what he or she thinks) and the answer will come to you. If the answer is a strong and unequivocal 'Yes', then you almost certainly don't need to look any further for the meaning of the sea symbol.

Are you thoroughly melancholic or have you been pushed by life into a deep depression; have your problems or sufferings become just too much for you? Then for you the sea possibly means the womb and the dream possibly expresses your (unconscious) desire to retreat from life and re-enter the womb, where existence was unproblematic, where no choices or decisions had to be made and all was warm and cosy. On the other hand, for the same depressed or confused person, the sea may represent potential for new life and the dream may mean that new possibilities are offering themselves to you. Water is both destructive and life-giving, according to what form it takes. Your dream will surely give you a due as far as this is concerned; just pay attention to the emotional charge – negative or positive – associated with the sea in your dream. Bear in mind, however, that even where the sea has a threatening aspect (dashing your body against the rocks, for instance, or drowning you, or inundating the whole land) the overriding message of your dream may be a positive one. Just as in the Flood myths the water destroys the old world as a prelude to the creation of a new and better world (a piece of water symbolism that is repeated in the religious ceremony of baptism), so the destruction of your old self or old lifestyle may be the essential and necessary precondition for the appearance and development of a new and improved, more satisfactory and more satisfying self or lifestyle.

Are there signs in your recent life that you are being drawn away from what you are beginning to regard as unsatisfactory, superficial, futile or meaningless preoccupations (promotion; possessions; doing and getting) towards a more contemplative, receptive search for the meaning of life? If so, the sea may represent the One behind or within the Many; the Ultimate Reality of which the multitudinous variety of life-forms are more or less ephemeral manifestations or incarnations. Or – and some would say this effectively amounts to the same thing, since the One or God or Ultimate Reality is discoverable within yourself – are you fed up with being pushed and pulled by emotions which only result in conflict and tension, and do you long for your real self (beneath the mask you wear for the world) and the real love that is deep within you? Then the sea may represent for you the depths of your own self, at present still unconscious and waiting for you to put your consciousness into it – perhaps by meditation or dream interpretation or both.

Finally, have you recently been to the seaside or been out in a boat, or read or watched on television something about the sea? If so, that may be the only significance of your dreaming of the sea. But then again it may not be! Perhaps seeing the sea or reading about it had a powerful effect on you because it 'chimed in' with some deep preoccupation with mother, or femininity, or a dissatisfaction with your present lifestyle. If it is foolish to suppose that a dream image always carries a profoundly mystical meaning; it is equally foolish to suppose that it always has only the most trivial explanation.

Trivial meanings are usually non-symbolic meanings. A dream image that is non-symbolic is one that refers to nothing beyond itself. Take, for example, the image of a train speeding into a tunnel. In a Freudian interpretation this would mean sexual intercourse. This is a symbolic meaning. But if your dream was simply a recollection and reliving of part of a train journey you had had during the day, the train-and-tunnel image is not symbolic: it does not mean anything other than a train going into a tunnel. However, even if the dream is a repetition of part of the day's experiences, it may also be symbolic. Why did your dream conjure up just this particular image? Was it because, in looking for something to make its point forcibly, your unconscious chose something from your recent experience? In that case, the dream was only superficially and accidentally a recollection of something that happened during the day; at another level it was symbolic. You would then have to ask yourself what the tunnel symbolized. A tunnel doesn't have to be a vagina. It could be a symbol of death, or of some frightening transition from a way of life to which you have become accustomed to an as yet unknown new mode of life.

In the dictionary I have sometimes included a possible non-symbolic meaning of an image. On the whole, however, I have left it to you, the reader, to bear in mind that any dream image may have no symbolic meaning attached to it at all but be a perfectly straightforward representation of an actual person or thing or event or situation.

The rest of the Introduction is designed to give you further assistance in working out which of several possible meanings of a dream symbol is likely to be the right one for you. Under the sections on Jung and Fritz Perls (Gestalt psychology) details are given of some special techniques for identifying with each item of a dream in turn, so as to uncover the meaning of each item that is the right meaning for you. In addition to such techniques, the rest of this Introduction will help you to make more intelligent and effective use of the dictionary by giving you an understanding of different approaches to dream interpretation and some background knowledge of relevant psychological theory – not so superficial as to be useless or harmful, but not too detailed for easy consumption.

A person who has a map and a knowledge of map-reading is more likely to succeed in finding his or her way across a strange terrain than someone who trusts to luck and so-called commonsense. I can't quite claim to be giving you anything as precise as a map of your dream world. To ask for that would be to ask for the impossible: only you can make the map as you go along, from dream to dream. What this Introduction – and indeed the whole book – tries to do is to show you how you can develop the skills to make your own map.

Freud on Dreams

Sigmund Freud and Carl Gustav Jung represent strongly contrasting approaches to dream interpretation. Some would say that Freud offers a more superficial or more blinkered approach and Jung a more profound mode of interpretation. Personally, although I share this view to some extent, I think there is a great deal to be learned from both these men and that both should be taken account of, precisely because they are so different from each other.

If I give more space in this Introduction to Freud and Jung than to later writers on dreams, there are good reasons for this. One is that Freud and Jung are less readable than some more recent writers such as Ann Faraday (whose books *The Dream Game and Dream Powers* are essential reading) and Strephon Kaplan-Williams (whose *Elements of Dreamwork* is possibly the best of all dream books). Another reason is that Freud and Jung have had such a tremendous influence on the field of dream analysis.

Sigmund Freud (*1856–1939*) was the first great modern pioneer of dream theory. *The Interpretation of Dreams* was first published in 1909, and is the most important of his writings on dreams. If you feel drawn to read Freud, you might also try one or more of the books listed in the Bibliography.

Parts of the mind

Freud saw the human mind or psyche as consisting of three elements, which he named the ego, the super-ego and the id. The id is the instinctive drives. Freud called it 'the pleasure principle', because our instincts always aim at pleasure. The super-ego corresponds roughly to what we commonly call 'conscience', and Freud himself referred to it as 'the moral principle'. However, it is important to bear in mind that Freud saw it as having a social origin: it represents the prohibitions and taboos as well as the values and ideals – the norms – of society. These norms are presented to the child first by its parents and later by other authority figures – teachers, for example, or just other grown-ups. These social pressures become internalized in the child and start to function as parts of his or her individual personality or psyche. (Freud called this process of internalization 'introjection'.)

Id and super-ego may quarrel. What id demands may be prohibited by the super-ego, and the result is conflict or tension in the depths of the self. I say 'in the depths of the self' because both id and super-ego function largely at the unconscious level. Resolving the tension and acting as referee between the rival claims of id and super-ego are functions of the ego. The ego is the conscious self. Freud calls it 'the reality principle' because it is the part of the mind that takes account of external reality. The ego therefore has the daunting task of holding in balance the claims of id, super-ego and outside world. In fact, it is almost impossible for the ego to satisfy the demands both of the id and of the super-ego, and the claims the external world makes on us, and maintain peace and order in the psyche, and ensure a successful or fulfilling life for the individual. That is why Freud himself said that most human beings are in some degree neurotic: in other words, most of us to some extent lack inner harmony or psychological balance.

What happens in dreams

According to Freud, in dreams the id (your instincts and desires) tries to communicate with the ego (the conscious part of yourself). When you sleep, the ego relaxes. Sleep is a withdrawal from the external world, so in sleep the ego goes off-duty, as it were. This means that, with lowered resistance from the conscious mind, the contents of the unconscious may begin to express themselves, coming up as dreams.

However, the super-ego also operates largely at the unconscious level and is therefore still on duty when you sleep. Therefore, if what the id is trying to tell the ego is in conflict with the moral/social values embodied in the super-ego, the latter will intervene and censor the message that the id is sending to the conscious mind. The result is that the message from the unconscious comes through to the conscious mind only in a disguised or distorted form.

Freud distinguished between the 'manifest content' of a dream and its 'latent content', or 'dream thoughts'. The manifest content is the actual dream: the characters, scenes and events that make up the dream story. In other words, it is what you would write down when making a record of the dream. The latent content, on the other hand, is what the dream is trying to tell you: the dream's message or meaning.

According to Freud, most dreams are disguised messages and therefore have to be decoded. This is especially the case when the thing that the id is trying to bring to the attention of the conscious mind is a desire that has been 'repressed', that is, banished from consciousness at some earlier date because it offended 'the moral principle', the superego, and caused too much trauma for the ego to handle. For example, a wish for the death of someone close to you (a parent, or brother or sister, or partner) is more than likely to be repressed on account of the guilt-feelings it arouses. Similarly, sexual desires are often repressed because they disgust or offend the super-ego. When such desires express themselves in dreams, therefore, they may be obliged to disguise themselves as fears: for instance, instead of dreaming of killing someone, you may have a dream in which you are filled with anxiety about that person's health.

The desires we repress are usually quite natural and normal. By that I do not mean to say that an act such as murder is good and permissible. What I mean is that a desire to murder, though it would not exist in an ideal world, may be explicable, given the particular circumstances and our own individual history; and what causes that desire is the frustration of another, altogether good desire, namely, the desire for self-fulfilment. The desire to be oneself, to be one's own person and to have the freedom and independence to fulfil one's own 'destiny', is a very proper and natural desire, and if frustrated it is likely to produce resentment. For example, pregnant women sometimes wish the child would not be born. This usually means that, although they do want a child, they cannot help feeling from time to time some degree of resentment at the prospect of losing their freedom. Again, it is not sexual desire as such that causes rape; but frustrated sexual desire might well lead to it.

This does not mean that you should give your instincts *carte blanche*. Rather, you should get to know what is going on in your unconscious, which means bringing the contents of the unconscious into your conscious mind. This is what dream interpretation will do for you. Having done that, you then have to find an appropriate outlet in your life for those desires that have hitherto been kept under lock and key.

Don't be afraid of these 'forbidden' desires. They are to be feared only if they are kept repressed. Allow them a proper mode of expression in your conscious life, and they will actually enhance the quality of your life by filling out your personality and perhaps remedying some previous lopsidedness. Keep them repressed, however, and they may eventually explode, and may even take possession of the whole psyche, with disastrous consequences.

Now do you see the importance of dreams, and how vital it is to take notice of them? Your dreams are messages from your unconscious, telling you what you should be giving your conscious attention to there.

It is well known that Freud tended to think that nearly all neuroses, imbalances or conflicts in the psyche were due to the frustration of sexual desires. This exclusive concentration on sexuality has rightly been criticized, but there were reasons for Freud's over-emphasis and it is important to bear these in mind. On the one hand, the sexual drive is one of the strongest and most insistent of all human drives; on the other hand, it is the one that has the strongest taboos placed on it by society. Therefore, reasoned Freud, it is in the area of sexuality that we can most expect to experience frustration and conflict. It is our sexuality that gives our poor ego the most trouble in its efforts to maintain a precarious balance between the individual's demands for instinctual satisfaction and society's demands for conformity to its codes of conduct.

The desires that express themselves in dreams are, therefore, according to Freud, almost invariably of a sexual nature. If your dreams have a sexual manifest content – if, for example, you see naked bodies and perform sexually with pleasure in the dream – your dream is unmistakably expressing sexual desire. But even if the manifest content of a dream appears to be quite devoid of sex, Freud says you may be sure that the meaning of the dream is sexual. Neuroses, which are always the product of an unresolved conflict between the rival claims of id and super-ego (that is, between instinctive drives and society's prohibitions or 'conscience'), are most likely to have a sexual origin. Therefore, insofar as dreams are expressions of the id and are to be seen as symptoms of neuroses, it follows that most dreams will have to be interpreted in sexual terms. So argued Freud.

However, despite his tendency to see sex in everything, Freud admitted that some dreams do not have a sexual meaning. He also warned against assuming that a dream symbol could have only one possible meaning. Thus, for example, a bridge in a woman's dream is usually – for Freud – a sexual symbol (as we shall see later), but he also allows that a bridge image may have non-sexual meanings: for instance, it may symbolize a transition, a passing from one stage of life to another.

Typical Dreams

Freud lists several categories of what he calls 'typical' dreams. For example: dreams of falling or flying or swinging, which express a desire for the freedom of childhood; dreams of being naked, which reflect a nostalgic longing for the freedom from inhibitions which characterizes early childhood; and dreams of the death of a brother or sister, or parent, or child, which express the quite common repressed feelings of jealous hatred towards a brother or sister etc.

In all these 'typical' dreams there is no disguise: the wish is expressed straightforwardly in the dream story. In the last example, says Freud, the dreamer finds the wish so inconceivable that he or she will speedily dismiss the dream as nonsense – 'just a dream' – and so there is no need for the dream message to be disguised or distorted in any way. Sometimes such a dream is brought about by the dreamer's actual anxiety concerning the health or well-being of the person who dies in the dream. This genuinely felt anxiety is, nevertheless, says Freud, a way of concealing a more deep-seated hatred for the person, but the dreamer will usually be content with making a connection between the dream and the feelings of anxiety and leave it at that, without probing any deeper.

Another example of a typical dream is failing an examination or test. These dreams, says Freud, express a more or less generalized fear of failure or disaster, a fear which stems from an unresolved Oedipus complex (see pages 28–33) and a consequent continuing fear of punishment. Such dreams are more likely to occur if you have parents who were too strict or demanded that you should conform to impossibly high standards of behaviour.

Anxiety

Many dreams seem to express anxiety. Freud believed that most of these dreams were really distorted or disguised wish-fulfilments. Their distressing manifest content is the disguise forced upon a repressed desire by the internal censor (the super-ego), so that anxieties are wishes in disguise and dreams are disguised fulfilments of a repressed or suppressed wish.

It is important that any element of repressed desire expressed as an anxiety must be identified. For instance, if in a dream you are frightened by a ferocious dog, the dog may symbolize the 'animal' within yourself – including your sexual desires. And in that case what looks like physical fear is actually a disguised expression of moral fear, which in turn is a cover for a neurotic fear – a fear of something in your own id which has caused you to repress something (sexual desire, or whatever). In other words, what you are frightened of is what your id wants. That means you have a conflict that must be resolved, and that can be resolved only by accommodating in the most appropriate and sensibly balanced way both the super-ego and the id.

In this connection bear in mind what Freud said about the super-ego. An over-developed and dominant super-ego, he warned, is not a good thing. The stronger a person's super-ego, the stronger the instinctive desires that he or she is attempting to keep suppressed or repressed. For that reason a Freudian psychologist might say that the fanatical anti-pornography crusader is typically a person with very strong and much feared – and therefore suppressed or repressed – sexual desires.

Suppression and repression

The difference between suppressing a desire and repressing it is that suppression is done consciously and repression is done unconsciously. Neither suppression nor repression, however, is a satisfactory solution to a personal problem. Both result in an inflated super-ego and a more troublesome, shackled and frustrated id.

By looking at your dreams carefully and, above all, honestly, you can get to know what repressed desires you are carrying around with you. And that puts you into a position to work out for yourself a strategy which will allow these desires satisfaction and fulfilment in ways that will enhance your well-being and happiness and restore peace and harmony to your psyche.

An unbridled satisfying of each and every desire is likely to play havoc with the psyche, pulling it in all directions and destroying its harmony and peace, and reducing rather than enhancing your happiness, as well as seriously damaging your effectiveness. Such a complete lack of control usually goes hand in hand with a complete ignorance of what forces are at work in one's unconscious depths. Sooner or later what is repressed will insist on having an outlet, and if there is no knowledge and therefore no rational control of what has been repressed, the latter may take possession of the psyche, destroying what is good and beautiful in it and almost inevitably doing hurt to other people, too.

Understanding your dreams, therefore, is a duty you owe both to yourself and to your fellow human beings.

Decoding dreams: the dream-work

The problem, according to Freud, is how to decode the dream messages, which have been disguised by the internal censor (the superego). Freud provides some clues in his account of what he calls the 'dream-work' – those unconscious processes that distort the original message of a dream. If we know what tricks the censor uses, we can easily work out what the original message was.

Freud describes three techniques used by the internal censor to disguise the message of a dream: 'condensation', 'displacement' and 'representation'.

CONDENSATION

A dream story is usually a condensed or compressed presentation of something that the conscious brain might have to use many words to express. The purpose of this condensing is, according to Freud, to make a more forceful impact on the conscious mind – in much the same way as an arrowhead, by virtue of the fact that it is condensed into a point, has the power to pierce its target.

Condensation may take several forms. For example, a piece of conversation in a dream may have been put together from bits taken from two or more actual and remembered conversations. Similarly, several real happenings or occasions may become fused together into a single event. Again, words or names (of people or places, for instance) may be combined in a dream to make composite words. For example, 'Blakeson' appearing in a dream may be an amalgam of real-life names Blake and Wilson.

Bear in mind, however, that what looks like the opposite of condensation may occur: one item in the dream thoughts (the latent content) may be represented by more than one image in the manifest content. Sometimes, when looking over a series of dreams you will find that a message you were unable to interpret in one dream crops up in a different form with a different image in a later dream.

DISPLACEMENT

This is where some change of emphasis takes place between the latent content and the manifest content of a dream. What was the crucial point in the latent content may appear in the manifest content as a purely incidental or peripheral detail of the story, and vice versa.

REPRESENTATION

Ideas in the dream thoughts (latent content) may be represented by visual images in the manifest content (the 'story') of a dream. For example, distance in time may be represented by distance in space. Very small – distant – figures in the dream story may represent someone or something from the more or less remote past.

Where two dream thoughts or ideas in the latent content are logically connected, they may be represented in the manifest dream by two events taking place simultaneously. Where there are two parts of a dream, or two dreams occurring one after the other, the latent content of the smaller one may contain the cause of whatever is depicted in the larger one. Again, where a dream image undergoes some transformation in a dream, whatever is represented by the first form of the image may have to be understood as the cause of whatever is represented by the second form of the image.

Representation by symbols is far and away the best known and also the most controversial part of Freud's account of the 'dream-work' – controversial because of its association with Freud's alleged tendency to see sex everywhere.

Boxes, chests of drawers, cupboards, ovens, receptacles of all kinds, caves, aircraft hangers, rooms – in fact, anything hollow is to be understood, says Freud, as a symbol of the womb or of woman. These symbols will normally occur in a man's dreams. Similarly, a suite of rooms appearing in a man's dreams means the dream is to be seen as representing the man's (unconscious, perhaps repressed) urgent desire for sexual satisfaction: the suite of rooms is an image of a brothel, where there are several rooms, each with a sexually available woman in it. (Freud believed that man was by nature polygamous.)

A landscape with hills and woods is a dream's disguised representation of the female body and female genitals: hills are breasts, a wood is the pubic hair. A bridge, on the other hand, symbolizes the male organ, which in sexual intercourse forms a bridge between the man and the woman.

Man or men may be represented by a tie (a symbol of the penis), and ploughs, hammers, knives, arrows, guns or anything else that is sharp or penetrating may represent the male organ. The latter may also be represented by a hand or foot, whereas the female sexual organ is sometimes represented by a moth, ear or eye. A hat is another symbol of genital organs, this time either male or female.

Freud lists various symbolic representations of the sexual act: climbing steps or a ladder, or climbing up a wall; going through a tunnel, for example, in a train or car; riding a horse; or (in a woman's dream) being run over.

If a woman dreams of being plagued by vermin, this, according to Freud, is a symbol of pregnancy.

I've already mentioned the protestations of Freud's critics: must a tie, or a tunnel, or motoring through rolling countryside always have a sexual meaning? Of course the answer is no, and Freud himself warned against supposing that a symbol could have only one meaning.

The important thing is to be honest and open when interpreting your dreams. Do not evade or dismiss a particular line of interpretation because you find it unpleasant. The unpleasantness or shocking quality of an interpretation may well he an indication that it is the correct interpretation. After all, if a dream is expressing something you have repressed, you can expect it to refer to something painful or distressing: the things we repress are things that disgust or frighten us. You may find Freud's insistent emphasis on sexuality distasteful, but don't be too hasty in rejecting any plausible interpretation of a dream. You should never assume that you have got the correct interpretation if you have not seriously considered alternatives.

Sometimes, on waking up immediately after a dream, the conscious or partly conscious mind adds something to the dream. According to Freud, this is always a further attempt at concealing the true message of the dream – though sometimes it may amount to no more than an abrupt dismissal of the dream (as when we wake up and say, 'Thank God! It was only a dream').

In my own experience, however, conscious or semi-conscious additions made as one is waking from a dream may actually be genuine interpretations of the dream – or at least genuine attempts to interpret the dream. These are not always to be dismissed as just another trick on the part of the censor to mislead you and steer you away from the true meaning of the dream. On the contrary, especially if you have got into the habit of examining your dreams, you may find that what is in your mind as you wake from a dream is, in fact, a correct interpretation. On the other hand, you must not let this serve an an excuse for not asking yourself if there might be other – or additional – meanings in your dream.

In this connection it is worth noting that some dream experts actually recommend that, on going to bed, you should resolve to wake up immediately after a dream and, instead of writing down what you can remember, continue the dream in your conscious mind, working out various possible sequels to the plot, or filling it out with further detail.

There's a lot to be said for this technique, but, if you try it, beware of the danger of letting your mind wander. Otherwise, you might find that you have forgotten the dream you started from. This technique can be a subtle trap for those who are too lazy to get up and write their dreams down on paper.

Freud's techniques of dream interpretation

Freud did not advise people to write down their dreams. In fact, he advised them not to write them down, but instead to tell them to a psychoanalyst (that is, a psychotherapist of the Freudian school). Personally, I have grave doubts about this advice. I find it difficult to believe that many people would remember their dreams, even if they went to an analyst daily. For me, writing down your dreams is the only sure way of preserving them.

Freud's technique of dream interpretation is based on what he called 'association'. By this he meant that you should take each item of a dream in turn – each person or object or scene or event or name or colour, or whatever – and tell your analyst what you associate with it. For example, if the dream item is a whale, you must say the first thing that comes into your mind when you think of a whale. Let us suppose the first thing you associate with a whale is the ocean, or deep water. Then you must say the first thing that comes into your head when you think of the ocean or deep water. And so on.

Using the method of association you will eventually, said Freud, reach something that 'rings a bell'. The 'bell' may be an alarm bell – you may uncover something that terrifies you, some emotion or emotionally charged event from your past that frightened you at the time and therefore caused you to suppress or repress it. That is why Freud said that the more you resist expressing a particular association, the more likely it is that the association points to something in your unconscious that you need to face up to. And that would be the purpose of your dream.

This method of association is certainly to be recommended. Even if you are not consulting a psychotherapist, the method can still be effective and successful – so long as you are honest and determined.

The materials and sources of dreams

According to Freud, the various items of a dream – the persons, objects, scenes, events, names and so on – usually come from your recent waking-life experiences, and mainly from the events of the preceding day.

I think that Freud overstates his case here. It is all right as far as it goes: many dreams do get their materials from the dreamer's recent experiences, and nearly all children's dreams are a reliving of the day's happenings, but many dreams contain items from the dreamer's very remote experience, and occasionally dream items may even come from outside the dreamer's experience.

In any case, even where the materials of a dream come from your very recent experience, the source of the dream may lie in your remote past.

Indeed, Freud claimed that nearly all mental conflicts, and therefore the sources of the dreams that give expression to such conflicts, can be traced back to early childhood. Freud's heavy emphasis on the first five years of life as the breeding ground for the vast majority of the neurotic anxieties that plague us as adults has been rejected by many of Freud's followers – the so-called 'neo-Freudians' – as well as by non-Freudian psychologists. What these people say is that the original cause of a mental disorder is just as likely to be found in painful and frightening experiences in adult life. In other words, they object to Freud's exclusive emphasis on early childhood. Some neuroses may have childhood causes, but we should also be prepared to look for other possible causes, such as cultural factors (social or religious taboos, for example) that come to bear on people during and after adolescence, or personal experiences during or after adolescence.

Some psychotherapists advise their patients not to bother about the past at all, to forget the past and live only in the present. Our hang-ups, they argue, originate in our emotional reactions to events in the past. Consequently, as long as we allow ourselves to be tied to the past – always harking back to this or that painful episode, this or that injustice suffered by us, or this or that guilt-producing thing we did ten or twenty or thirty years ago – we are letting our neuroses tighten their hold on us. The only way to get free of our anxieties and depressions and pent-up anger or guilt – and all the other things that make our life unhappy and unprofitable – is to liberate ourselves from the past, by refusing to live anywhere except in the present moment.

This stress on living only in the present is something I personally favour. By 'living only in the present' I mean cutting out all thoughts of the past that have ceased to be focused entirely on the positive purpose of facing up to our hang-ups and have instead become a mere idle, negative dwelling on the past, which only reinforces the past's paralysing power over us.

However, my advice to you, the reader, is to acknowledge and apply to yourself whatever truth there is in both sides of the argument. Careful and constant attention to the sort of symbols that crop up in your dreams, combined with honest self-appraisal, will usually guide you along the path that is most appropriate for you. Keep an open mind about the actual date of birth of whatever mental trouble your dreams are bringing to your attention. By all means search for the experience that first prompted you to repress this or that emotion, and your dreams may well assist you in this search for the starting-point. However, when you have finally succeeded in identifying and facing up to that experience, what you then have to do is to dissolve it, let go of it. Dwelling on it only reinforces its hold on you. Undissolved fear or anger starts off as a fog that obscures and darkens our view of reality; it finishes up as an encasing and asphyxiating block of concrete.

Once identified, the original cause of your trouble will be seen to be not nearly so bad as you thought. For example, you will realize that that thing you did in your teens which has ever since filled you with guilt feelings and self-hatred, was not so bad after all – or, no matter how bad it was, it was understandable and inevitable in the circumstances. The same applies to that anger that you repressed long ago but has ever since been seething under the surface and perhaps sometimes breaking through the surface in violent outbursts, usually on the most inappropriate occasions and directed against innocent victims. By all means track that anger down to the moment when you first felt it and, being frightened or 'morally offended' by it, repressed it. But you will invariably find that the anger begins to dissolve once you look dispassionately and objectively at its cause and you are able to acknowledge that no one was really to blame – because everyone involved (including you) was only doing his or her best.

Freud tells us that a neurosis that has its first cause in early childhood may nevertheless remain dormant until some adult experience triggers it off. It is rather like a gun, which may remain loaded and even cocked for a long time before it is actually fired. To that we may add, once an experience has triggered off the irrational tear or guilt-feeling or anger, there is a tendency for further experiences to trigger it off again, until eventually almost any experience can set it off. In this way a neurosis becomes more and more reinforced.

A neurosis is, according to Freud, an inappropriate, distorted and unsatisfactory way of expressing a desire or emotion that you have repressed. Dreams are one form of such distorted, disguised expression. Paying attention to your dreams, therefore, means paying attention to any repressed desires or emotions you may have. It is therefore a therapy, a way of healing yourself, in which the cure consists in first facing and then throwing away your past. By 'throwing away' I do not mean suppressing or ignoring the past – that is the best way to start or prolong a neurosis. Rather, I mean that the actual process of facing your irrational fear or anger or whatever, will make it disappear – perhaps not overnight, but bit by bit, little by little.

I feel I ought to say something about Freud's theory of infantile sexuality, fixation, regression and the famous Oedipus complex. You may be tempted to dismiss these parts of Freud's theorizing as too farfetched, irrelevant, or even just plain repugnant. If that is the case, let me plead with you to put any prejudice aside, at least long enough to learn what Freud actually said on these topics and how it might be relevant to understanding some of your dreams.

Infantile sexuality

We have already seen that for Freud, adult dreams that derive from events and experiences in early childhood are very important. 'Early childhood' here means the first five or six years. In those early years you may have had intensely emotional experiences which you then repressed – perhaps because they made you feel guilty, or frightened of punishment or dreadful consequences. We have also seen that repressed emotions do not go away: they linger on, in the unconscious. And they may be the clue you need for understanding your present attitudes and behaviour, your tensions, explosive anger, and so on.

Now let us go a little further. A traumatic experience in the early years may stunt a person's sexual development, so that he or she never attains normal adult sexuality. This theory needs to be explained, and its explanation requires that we should take a look at what Freud called 'infantile sexuality'.

What we usually mean when we use the word 'sex' is adult sexuality in which sexual organs are aroused and there is – typically, though not always – an act of penetration which gives intense pleasure to both parties. Freud argued that this adult sexuality developed out of something that was already present in early childhood called 'infantile sexuality'. It is important to be clear about what Freud meant by this phrase. He is using 'sexuality' here in a very broad way, to mean the desire for, and experience of, sensuous pleasure. In the newly born baby this sensuous pleasure is felt throughout the body, both internally and on the skin surface. Later, it becomes focused on particular parts of the body: mouth, anus and genitals in that order.

Pleasure at the mouth is first felt when sucking at the mother's breast: the source of nourishment is the source of pleasure. The baby's oral pleasure may also be found in biting as well as in sucking. Other objects of sucking and biting, says Freud, are mere substitutes for the nipple.

Pleasure at the anus comes next, and is found either in emptying the bowels or in holding the faeces back.

Finally, pleasure at the genitals comes from touching, pulling and playing with the penis (in the case of a boy) or the walls of the vagina (in the case of a girl).

All this happens before puberty, which is the time when adult sexuality begins.

Fixation

Now, the interesting thing about all this, as far as understanding our dreams is concerned, is that we don't all 'make it' to normal adult sexuality. Many of us have sexual hang-ups of one kind or another, and in these cases what happens, according to Freud, is that we get stuck ('fixated') at one or other of the three infantile stages of sexual development.

Freud said there are easily recognizable clues to what sort of fixation a person may be suffering from. These clues take the form of certain personality and behavioural characteristics, which differ according to the stage at which fixation took place.

Fixation at the sucking stages tends to produce a dependent sort of adult. It may show itself in thumb-sucking or smoking or over-eating. People with these characteristics have not succeeded in becoming properly independent of their mother, have not learned to stand on their own two feet.

Fixation at the biting stage gives rise to an aggressive personality, or sarcastic and critical (orally aggressive) or cynical. It is possible for someone to get stuck in a more general way at the mouth phase of sexual development, in which case he or she may display something of both sets of characteristics – the dependent and the aggressive.

Fixation at the anal expulsive stage, the stage where pleasure is found in expelling faeces, will tend to produce an untidy, wasteful and extravagant (perhaps extravagantly generous) person.

Fixation at the anal retentive stage, where pleasure is got from withholding the faeces, will produce a neat, perhaps compulsively fastidious person; mean and miserly, perhaps a collector (of stamps or butterflies or whatever); stubborn and very independent.

(Hence the importance of correct potty training! Too much stress on it may cause a child to hold his motions back; too little stress on it may bring about a fixation at the anal expulsive stage. A nicely balanced parental attitude towards potty training will help the child to become a balanced person: generous [neither mean nor extravagant] and creative. With regard to creativity, this may take an artistic form: having pleased its parents by producing excrement in its potty, a child may later on in life continue this process of producing things to please people by creating works of art.)

Fixation at the pre-adult genital stage of development may show itself in adult life in either exhibitionism or auto-eroticism. Exhibitionism means displaying your genitals – uninvited – to someone of the opposite sex and represents an unconscious wish that the other person will offer you his or her genitals. Young children display their genitals without the least embarrassment; but in adults exhibitionism is an abnormal substitute for making love.

Regression

Another psychological mechanism Freud described is what he called 'regression'. Strong childhood fixation and/or adult frustration followed by regression is what leads to neurosis, according to Freud. 'Neurosis' is Freud's word for any mental disease or – perhaps better – mental dis-ease: any kind of distress or unease (for example, an unresolved conflict) in the psyche.

Regression is where everything is going along nicely until some frustration occurs in our adult sexual life and causes us to retreat to an earlier – infantile – phase of our sexual development. We all know how adults may sometimes display infantile behaviour of a non-sexual kind: for example, going into a tantrum and stamping the floor or banging the table. This, too, is a regression to early childhood, and is brought about by some frustration with which the person cannot cope in a rational and grown-up way.

Freud's notion of fixation and regression was almost certainly inspired by his reading of Charles Darwin. Darwin, speaking about evolution, described a phenomenon that he called an 'arrest in development', and declared that anything that is regarded as pathological or abnormal in a more evolved form of life appears as a normal and permanent condition in some earlier, less evolved forms of life. In the same vein, Freud tells us that abnormal sexual behaviour in a human adult corresponds to what is normal in human infants.

Regression may take several forms, including auto-eroticism, which means finding pleasure of a sensuous kind in your own body. This is usually manifest as masturbation, but over-eating, over-drinking and smoking may also be forms of auto-eroticism – ways of getting sensuous pleasure without another person.

Auto-eroticism plays a part in what is generally agreed to be normal sexuality. However, where the balance tips over heavily on the pleasure for-self side of the scales, sexuality becomes abnormal. This is often the case with men who frequently ejaculate immediately on entering – or even before entering – the vagina. Premature ejaculation is due to the man's state of excitement (as distinct from passion or love), which indicates that he is unduly preoccupied with his own body-pleasure. In other words, he is still behaving like a very young child.

The Oedipus complex

This is another topic that may provide useful hints for your dream interpretation and self-understanding – so long as you relinquish (for the time being, at least) any prejudices you may have about it. Freud believed that 'the whole progress of society' depends on the 'opposition between successive generations'. Certainly, as far as the individual is concerned, some liberation from the authority of parents is necessary if a person is to unfold his or her own 'destiny' and live in accordance with the ground-plan contained in his or her unique psyche or self. It is these considerations that make what Freud said about the Oedipus complex so important, especially since many of us fail to achieve that freedom from parental influence which is the freedom to be ourselves and to enjoy ourselves (literally).

Freud believed that every young child goes through a phase where he or she develops an incestuous desire for the parent of the opposite sex. He arrived at this conclusion partly because many of his female patients spoke of acts of incest committed on them in their childhood. Freud found it impossible to believe that the staid, respectable, middle-class fathers of these patients could have committed such acts, and he therefore interpreted these stories as wish-fulfilling fantasies.

Nowadays we know very well that incest – between fathers and daughters, at least – is quite common, and we might therefore be more ready than Freud was to take those patients' stories literally. However, this does not necessarily negate all that Freud concluded about the Oedipus complex.

The Oedipus complex in a young male child (roughly, between four and seven years old) means a desire for his mother and consequent feelings of envy, resentment and hatred towards his father, whom he sees as a trial. The child also fears that his father might punish him by castrating him. Normally, the Oedipus complex resolves itself at or before puberty. In many cases, however, traces of it persist into adult life. There may be a fixation on the mother, so that the man finds it difficult to love another woman for herself: other women are only a more or less adequate substitute for his mother. It may be that feelings of guilt associated with the child's sensuous attraction to the mother linger on. If so, the grown man's attitude and approach to sex may well be poisoned and his sexual relations sullied and spoilt. He may continue to be dominated – unconsciously – by an internalized ('introjected') father figure taking the form of a severe super-ego which will blight the whole of his life – not just his sexual life – with its prohibitions and threats of disaster.

In a young female child the Oedipus complex takes a different form. Whereas for the young boy castration is a mere fantasy, for the young girl it is perceived as an accomplished fact: comparing herself with the males she sees around her (brother, school-mates, or father), she imagines that her own penis must have been cut off. This, according to Freud, gives rise to what he calls 'penis-envy', which is one of the root causes of women's feelings of inferiority: the young female sees herself as an incomplete male!

Freud said that a young girl might react to this imagined castration in one of several different ways:

1 She might see her inferiority as strictly sexual and consequently – so as not to be forced to feel inferior – avoid sex altogether. This sexual inhibition, it should be noted, is not a result of conscious thought; it is an unconscious reaction.

2 She might avoid clitoral sex. Seeing her clitoris as an inferior penis causes her to lose her pleasure in it.

3 She might take a lesbian mate.

4 She might concentrate on a career where she might be man's equal.

5 She might resolve the Oedipus complex. As with a young boy, so with a young girl, the first object of love – after the auto-erotic stage has been outgrown – is the mother. But it is the mother whom she imagines as having castrated her – as a punishment for her unacceptable incestuous desire. The girl's love for her mother therefore turns to hatred, and her father now becomes the object of her love. This turning to the father is her entry into the Oedipus situation; but, says Freud, it also paves the way for normal femininity: from now on the desire for a penis ('penis-envy') will be satisfied by taking possession of a man's penis in a normal heterosexual relationship.
6 She might fail to resolve the Oedipus complex and remain (unconsciously) in love with her father – in which case the men in her life will tend to be father-substitutes.

Defence mechanisms

A word about what Freud called 'defence mechanisms' may be helpful to you in your efforts to achieve the self-scrutiny that is fundamental to correct and fruitful dream interpretation.

We have seen that, according to Freud, some degree of tension is inevitable between what society requires of us and what our instinctive nature demands in the way of self-gratification. Remember that, according to Freud, if the ego is not in control, then either the id will destroy or damage the psyche. or a neurosis will come about as a result of the super-ego refusing to allow the id adequate satisfaction. In its endeavours to maintain inner harmony and reduce the tension between the conflicting demands of society (super-ego) and instinct (id), the ego sometimes resorts to short-term solutions which in the long run are far from satisfactory. These are the so-called 'ego-defences' or 'defence mechanisms'. Here is a list of them:

1 ***Repression.*** As we discussed earlier (page 19), this means expelling from consciousness any natural desire that offends your super-ego, which is that sense of right and wrong that you have picked up from parents and, later, from society at large and which you have then internalized ('introjected') as 'conscience'. The unsatisfactory nature of this solution lies in the fact that repressed desires do not disappear: they remain active in the unconscious layers of the mind and, since they are denied even a controlled and regulated expression, they may at any moment explode in uncontrolled and even violent forms of expression. The rapist, for example, is a product of sexual repression.

2 ***Regression.*** This, too, we have already looked at (pages 27–28). Adults sometimes behave like children: for example, stamping and screaming as a means of getting their own way; or wives threatening, in response to a

minor marital dispute, to go home to mother. As children they may have succeeded by such means in getting what they wanted; but that sort of behaviour in adults suggests immaturity, a refusal to grow up and confront life's problems and assume responsibility for one's life. Regression is often triggered by some frustration in an adult's sexual life, but any other kind of frustration in a situation or a relationship may have the same effect.

3 ***Projection.*** This means treating as external what is really internal. For example, we all tend to disown our faults and see them instead in other people; we accuse others of doing what we ourselves have done or would like to do. An adolescent girl's complaint that boys are always ogling her may just be a piece of (unconscious) wishful thinking. In other words, she may be projecting on to other people a desire she refuses to acknowledge in herself (because some experience has caused her to repress it). Similarly, 'He's arrogant' may really mean 'I feel inferior.'

Projection may result in the scapegoat syndrome, where either the individual or society as a whole puts the blame for all misfortunes on someone else, refusing to look inside for the causes.

4 ***Rationalization.*** This means inventing excuses for yourself. For example, a lazy student may come up with the pseudo-justification 'Too much reading is bad for the eyes.' The frigid spouse who is actually suffering from a neurosis caused by repression of his or her sexual desire may rationalize the inhibition with comments such as 'There are more important things in life than sex' or 'Sex isn't everything, is it?'

5 ***Compensation.*** This takes place where the natural outlet for an instinctive drive is replaced by some less direct means of expression. For instance, someone who is physically unattractive or who feels unattractive may become a workaholic; for a childless couple a pet dog may be a compensation; over-eating or smoking may be a way of trying to compensate for a frustrated desire for love or sex.

6 ***Sublimation.*** This is similar to compensation, but the word is usually used where the substituted outlet for an instinctive drive is a somewhat sophisticated or elevated one. For example, Freud thought that all forms of art were the product of sublimated sexual energy.

7 ***Displacement.*** This is scarcely distinguishable from compensation. Freud gives rather surreal examples: a person's desire to devour (destroy?) his or her parents may be expressed in eating meat; if the desire has been repressed

it may express itself in vegetarianism. Both are cases of displacement. (Incidentally, this would seem to be one of those all too frequent instances in Freud's theorizings of 'Heads I win, tails you lose': since everyone is either a meat-eater or a vegetarian, it would appear that everyone must have an unconscious desire to devour his or her parents. In practice, no self-respecting psychoanalyst would base a diagnosis simply on meat-eating or vegetarianism. If, however, you were a fanatical meat-eater or a fanatical vegetarian, a psychoanalyst might see it as pointing the way to a diagnosis, particularly if there were other characteristics pointing in the same direction.)

8 ***Identification.*** This word has become a part of our everyday vocabulary. Identifying with a hero – pop star, film star, footballer or whatever – is a well-known phenomenon. To be identification, however, and not just hero-worship, it must include seeing oneself as the admired person, adopting his or her dress-style, hairstyle, and attitudes and values. Children sometimes imitate their parents as a means of getting what they want, so identification may in some cases be a form of regression.

9 ***Reaction-formation.*** This is an attempt to redress the balance in the psyche, but with a vengeance! It is a heavy-handed over-compensation. If a particular instinctive drive produces anxiety, the ego may concentrate on (over-) developing its opposite.

For example, Freud came to believe that there were just two basic and opposed instinctive drives – the life-instinct (which he also called 'Eros') and the death-instinct ('Thanatos'). The life-instinct includes not only sexual desire but also any desire for life or for its preservation or enhancement. The death-instinct is its opposite: a drive towards death, a desire to return to the womb (that is, a wish that one had never been born). Now, if some experience causes a person to repress or suppress any part of the life-instinct (for example, if frightened by his or her sexual desires), there may take place a strong upsurge of the death-instinct (for example, in the form of a renunciation of all ambition, all desire to achieve or do or even be anything). This would be a case of reaction-formation. Perhaps a more common instance is where fear of one's strong sexual desires leads one to become a stern campaigner against pornography, prostitution, sex outside marriage, sex education in schools, etc.

10 ***Symptoms.*** Even physical symptoms may be seen as a kind of defence mechanism. Like most dreams, they can be disguised expressions of a repressed desire: for example, a paralysed arm or leg may express a soldier's repressed desire to get away from the front line; a man's inability to get an

erection may be a disguised expression of his desire to punish his partner. In other words, symptoms are attempts to prevent a repressed desire from causing a painful and intolerable disturbance in the psyche.

11 *Neuroses and psychoses* may also be seen as defence mechanisms. Freud describes a neurosis as an unstable, precarious attempt to satisfy an instinctive drive or desire that has been inhibited or repressed. For example, a phobia (irrational fear) about knives may conceal deep-seated destructive wishes, for which it provides a substitute obsession.

Further, Freud declares that every neurosis represents a withdrawal from the real world into a world of fantasy. This withdrawal is accomplished fully in a psychosis, which is simply a severe form of neurosis in which the person loses the ability to distinguish between fantasy and reality. The withdrawal is from a situation or relationship which is felt to be both intolerable and unavoidable: for instance, a woman who is pressed – by parents or circumstances – into a marriage for which she feels unready may (unconsciously) fall into a neurosis as a way of escape.

On using Freud

Take from Freud whatever you find useful for throwing light on your dreams. Always be on the look-out for repressed wishes, especially repressed sexual desires and repressed hostile wishes towards parents, partners, brothers or sisters. On the other hand, do not suppose that all your dreams contain disguised wishes. Some dreams express anxiety, others give warnings, or offer solutions to problems; some may reveal deep untapped resources of your personality. In fact, disguise (as distinct from symbolism) is much less common in dreams than Freud supposed. Some dreams are straightforward representations of recent events (for example, an encounter with your boss, or your father), sometimes with the purpose of urging you to give your conscious attention to the relationship and its problems and tensions; other dreams express some hidden desire without any disguise at all.

We have seen that Freud sometimes gives the impression that all dreams are expressions of the gratification of sexual desire. If you are reluctant to interpret a dream sexually, be on your guard: your reluctance may itself be an indicator of repressed sexuality. On the other hand, where a dream allows other kinds of interpretation as well as a sexual one, try them all and see which of them 'fits' best. It may be that a dream can properly be understood at more than one level. And where a dream is obviously sexual, what is important is the attitude to sex or the feelings that are revealed in the dream.

Jung on Dreams

To move from Freud to Jung is to enter a very different world. Carl Gustav Jung (1875–1961) was at one time a disciple and colleague of Freud but later rejected much of Freud's teaching. To distinguish his own approach from Freud's he used the title 'analytical psychology', as against Freud's 'psychoanalytical psychology' or 'psychoanalysts'.

Some of you will find Jung more to your liking, others Freud. What I recommend, however, is that you keep an open mind and see which approach fits you and your dreams better. It is more than likely that some of your dreams will naturally call for a Freudian kind of interpretation, whilst others will be more adequately interpreted in a Jungian way.

JUNG VERSUS FREUD

How does Jung's style of dream interpretation differ from Freud's? For a start, Jung rejected Freud's heavy emphasis on sexuality as the source of all psychic disorders and consequently almost the one and only key to unlock the meaning of dreams. Secondly, Jung saw the unconscious as much more than a mere dustbin, a receptacle for rejected emotions and desires. For Jung, dreams are not to be understood as simply showing what is wrong in the psyche. Certainly they do that, and that is an important and valuable function in itself, but they can also do much more than that. The unconscious contains all we need to know about the causes to our psychic troubles: it can tell us why we are as we are – victim or martyr, sexually impotent, or whatever – but it can also show us the remedy for our disorder. And it does both these things through dreams.

The unconscious, says Jung, is not concerned merely with putting right the things that have gone wrong in us. It aims at our well-being in the fullest possible sense; its goal is nothing less than our complete personal development, the creative unfolding of the potentialities that are contained in our individual 'ground-plan' or 'destiny'. This means not just healing but wholeness.

For Jung, the unconscious is not merely a bundle of instincts centring on hunger, sex and survival. It also contains the secret of life's meaning, which is hidden from the conscious intellect. The unconscious will reveal that secret in our dreams – if only we are receptive enough, which means being humble enough.

Jung also does not go along with Freud's idea that there is a censor at work when we dream, causing disguise or distortion between the latent content and the manifest content (i.e. between the dream message and the actual dream story). According to Jung, what the unconscious is saying to us in our dreams is presented in a totally undisguised way. If we cannot understand our dreams, therefore, it is only because in the modern world we have lost touch with the language of symbols, which is the language of dreams. Anyone who is at home in the world of symbolism – as so-called 'primitive' people were and are – will have no great difficulty in understanding dreams.

Freud saw the symbols in a dream as concealing the dream's message, keeping it from the dreamer's conscious attention. For Jung, on the other hand, dream symbols are both 'expressive' and 'impressive': they express what is going on at an unconscious level of the psyche; and they make an impression – leave their imprint – on the dreamer, influencing the direction of his or her personal development from that moment on. For example, a withered tree in dreams may symbolize – 'express' – a life that has been lived too intellectually, too much in the head; and the impression that symbol makes on the dreamer may bring about a reshaping of his or her personality by re-rooting the dreamer's life in instinct or Nature.

Jung did not use Freud's method of free association. That method, said Jung, would always lead us to a 'complex' (Jung's term for what Freud called a 'neurosis'), but the complex it led us to might not be the one that was the source of the dream. Indeed, a dream may sometimes point away from a complex in order to show the dreamer a part of the psyche that might, if used and developed, liberate him or her from the complex.

Free association means not exercising any control over the series of associations. Starting with one word or event in a dream, you say (or write down) whatever you immediately associate with it; then what you associate with that; and so on. By the time you reach the end of the chain of associations – or rather, by the time your feeling-reactions suggest you have reached some revelation of your inner state – you may be miles away from the dream with which you started.

Jung's method, on the other hand, never loses sight of the dream. This method – he calls it 'amplification' – is to take every item in a dream (words, persons, objects, etc.) and associate with each in turn: you simply say or jot down whatever the particular item suggests to you, or what recollections it conjures up for you. For example, if a red flower appeared in your dream, you must ask yourself (a) what a flower means to you; (b) what red means for you; (c) if the flower has a definite shape or structure – circular, say, or divided into four segments – you must ask yourself what that shape or structure means or suggests to you; (d) if the dream flower is fragrant, what does that particular aroma mean to you? When you have associated in this way with all the items in your dream, you must then associate with the dream as a whole.

What Jung calls 'active imagination' is a set of techniques for helping you to associate, helping you to discover what this or that item in a dream means to you. As the title suggests, all these techniques involve some sort of activity, and all put your imagination to work. One of these techniques is to draw or – preferably – paint your dream symbols. Another is to imagine that you are an actor and your job is to be this or that person who appeared in your dream, to get inside and identify with that person. (A person in a dream is nearly always some part of yourself, usually a neglected part. The ability to identify and to empathise with that part of yourself is therefore obviously worth developing.) Jung himself even went so far as to build actual physical models, as life-size as possible, of objects appearing in his dreams.

A rather different form of 'active imagination' is meditation: that is, exploring your unconscious mind by putting your consciousness into it. If, during your meditation, you visualize the items that appeared in your dream, one after another, these may actually guide your conscious self in its exploration of the unconscious, leading it towards what it most needs to know at that time.

Jung insisted more strongly than Freud that the meaning of any particular dream symbol is not necessarily the same for different people, or even for the same person at different stages of his or her life. The only sure way of getting the meaning that is applicable to you here and now is, says Jung' to use the 'amplification' method.

This warning has been heeded in compiling this dictionary. In nearly all cases more than one possible meaning of a symbol is given; and in these cases it is left to you, the individual reader, to work out for yourself which of the given meanings is the most appropriate one for you. If a dream symbol has strong associations for you which suggest a meaning not given in this dictionary, don't let that put you off: I don't claim to have given all possible meanings of every symbol. On the other hand don't be too ready to reject the meanings given in the dictionary, especially if one of them makes a strong impact on you. A strong impact may be either strong and pleasant or strong and unpleasant; if what you want is the truth about yourself rather than comfort, you should pay particular attention to any suggested interpretation that strongly offends or disgusts you.

In his work on dream interpretation, Jung distinguished between younger and older people: up to about the age of thirty-five years, he said, a Freudian interpretation might suffice, but not in the second half of life. This should not be taken too strictly or narrowly. Jung does not mean that no one over the age of thirty-five has sexual problems and we can therefore forget about Freud when we reach the halfway mark in our life. Nor does he mean that no one below the age of thirty-five has any problems of a non-sexual nature. What Jung means is that, for instance, most people in the first half of life are generally preoccupied with outward things – success in their job and a satisfactory sexual life, buying/renting and furnishing a home, and the self-image they present to the world. After thirty-five or so, there is a tendency for people to start looking inwards and ask themselves whether they are going in the right direction and whether the set of values they have lived by is really the right one. People in the second half of life often begin to take death more seriously and consequently become more deeply and constantly concerned with the question of the meaning and purpose of life.

For these reasons, says Jung, the same dream symbol may have a different meaning or a different level of meaning, according to whether the dreamer is in the first half of life or the second. As a simple illustration of this, let us take the sun. In a child's dream this will probably have no symbolic value at all: it will most likely be just a straightforward reliving of the child's experience of the sun during the day. In the dreams of a young adult the sun might symbolize the dreamer's father, or possibly the 'light' of reason. For an older adult the sun could be a symbol of the dreamer's true self, or of that indefinable something that some people call 'God' or 'Nature' or 'Ultimate Reality' or '(the source of) Truth'.

All this will become clearer when you read about what Jung called the 'individuation process' (pages 44–55). Meanwhile, let me warn against a too doctrinaire application of Jung's distinction. It would be ridiculous to suppose that no one under the age of thirty-five has ever been concerned with the deep questions of life; and it would be even more foolish to equate middle age with personal maturity, or old age with spirituality and deep wisdom.

Although Jung had no time for institutionalized forms of religion, he did not share Freud's dogmatic atheism. Freud rejected all religions and metaphysical ideas as pernicious illusions and a neurotic form of escapism, a withdrawal from the real world into a world of fantasy. 'Religion,' he said, 'is the universal obsessional neurosis of mankind.'

Jung, on the other hand, came to the conclusion that what most of his patients in the second half of life were suffering from was basically a lack of religion. For Freud, religion was a neurosis; for Jung, religion was therapeutic – it was the ultimate cure for the troubled human psyche. The quest for one's own authentic self and the quest for God are, for Jung, one and the same quest.

Moreover, Jung tells us that he frequently found the symbols of religion – its mythologies and rituals – in the dreams of people in the second half of life. As we have seen (in the case of the sun), a potentially religious symbol may appear in a dream without any religious meaning at all (or, in some cases, with just a trace of its religious significance). However, according to Jung, in the dreams of middle-aged and older people these symbols appear more frequently with their full religious meaning. And indeed Jung sometimes speaks as if all symbols have a religious function: 'It is the role of symbols,' he says, 'to give a meaning to the life of man.'

To pave the way for a better understanding of Jung's approach to the interpretation of dreams, we need to look at what he calls 'the process of individuation'; and as a preliminary to understanding that, we need to know something about Jung's 'psychological types' and his view of the unconscious.

Psychological types

Jung divides these into 'attitudinal' end 'functional' types.

ATTITUDINAL TYPES

Everyone now is familiar with the terms 'extrovert' and 'introvert'. These words were first coined by Jung, to distinguish what he saw as two basic psychological types.

The introvert's first reaction to any situation is to back away from it – or, at least, to want to back away from it – 'as if with an unspoken "No"'. The introvert does not welcome new faces or new situations; rather, he or she is afraid of them, even though he or she may in time learn to control and conceal this fear, for the sake of politeness or for the sake of 'getting on' with people. The introvert will tend to find his or her values and standards, and direction in life, not from other people – the outside world – but from an inner world of private thoughts and feelings.

The extrovert, on the other hand, meets every new person, every new situation, with a 'Yes', moving towards them with open arms, welcoming and trusting. He or she finds his or her bearings and direction in life chiefly by reacting to the world outside – what other people say or think or do. One consequence of this gregariousness is that the extrovert tends to be a conformist, accepting without question the values and standards of society at large or of his or her own particular socio-economic group.

Please note that, although it is possible – and useful – to distinguish these two types, and although most people fall unmistakably into one or the other category, there is probably no one who is either 100 per cent extrovert or 100 per cent introvert.

FUNCTIONAL TYPES

Roughly speaking, to classify people according to 'function' means grouping them in accordance with their predominant way of making sense of things. Jung distinguishes four main functional types:

1 ***The thinking type.*** If thinking – the use of reason – is where you function most strongly, confidently and successfully, then thinking is what Jung calls your 'superior' function, and you belong to the thinking type.

2 ***The intuitive type.*** If you are the intuitive type, your strongest psychic faculty is intuition, which means that you 'know' things in a direct, immediate way, without the need for reasoning.

3 ***The feeling type.*** The word 'feeling' as used by Jung includes moral feelings, as well as all other kinds of sentiment (for example, love and tenderness). In this sense, 'feeling' must be clearly distinguished from sensation, which is a physical thing. If feeling is where you function best, you are of the feeling type.

4 ***The sensational type.*** To belong to the sensational type does not mean that you cause a stir wherever you go! It simply means that your strongest –'superior'– psychic function, your favoured way of relating to reality, is physical sensation.

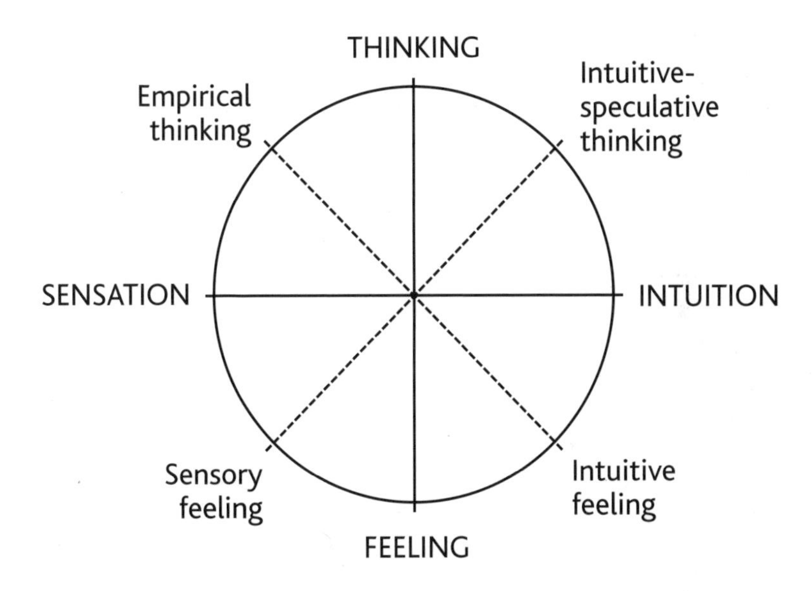

The diagram is adapted from Jacobi, *The Psychology of C.G. Jung*, revised ed., Yale University Press, New Haven and London, 1973.

In connection with what follows, you may find it useful to consult the diagram above. This shows the way things are for the thinking type – with 'thinking' at the top. If you are the sensational type, you will have to turn the page round till 'sensation' is at the top, and so on.

If your superior function is thinking, then feeling will tend to be your 'inferior' function – which means that your feeling capacity will be undeveloped and unorganized and will function only inefficiently and ineffectively. Scientists will normally belong to the thinking type; and it is interesting to note that Jung was more than a little apprehensive about giving scientists too much say in political and social policy-making. The reason for his fears is that people who belong to the thinking type cannot be trusted to make wise judgements – that is, judgements that will be the right ones in terms of human happiness and well-being.

By turning the diagram round till your superior function is at the top, you will see which is your inferior function, the one that is the least reliable and the most in need of development.

You will see from the diagram that, in addition to the four main functional types, there are four intermediate or mixed types. If, for example, like Jung himself, you are strong in a kind of thinking which is not pure reasoning (rational thinking) but contains a large intuitive ingredient, you will belong to the intuitive-speculative thinking type. In that case, your inferior function will be that of sensory feeling, which might include such things as awareness and appreciation of beauty and the making of value-judgements based on such awareness and appreciation – as distinct from more purely 'conscience'-based judgements.

Persona

'Persona' is another word coined by Jung that has now become part of our everyday language. It is a Greek word meaning 'mask'. In Greek theatre the actors wore masks to show which character they represented. Jung uses the word to mean the self-image with which we face the world.

A young person's main task is to identify and develop his or her superior function, the function that is most solidly rooted in his or her particular constitution and will therefore best serve him or her in meeting the world's demands – the need to make a living, for example, which involves the need to develop some kind of skill. It is in this connection that the persona is constructed. The persona is the self-image you create in your attempt to bring about as happy a marriage as possible between what society requires and the internal requirements of your own psyche.

The persona should ideally be based on your superior function. Unfortunately, however, this is not always the case: your persona may have been forced on you by your parents, or by your education, or by the pressure of your peer-group. For example, your parents may have pushed you into academic achievement, forcing you to build a thinking-based persona, whereas your natural (God-given) superior function was, let's say, the feeling function.

If there is a misfit between your persona and your real superior function, you will soon know about it. Some sort of neurosis or complex will soon show itself: you may become a person who never seems to have any luck; or you may become a victim of the 'bull-in-the-china-shop' syndrome – always 'putting your foot in it' or blundering from one disaster to another.

Again, you may identify with what Jung calls 'inner figures' – the hero(-ine), the saviour, the martyr, the outcast, the avenger, and others. This means that you suppose that it is your destiny to play the hero, the martyr, or whatever. There are great dangers in this. For instance, if you have too high an opinion of yourself and entertain grandiose ambitions out of all proportion to your real capacities, you may begin to have dreams of (flying and) falling. These dreams will be warnings from your unconscious, telling you that, unless you take a more realistic view of yourself and reformulate your ambitions in accordance with your real (and not your imagined) capabilities, you are heading for a fall – which might be an external disaster (e.g. losing your job) or an internal one (e.g. a mental collapse), or indeed both.

(Notice the difference between a Freudian and a Jungian interpretation of dreams of falling, or flying and falling. For Freud's interpretation, see page 18.)

Even if you successfully identify and develop your true superior function, you can still make trouble for yourself! Concentrating too much on developing your superior function produces a lopsided personality; and this lack of balance will tend to cause inner tensions or conflicts in the second half of life. The persona must not become an iron mask; it must always allow for growth. For example, you must not identify too exclusively with your occupation – like the sergeant-major who is never off duty, even at home with his family, and even after retirement. If you are only a solicitor or accountant or whatever, you have discovered and developed only a very superficial part of the total psyche; and the extent to which you depend on your job for self-esteem is itself a measure of how little you have explored your psyche and consequently how under-developed your personality is.

Moreover, neglected functions – the parts of your psyche that you have left in a crude undeveloped state will sooner or later rise in revolt and express themselves in uncontrolled and unacceptable ways.

The unconscious

Jung took an altogether grander view of the unconscious than Freud. Whereas for Freud the unconscious was principally a bin for receiving the conscious mind's rejects, for Jung the unconscious fulfilled a positive role, performing a therapeutic function by showing the conscious mind what needs to be done to get rid of unease and unhappiness and to achieve fuller satisfaction in life.

One very important feature of the unconscious, according to Jung, is that it compensates for the one-sidedness of the conscious mind. For example, if you are an extrovert at the conscious level, you will be introverted at the unconscious level, and vice versa. If at the conscious level you are a thinking type, at the unconscious level you will be strong in feeling; and so on.

What this means is that, in order to round out your personality, you must bring the unconscious part of your psyche into your consciousness. And this is precisely what happens in dreams. Dreams are the channels through which the unconscious enters consciousness – if you let it. Dreams carry messages from the instinctive to the rational part of the mind. Pay attention to your dreams, therefore, and you will increasingly find yourself acting in accord with your whole psyche, not just one bit of it.

The unconscious aims at personal wholeness, and wholeness means healing. To base your life on the dictates of the conscious mind alone is appropriate for the earlier half of adult life – until you have got yourself established in an occupation that suits you – but for unconditional happiness and well-being you need to base your life on the inner necessities of your total psyche.

Do you think you – the conscious ego – know best? No, says Jung; the unconscious knows best. It knows what is good for you. It contains the wisdom and the faculties and the energy you require for a completely happy and self-fulfilling life.

This does not mean, however, that the conscious ego should let the unconscious take over the psyche and rule the roost. As well as containing deep wisdom and inexhaustible energy, the unconscious may also contain forces that, if unleashed, would destroy the psyche – that is, produce madness. Such forces Jung referred to as 'complexes'. Complexes are 'psychic entities that have escaped from the control of consciousness and split off from it, to lead a separate existence in the dark sphere of the psyche, whence they may at any time hinder or help the conscious performance.' They correspond to the good and bad spirits which, in religious mythology, may set up house in a person's soul. These complexes hinder the person (the spirits are bad) if they are not integrated with consciousness, not brought into the light of consciousness and not allowed appropriate and creative expression under the control of the conscious mind, the ego.

Neurosis or psychosis (severe neurosis) occurs when contents of the unconscious mind flood the conscious mind – when, to use mythological language, spirits take possession of the person (as with the 'demoniacs' of the New Testament: people 'possessed' by demons).

The question of which knows better, conscious or unconscious, becomes clearer once we distinguish between consciousness and reason. Reason –

rational thinking has its uses: for making money as well as for building bridges or bombs. But mere reason will not reveal the truth about yourself and your 'destiny'. For that you need to explore the unconscious depths of the mind. And it is not the rational mind that explores the unconscious. The rational mind rejects the unconscious. It is consciousness – the conscious mind – that does the exploring, not in its rational mode, but in the mode of pure awareness, where the mind cuts through abstract reasoning to an immediate experiencing of reality. Reason conceives – imagines and speculates; pure consciousness perceives reality directly. Reason knows about things; pure awareness knows the things themselves, experientially.

In this connection it is interesting to note that some existentialist philosophers, notably Jean-Paul Sartre, rejected depth psychology out of hand. Depth psychology is any psychology that accepts that the human mind has an unconscious dimension. Sartre rejected this notion of an unconscious part or function of the mind because he believed that the individual human being must accept responsibility for himself or herself. To be responsible, however, is to be free: we cannot properly hold a person responsible for his or her action if we are convinced that he or she was not free to choose to act otherwise than he or she did. And lots of people – most people, in fact, argued Sartre – seek to shrug off their responsibility by pretending that they are not free agents: that society is responsible for what they are, or that heredity determines all that a person is or does, or that we are all in the grip of unconscious forces that are beyond our control.

The truth of the matter would seem to be that Sartre is both right and wrong. He is surely right in insisting that each individual has the power to be other than he or she is. He is wrong, however, in assuming that that power resides in the reasoning faculty. Consciousness, not reason, is the key. And consciousness can open up possibilities for being other than one is only by entering the unconscious depths of the psyche, or by letting them enter consciousness.

What Jung is recommending is not that the conscious mind should become the slave of the unconscious, or vice versa. Neither the conscious mind nor the unconscious should be subjugated by the other. On the contrary, conscious and unconscious should come together in a marriage of equal partners. That is the way to salvation, or healing, or wholeness.

Personal and collective unconscious

Jung distinguishes between more superficial and deeper layers of the unconscious mind and calls them respectively 'the personal unconscious' and 'the collective unconscious'. The personal unconscious consists of those things that have been repressed, rejected from consciousness; it is therefore something that is built up during the individual's lifetime. The collective unconscious, on the other hand, is older than the individual and indeed older than consciousness: it consists of 'the whole spiritual heritage of mankind's evolution born anew in the brainstructure of every individual'. (Do not be misled by the words 'brainstructure': the collective unconscious should not be thought of as situated in the head; it includes emotions and instincts and, although it cannot be pinned down to any particular location in the body, it might be more helpful to think of it as in the solar plexus region rather than in the head.)

ARCHETYPAL IMAGES

When looking at your dreams you will probably find that most of them are communications from your personal unconscious, especially – says Jung – if you are in the first half of life. If, however, your dreams contain what Jung calls 'archetypal images', they may well be coming from the collective unconscious.

Jung describes these archetypal images as 'self-portraits of the instincts'. To put it another way, 'archetypes' are the instinctive forces and instinctive strategies or ways of behaving; 'archetypal images' are the symbols through which these instinctive things show themselves in dreams.

Archetypal images include symbols that occur in mythology: God, Earth Mother, death and resurrection/rebirth, and many more. They are older than you, the individual. They belong to the collective unconscious. On the other hand, an archetype may have numerous images, some of them stemming from the deep collective unconscious, others from the more superficial personal unconscious. The Feminine is such an archetype. Here are a few of its many and various images: your own mother; your grandmother; a cow; a cat; a witch; a fairy; a cave; the sea; night. Any one of these symbols appearing in your dreams might be from either the personal or the collective unconscious. As a general rule, says Jung, the more definite the image, the more likely is it to have come from the more superficial layers of the unconscious; the more indefinite the image, the more likely is it to have come from the deeper layers. (For possible meanings of the various symbols of the Feminine, see entries in the dictionary: *mother, cow,* etc., as well as *woman*.)

Individuation

What Jung has to say about individuation is of supreme importance for anyone who is interested in personal growth or, indeed, in personal happiness. By 'individuation' Jung means self-realization, or full and balanced personal development. It can be achieved by exploring your unconscious and paying attention to it when it 'speaks' to you in your dreams.

According to Jung, the unconscious expresses itself also in folktale and myth; and all myths, he says, revolve around the theme of individuation.

Myths are, so to speak, signposts showing us the way to fuller self-realization. In describing the four stages of the individuation process, therefore, I shall mention some of the mythological images that represent these different stages. Of course, as I have said already, mythological images may appear in dreams. (In fact, there is some evidence – among North American Indians, for example – that myths originated in dreams: special dreams of special people, namely, the tribal 'holy' men or woman.)

STAGE ONE: THE SHADOW

The first step is taken towards self-realization when you meet your 'shadow'. This is so called because it is the 'dark' side of your psyche, the parts of yourself that you have not previously brought into the light of consciousness. It is, for this reason, the 'primitive' (undeveloped or underdeveloped) side of your personality. It is also the 'negative' side of your personality, insofar as it is the opposite of whatever you have hitherto regarded as making a positive contribution to your well-being.

In dreams your shadow may be represented either by some figure of the same sex as yourself (an elder brother or sister, your best friend, or some alien or primitive person) or by a person who represents your opposite. A clear example of this in literature is Robert Louis Stevenson's *The Strange Case of Dr Jekyll and Mr Hyde,* in which Mr Hyde may be seen as Dr Jekyll's unconscious shadow, leading a separate and altogether different life from the conscious part of the personality. The werewolf motif features in the same way in literature (e.g. Hermann Hesse's *Steppenwolf*) and in folklore. In pre-literate societies this 'other' side of the individual's personality was sometimes depicted as a 'bushsoul', having its own separate body – usually that of an animal or tree in the nearby bushland or forest. (It should be noted that in such a preliterate society the bush or forest or other wild or desert places surrounding the human settlement were powerful symbols of anti-nomianism, that is, of everything that constituted a threat to the established law and order in the human community. There is an obvious parallel here to the way the dark forces of the unconscious may be felt as a threat to the ordered life of the conscious ego.)

Cinderella is a shadow figure. She is ignored and neglected by her elder sisters. They go out into the world, but Cinderella is shut up indoors. This represents the contrast between the conscious ego (which relates to the outside world) and those parts of the unconscious that have not been allowed any part in one's conscious activity. However, Cinderella eventually escapes from her imprisonment and marries the Prince. This marriage symbolizes the joining together of conscious ego (Prince) and shadow (Cinderella), which is the end result of the penetration of the conscious mind by the unconscious and/or the penetration of the unconscious by consciousness. Symbolically – in myths and in dreams – consciousness is usually represented as male, the unconscious as female; and the sexual penetration of female by male is therefore a common symbol of the descent of consciousness into the dark cave-like depths of the unconscious. (Here is a splendid example of the difference between Freud and Jung: whereas for Freud all – or very nearly all – dream images were symbols of sexuality, Jung asks us to entertain the possibility that the sexual act itself may be a symbol pointing to something beyond itself.)

Other symbols of the encounter with the shadow include the conversion motif. In the New Testament the Greek word that is translated as 'conversion' means literally 'a turning about'. And this is precisely what happens in the first stage of the individuation process: you start looking in the opposite direction – inside instead of outside – and this leads to the discovery and unfolding of a new dimension of yourself; new powers begin to work for you and you begin to experience 'newness of life'. 'You shall have life and shall have it more abundantly,' said Jesus; and this, Jung would say, is what individuation is all about.

Both the ritual of baptism and the many Flood myths may be seen as symbols of this first stage of individuation. Water is a common symbol of the unconscious. In baptism a person is plunged into water and is said to be 'born again' when he or she rises out of the water. This symbolizes the descent of consciousness into the unconscious and the resulting new and fuller life.

The same applies to stories of a great flood which destroys the face of the earth and then recedes, leaving one pure human being (e.g. Noah in the Jewish–Christian tradition; Markandrya in the Hindu tradition). If we take this as a symbol of individuation, what is destroyed by the flood-waters (the unconscious) is the persona, that makeshift self-image with which we start our adult life. This partial self must be dissolved to make way for the appearance of the whole self (represented by Noah or Markandeya).

In some cultures there are myths of a diver who plunges to the bottom of the sea and brings up treasure. The water, again, may be seen as a symbol of the unconscious, and the treasure as the new self one finds when previously unused psychic resources are given appropriate expression in one's conscious life.

The story of the Frog Prince tells of a young woman who is visited on three consecutive nights by a frog. On the first and second nights she is horrified, but on the third night she relents and lets the frog into her bed, and in the moment that she kisses him the frog turns into a handsome prince. For Ernest Jones (a follower and biographer of Freud) the story is an allegorical account of a young woman overcoming her fear of sex. For Joseph Campbell (a follower of Jung) the frog is just another example of the dragons and other frightening monsters whose role in mythology is to guard treasure. The frog, like them, represents the dark and frightening shadow; the treasure is the true self. The kiss symbolizes a person's acceptance of the shadow. And the result is the manifestation of the true nature of the shadow, as the bearer of one's true selflhood.

In order to reach the second stage of individuation you must resist two temptations. First, you must avoid projecting your shadow on to other people. Your shadow, because it is your dark side, may be quite frightening, and you may even see it as something evil. You may therefore want to disown it; and one way of doing this is to make believe that it is the property of someone else. On a collective level this is what leads to racism and the persecution of 'non-believers' (which in this context means people whose beliefs are different from our own). These are both examples of the 'them-and-us' syndrome, where we unload our 'dark' side on to some other group, which then becomes the scapegoat that carries the blame for everything that is wrong in our lives or our society. Commenting on Jesus's command to 'Love your enemy', Jung remarks: 'But what if I should discover that that very enemy himself is within me, that I myself am the enemy who must be loved-what then?' The answer is that you must learn to integrate the dark side of yourself, which means accepting it and allowing it proper expression under the control of your conscious mind. It will then cease to be dark and terrifying and hostile; instead, it will enhance the quality of your life, advance your personal development and increase your happiness.

The second temptation to be resisted is that of suppressing the shadow, which means putting it back into the cellars of the unconscious and locking the doors on it. Says Jung: 'Mere suppression of the Shadow is as little a remedy as beheading would be for headache.' Whatever pain or unease your shadow, may cause you, it consists of precisely those parts of your total self that you need to utilize if you are to achieve full personal growth. To suppress the shadow is merely to go back to square one; and sooner or later you will be forced to come to terms with this 'dark' side of yourself.

Usually, the first encounter with the shadow leads only to a partial acceptance of it, a mere acknowledgement of its existence. Certainly it is good to confess (what appear as) the less desirable – the 'dark'– aspects of one's personality: without that, no further progress can be made. But merely acknowledging these aspects does not take us very far. A lot more work is necessary. So let us take a look at the next stage of the individuation process.

STAGE TWO: ANIMA AND ANIMUS

This second stage means encountering what Jung calls the 'soul-image', which is one of the archetypal images. For a man this is the 'anima'; for a woman, the 'animus'. The anima is the feminine aspects of a male psyche:

for example, gentleness, tenderness, patience, receptiveness, closeness to nature, readiness to forgive, and so on. The animus is the male side of a female psyche: assertiveness, the will to control and take charge, fighting spirit, and so on.

Every man has a feminine component in his psyche; every woman has a masculine component in hers. Unfortunately, for many centuries, and particularly in the western world, it has been considered a virtue – 'the done thing' – for men to suppress their femininity; and until very recently women have been socially conditioned to think it unbecoming to show their masculinity. One result of this has been man's bad treatment of women. Man's fear and neglect of his own femininity have had dire consequences. Not only has he repressed the feminine in himself; but also, being frightened of women – who are 'the feminine' *par excellence* – he has suppressed them, kept them subordinate and powerless.

A further consequence of this suppression of femininity in a world dominated by men is war. Wars are the result of the lopsided development of men whose aggressiveness has not been balanced by love and patience and a feeling for harmony: that is, whose anima has been kept under lock and key. The macho male is violent and destructive.

Another consequence is mechanical, soul-less sex. Sex can be an invaluable aid to the achieving of personal wholeness and harmony; and it has been recognized as such in the Tantric mystic-meditative traditions of Hinduism and Buddhism. But sex can reach those heights only where there is worship: that is, where each partner acknowledges the worth of his or her sexual opposite. The macho male tends to reduce sex to a purely physical and emotional level, at which his partner is turned into a mere object.

For several reasons, therefore, it is imperative, both for individual and for social progress, that we learn to acknowledge and integrate our anima or animus, our soul-image.

Your soul-image will lead your conscious ego safely into the unconscious and safely out again. When Theseus needed to penetrate the labyrinth in Crete in order to slay the monstrous Minotaur, the fair Ariadne, with her thread, enabled him to go in and find his way out again. If we follow Jung and translate this story into psychological terms, the labyrinth is a symbol of the unconscious, the monster is the frightening and threatening aspect of whatever in our unconscious has been neglected and has therefore 'gone wild'; the slaying of the monster means 'taming' that wild, unruly force and bringing it under conscious control. The 'slaying' can be accomplished, however, only by love – only by accepting the neglected thing, honouring it and welcoming it into our consciousness.

The soul-image, then, is a mediator – a go-between or middle-man (or middle-woman) – who establishes communication between the conscious ego and the unconscious and reconciles the two. In the realm of religion there is the psychopomp, the one who guides human souls safely to the underworld; or – in some cultures – the shaman, who not only leads the souls of the dead to the spirit-world and makes the necessary introductions to spirits who will take proper care of the newcomers and get them ready for rebirth, but also carries the souls of sick people to the spirit-world for healing. The psychopomp and the shaman are animus or anima figures. The underworld or spirit-world is the unconscious. The unconscious has healing powers and by descending into it the conscious self can attain new life.

Your soul-image has characteristics which are the opposite of those possessed by your persona (the self-image you have constructed for the specific purpose of relating to the external world and for 'making your mark' in that world). For instance, if your persona is an intellectual one, your soul-image will be characterized by sentiment and emotion; and if you are the intuitive type, your soul-image will be earthy and sensual.

This means that if, instead of acknowledging and becoming acquainted with your own soul-image, you project it on to members of the opposite sex, you may be led into disastrous relationships. For example, an emotional man may choose a blue-stocking for his partner; or a sensitive woman may be irresistibly attracted by bearded intellectuals.

If, however, you accept and integrate your soul-image, it will make up the deficiencies of your persona and help you to become a fuller and more balanced person.

Let us look at some of the forms in which the soul-image may appear in dreams. 'The first bearer of the soul-image,' says Jung, 'is always the mother.' This applies to both men and women, and it means that the man or woman has not yet achieved liberation – independence – from mother. Therefore, the appearance of your mother in a dream – especially if she appears with possessive or devouring characteristics – may well be a symbol of your soul-image. If that is the case, bear in mind that the way to detach yourself from the suffocating influence of your mother is to integrate your anima or animus into your conscious ego. Accept your soul-image, respect it and welcome it as a creative contributor to your personal growth, and you will then find that your soul-image ceases to be represented in dreams by negative devouring mother figures and that you are gaining a proper degree of independence from your mother. (Incidentally, it doesn't make any difference if your actual mother is alive or dead. Even a dead mother may live on as a forceful presence within your unconsciousness.)

With the exception of the mother figure, the dream symbols that represent the soul-image are always of the opposite sex to the dreamer. Thus, a man's anima may be represented in dreams by his sister; a woman's animus by her brother. Some other symbols of the animus are an eagle, a bull, a lion, and a phallus (erect penis) or other phallic figures such as a tower or a spear. The eagle is associated with high altitudes and in mythology the sky is usually (ancient Egyptian mythology is the exception) regarded as male and symbolizes pure reason or spirituality. The earth is seen as female (Mother Earth) and symbolizes sensuous existence – that is, existence confined within the limits of the senses – plus intuition.

Some symbols of the anima include a cow, a cat, a tiger, a cave and a ship. All these are more or less obviously female figures. Ships are associated with the sea, which is a common symbol of the feminine, and are womb-like insofar as they are hollow. (At a launching we still say, 'Bless all who sail in her'.) Caves are hollow and womb-like. Sometimes they are filled with water, which is another feminine symbol; otherwise they are hollows in the earth, which – as we have seen – is a symbol of the feminine, and are the womb of the Earth Mother or vaginal entrances to her womb.

One common representation of the anima calls for special mention. This is the figure of the damsel in distress, frequently appearing in so-called 'hero' myths. Here a recurring theme is that of the hero rescuing a beautiful young woman and in some cases marrying her (e.g. the Greek hero Perseus saves the Ethiopian princess Andromeda from a sea-monster and later marries her). In a folktale variant of the same theme, the hero wakes a maiden from the sleep of death with a kiss (the Sleeping Beauty). In logical terms, the damsel in distress is the man's anima, which, because of neglect or repression, is – metaphorically speaking – either 'dead' or in danger of 'dying'. The rescue or kiss of life means that the man has now lifted his femininity out of its dark imprisonment and welcomed it – and, indeed, submitted to it – as an indispensable factor in his life and happiness.

After the prince has succeeded in waking Sleeping Beauty, all the other people in the palace – who had also been asleep for a hundred years – awake from their sleep. This may be seen as a symbol of how the 'waking' of a man's anima is the first step towards the 'waking' of all the 'sleeping' (repressed, neglected) aspects of his psyche.

Another anima figure is the seductive nymph. Ondine is one such. Ondine has no soul, and can gain one only if she can get a man to embrace her. There are many stories of mermaids who lure sailors to their underwater beds. Here we have a twofold message: Man, give life to your anima; but take care that you don't drown in your unconscious depths. Find the treasure that is there, then surface again. In other words, maintain conscious control.

A folktale animus figure is the dwarf. Dwarfs and other 'little people' work underground in mines, out of which they bring forth gold and other precious substances. This illustrates the way the animus, if cared for and nurtured by a woman (as Snow White looked after the Seven Dwarfs), will bring up from her unconscious many valuable things that will serve her well in her daily life and in her quest for self-realization.

Incidentally, marriage or sexual intercourse (or, in relatively modern and bowdlerized folklore, a kiss or embrace) symbolizes the union and intermingling of conscious ego and unconscious soul-image. It may also symbolize that complete union of the conscious and the unconscious which is the final stage of individuation. (A third possibility is that, where the anima or animus has not yet been distinguished –'rescued'– from the shadow, soul-image and shadow may be symbolized by bride and bridegroom.)

STAGE THREE: 'MANA' PERSONALITIES

Stage three is where a man meets the Wise Old Man and a woman meets the Great Mother. These archetypal images are symbols of power and wisdom. Jung calls them '*mana personalities*', because in primitive communities anyone having extraordinary power or wisdom was said to be filled with *mana* (a Melanesian word meaning 'holiness' or 'the divine').

Jung warns us that to be 'possessed' by these mana personalities is dangerous. It commonly results in megalomania. For example, a woman who allows her conscious mind to be invaded and subdued by the Great Mother will begin to believe herself able and destined to protect and nurture the whole world. Similarly, a man who allows himself to be taken over by the Wise Old Man is likely to become convinced that he is some sort of superman or great guru, filled with heroic power or with superior insight into the meaning of things.

These *mana* personalities are symbols of the power and wisdom that lie in the deep parts of our own psyche. But, like other things in our unconscious, they may be projected. For example, instead of making contact with this inner store of power and wisdom, we may choose to disown it and see it as the property of someone else, some national leader or some superman figure from modern mythology.

The right thing to do with the *mana* personality, however, is neither to project it nor to keep it suppressed, but to integrate it into your consciousness. This means enriching your life with a wisdom that is not accessible to intellect but comes from the unconscious. It also means that from now on, conscious and unconscious are no longer seen as opposites, but as two cooperating and complementary parts of one and the same psyche.

Jung speaks of stage three as the second liberation from mother (the first liberation from mother being stage two, when anima or animus is integrated into conscious life). This second and fuller liberation means achieving a genuine sense of one's true individuality.

Common symbols of the Wise Old Man include the king, magician, prophet or guru and guide. Common symbols of the Great Mother include a goddess or other female figure associated with fertility (e.g. a nude female figure with large breasts, or many breasts, or broad buttocks, or prominent vagina), priestess and prophetess. The words 'prophet' and 'prophetess' are used here in the sense of someone through whom a god or goddess speaks.

STAGE FOUR : THE SELF

This is the final stage of the individuation process and, says Jung, most people never reach it.

Jung sometimes calls this the stage of 'self-realization'; sometimes he uses the term to cover the whole of the individuation process. For the sake of clarity we might be tempted to call this final stage that of 'complete self-realization'; and there would be nothing wrong in that, so long as we remembered that it is a stage, albeit the last one, and that within this stage there is still some room for growth and development.

Stage four consists in encountering what Jung calls 'the Self'. The self has to be distinguished from the ego. The ego is the conscious mind. The self is the total, fully integrated psyche, in which all opposing or conflicting elements are united and coordinated. Bear in mind what Jung says about the relationship between conscious and unconscious: the unconscious contains the opposite characteristics or capabilities to those that are evident at the conscious level of the personality (e.g. if you are the extrovert type, your unconscious will be introvert). At this final stage of individuation conscious and unconscious become so thoroughly integrated into one harmonious whole that those things that were previously opposites and therefore – potentially, at least – in conflict are transformed.

In the case of (complete) self-realization, a person's consciousness will no longer consist simply of thinking (reasoning, 'working things out in the head') and fantasizing (just letting one's thoughts wander); it will include that immediate knowledge of reality which was formerly the property of the unconscious alone. In other words, the person's total psyche is now conscious and is now doing the knowing and the feeling and the experiencing.

Another way of putting this is to say that you are fully conscious of your body, and your body is fully conscious. And the consequence of this is a radical change in your view of life, your values and goals. You will feel completely at ease in your body. You will feel joyful and loving. You are now ***self***-centred, no longer self-centred. In particular, you will find such bliss in sheer consciousness and in just being, that you will cease to worry about achieving. You now have all you want.

Jung described this state of self-realization as follows:

> *This widened consciousness is no longer that touchy, egotistical bundle of personal wishes, fears, hopes and ambitions which has always to be compensated or corrected by unconscious counter-tendencies; instead, it is a . . . relationship to the world of objects, bringing the individual into absolute, binding and indissoluble communion with the world at large.*

As Jung describes it, this last stage of individuation resembles the state of consciousness reached by mystics through prolonged meditation. (What, after all, is meditation if not an exploration of one's total psyche?) Jung's 'Self' is a transpersonal reality – that is, although it is the ultimate reality of your own personality, it is not just that; it is something bigger, it is the ultimate reality of everything and everyone. It is what people have called God or – in the Eastern mystic-meditative traditions – the One behind the Many, the one underlying reality of which all existing things are manitesrations or (partial) embodiments.

Do not suppose, however, that self realization means being lost in or swallowed up by some greater reality (which might be suggested by the Indian image of a drop of water rejoining the ocean). Nor does selfrealization mean being swamped by the unconscious. (That would be a state of psychosis, a state of 'possession'.) Rather, it means that you are now fully conscious, but you realize that 'your' consciousness is also the consciousness that is everywhere, in all things (what in mystic-meditative traditions is sometimes referred to as 'cosmic consciousness'). The self is the ultimate in your experience of the psyche. Experiencing the self means knowing all there is to know about yourself; your life, your destiny, your meaning, and the meaning of life in general.

I have mentioned how, in this final stage of self-realization, opposites are brought together and thereby transformed. One particularly interesting aspect of this concerns the pair of opposites that we call good and evil. The contents of our unconscious may at first appear to us (that is, to the conscious ego) as evil – dark and menacing. But these same parts of the unconscious are capable of enriching and enlarging our personality. That is what they are for! The unconscious holds all those possibilities that will allow the individual to live a full life. Whether the contents of the unconscious are good or evil depends on whether or not they are integrated, taken seriously, respected and allowed appropriate expression in our conscious life.

The fourth stage of individuation is where the integration and mutual penetration of conscious and unconscious becomes complete. It is therefore the stage at which all that was (or appeared to be) evil has now become (or is now recognized as) good. If you like figurative and dramatic language, you can say that at this final stage of self-realization the Devil becomes God.

Alternatively, we might say that the Devil is now seen to have been God all the time, although we didn't realize it before. Yet another way of expressing the same point is to say that now the Devil no longer exists – because there is no longer anything evil in the psyche, and therefore no need to project that evil on to some external being.

When we come to look at symbols of this fourth stage of the individuation process, we see that most of them allow different interpretations: they can be symbols either of the final stage of self-realization or of the whole process of individuation from stage one to stage four, or of any one of those four stages. This is not really so bewildering as might at first appear. Any partial exploration of the unconscious is already a (partial) self-realization; and, as we have seen, Jung himself gives the title 'self-realization' not only to the last stage of individuation but also to the whole four-stage process.

Jung has been criticized for being too rigid and doctrinaire in dividing the individuation process neatly into four parts. The number four (and multiples of it) is a well-known symbolic number, signifying completeness, wholeness. Is that why Jung divided the individuation process into four stages? He was certainly very fond of fourfold divisions. He saw four primary functions in the human psyche: thinking, intuition, feeling, sensation. He claimed that every uninterrupted dream has four parts: setting the scene; stating the problem; movement towards a climax; the solution to the problem.

I would advise against a slavish acceptance of Jung's four stages. For some people stages one and two will coincide: their first awareness of their shadow may be accompanied by a feeling of their soul-image. Similarly, some people will find that stages three and four merge to some extent: the encounter with the deep wisdom and power in their unconscious will be simultaneously an awareness that the ultimate basis of their psyche is God, or that their psyche has a cosmic – not merely individual – dimension. And even stage four is only a completion of stage one: the whole of the process of individuation may be said to be a continued exploration of one's shadow, and the shadow does not fully disappear – is not fully integrated – until what Jung describes as stage four is attained.

The symbols of stage four commonly have their origin in mythology and religious ritual. Some express the ultimate oneness of the individual soul and God: for example, the 'birth' of a divinity – perhaps in the form of a child – in your soul, or psyche; or a holy being residing in the depths of your self – perhaps sitting on a throne; or a bridal couple, or a couple engaged in the sexual act; or a figure that has both male and female physical characteristics. These last two symbols, however, may also represent the integration of the soul-image (the 'marriage' of the masculine and feminine sides of the psyche) or the general inter-penetration of the conscious and unconscious parts of the psyche.

You will have to judge for yourself which stage of the individuation process is symbolized by these images if and when they appear in your dreams. This is not just a matter of where you think you are in the progress towards self-realization; a symbol may be telling you, not where you are, but where you should be going.

Any death-and-resurrection symbolism – a flood, or an immersion in water, being swallowed and later regurgitated by a whale, the sun being 'swallowed' by the sea (at sunset) and rising again at dawn, or the kiss of life raising a corpse, etc. – may be understood as representing the descent of the conscious ego into the unconscious and rising again as a new, transformed being. Again, whether such symbolism in your dreams means that you are near the end of the process of self-realization or that you are just beginning – or being invited to begin – must be left for you to judge.

Self-realization may be symbolized by other transformation processes, like the Ugly Duckling's transformation into a beautiful white swan, or the changing of a frog into a handsome prince.

Mandalas represent the self. A mandala is a square or a circle, usually with an obvious central point and sometimes divided into segments. It may be highly stylized, like the Hindu and Buddhist mandalas used in meditation (in connection with which they are known as yantras). For example, the Shri yantra (meaning 'supreme yantra') contains the plan of a temple with four walls and four doorways, together with upwardpointing and downward-pointing triangles representing respectively the male and female – or the conscious and the unconscious – components of the psyche, or the opposites that are believed to be united or intermingled in all reality. Any church or temple, or indeed any room – so long as it is square or circular – may be a mandala figure. So may a garden, especially if it is square or round and has a central point – for example, a fountain or a bird-bath, or a pool.

The number four is itself a kind of mandala and, therefore, a symbol of the self, since it represents the four sides of a square or the four principal geographical directions/points of the compass which in turn represent total reality, wholeness, completeness.

In any mandala symmetry is all-important. It symbolizes the order and harmony of a self-realized person.

On using Jung

All this talk about self-realization may seem too remote to interest you. If so, please bear in mind that every dream should be understood as saying something about your present situation. Symbols of self-realization may be pointing you to a goal that can be fully attained only in the future. Nevertheless, they are the response of the unconscious to your situation here and now: they are telling you what you need to do (or begin to do) now. There is nothing remote about the message of mandala dreams.

The same applies to dreams that bring up things from the past: their point and purpose is to tell you something that will solve your present problem. The American psychic Edgar Cayce even believed that some dreams bring up things from a previous existence; but the message of such dreams, he insisted, was always related to the present circumstances of the dreamer.

Broadly speaking, one might say there are two kinds of people in this world. The first is the 'self-made' type of person, or those who want to be self-made, whose sole and consuming ambition is directed towards worldly success. The second kind is those who want, not to make themselves, but to find themselves. Dream interpretation is probably going to appeal more to the second type of person than to the first. But dream interpretation is important for everyone, because everyone needs the kind of self-awareness that comes from paying attention to one's dream. Everyone has problems that can be solved only if there is a willingness to look inside oneself.

The first category – people who think and function generally in terms of what they make of themselves – divides into two sub-categories:

a the 'self-made', those who have 'made it', the outwardly successful; and
b the 'failures', those who have not 'made it' in the eyes of the world or in their own eyes.

Those in sub-category **b** will usually be filled with resentments and bitter discontent, or be kept going by some kind of hope – perhaps next week they will win the pools, or perhaps something will turn up for them out of the blue. This kind of hoping, however, is mere fantasizing; and the more fantasizing we do, the more we disable ourselves from doing and therefore achieving.

Those in sub-category **a** – the 'self-made' men and women – may eventually discover a deep craving that is not satisfied by material possessions, economic security or pride in material achievement. These things give them pleasure and happiness that last for a time, but not the inner well-being and joy that are independent of possessions and are not affected by stock markets or bank balances.

The second broad category of persons – those who are more concerned with finding themselves than with making something of themselves – are the people who are ready for what Jung calls the 'individuation' process, the journey into themselves that wild lead them to a wealth of wisdom and joy, and eventually to the core of themselves which some people call God, a realization of their oneness with Life or Nature, or the Transcendent.

(What you call this ultimate thing – how you name it – doesn't much matter. In fact, insistence on this or that name is sheer dogmatism, the same sort of dogmatism that has at times poisoned any number of organized religions. Interestingly, Jung rejected all forms of institutionalized religion because – he said – they took the symbolic poetry of myths and hardened it into intellectual dogma, which then became a substitute for the actual experiences of reality that were the starting point of religion and its *raison d'être*. In other words, Jung was against religions, but only because they hide religion from people. The experienced reality is the important thing. And those who have experienced that reality tell us that it has no form or shape, which means that it cannot be perceived by any of the five senses. It can only be 'felt', experienced directly, without any intervention of the brain – which is fed by sense perceptions. In this experience even the distinction between knower and known disappears: you are it, it is you. In short, this is a mystical experience.)

Obviously, then, people in our second category are more likely to be attracted by Jung's approach to the interpretation of dreams. But even people in our first category may eventually feel themselves ready for the most thoroughgoing exploration of their inner world. Nor is the Jungian approach just for those who are looking for the deepest layer – or, rather, the centre – of reality. It is also for anyone who feels the need to get to know more about themselves.

Gestalt Psychology

It is a mistake to be too intellectual in your dream interpreting or in your use of this dictionary. It should not be used in the way you would use the *Oxford English Dictionary*, taking in the meaning of a word with your brain alone. Bear in mind what has been said before about identifying with each dream image. That is a matter of feeling and awareness, not of thinking. What Jung calls 'active imagination' is a process of experiencing each dream symbol within yourself.

This aspect of dream interpretation is particularly stressed in Gestalt psychology, founded by Fritz Perls, who insists – as did Jung – that your dreams are about you and you alone. Consequently, says Perls, you should see every part of a dream as a part of yourself, some aspect of your personality. In other words, no part of a dream should be projected: every part of a dream is a part of you, and you must not try to pretend that it represents someone else.

For instance, if a dream contains children and adults, someone of the opposite sex, a wise and saintly old man and a ferocious wolf, you might be tempted to identify with the adults and then ask what is being 'said' to you by the other characters in the dream, thus seeing these other characters as external to yourself. Any such temptation, says Perls, must be resisted. Certainly, all the characters in a dream (and not only characters, but objects and places, too) have something to say to you; but in each and every case, what is doing the 'talking' is a part of yourself.

The wolf; for example, is probably your own animal nature addressing you: a part of your unconscious mind speaking to your conscious ego. Similarly, the wise and saintly person is not (a symbol of) someone outside you. Even if it is the image of someone you have actually known, the appearance of that image in your dream is to be seen as (a symbol of) something inside you – the intuitive or instinctive wisdom that is contained in the depths of your unconscious.

As for the children in the dream, they probably represent either some lingering remnants of childish behaviour or the innocent love of life (which you may have lost and is now demanding a place in the sun, i.e. a role in your conscious life). The same applies to that person of the opposite sex in the dream. Even if he or she has the features of someone known to you, his or her function in your dream is a symbolic one: to represent to your conscious ego either your soul-image or your shadow, or possibly your Wise Old Man or Earth Mother – all of which are parts of your own self, parts that your dreams are telling you to activate and employ in your conscious day-to-day life.

The roots of this approach to dream interpretation may be seen even in Freud. Freud's theory of the human psyche is a dramatic theory: id, ego and super-ego are conceived of as interacting like the characters in a play. The Gestalt approach to dream interpretation is simply inviting you to fall into the role of each of these in turn so that, instead of disowning some part of yourself (because it makes you feel dirty and ashamed, or whatever), you accept it by identifying with it and pay attention to what it has to say to you by actually being it and expressing it – in role play.

The Gestalt approach to dream interpretation (and to therapy in general) is typically a group approach: their 'encounter' groups are well known. The basic idea is that you take each component of your dream in turn and act it out in front of the other group members. They will then encourage you to go further into the 'character' with which you are trying to identity and so help you to overcome any resistance you may have to uncovering that hidden part of yourself that is represented by the particular dream item. You will also be helped, by the group's promptings and questions, to understand why you repressed that hidden part of yourself. As Freud pointed out, the more resistance you display towards identifying with something in your dream, the more you can be sure that that something is a part of yourself that you have disowned, and that you badly need to reclaim it and reinstate it in your life.

Another technique instituted by Perls – again, an extension of Jung's 'active imagination' – is that of getting a dialogue going between two elements (people or animals or objects, or even colours or smells) in a dream. The most efficient way of doing this is to place two chairs so that they face each other, and sit in one chair while you take the role of one element in your dream (a girl, for instance) and in the other chair when you are in role as the other element (a boy, say, or a snake). This movement from chair to chair assists in making a complete changeover from the one 'character' to the other. As the snake, you might find yourself trying to convince the girl that you are not the horrifying and evil thing she thinks you are, but a positive natural power than can enrich her life. As the girl, you might find yourself expressing and giving reasons for feelings of horror and fear towards the snake, and this might eventually lead to a discovery of a sexual anxiety.

These dialogues between two dream items will often be dialogues between what Perls called 'topdog' and 'underdog'. That means that one of the components of your dream will stand for some repressed or neglected or undervalued and underemployed part of your personality, and another component will be that part of you – the conscious ego or the super-ego (conscience) – that has been frightened or shocked and disgusted by the other part of you and has therefore repressed and disowned it. In this sort of dialogue the 'underdog' will express its point of view and claim its rightful place in your conscious life; and eventually the dialogue should conclude in some sort of cooperative agreement between the two previously conflicting parts of your personality.

The way to get rid of trouble in the psyche is not to get rid of the troublemaker (which, to repeat an earlier image, would be rather like chopping off your head to get rid of a headache) but to acknowledge the rights of that part of you that is causing the trouble: it will cease to be a troublemaker and become – what it always was potentially – a creative contributor to your happiness and total fulfilment.

Perls, it should be noted, was reluctant to talk about 'the unconscious'. Instead, he spoke of parts of the personality that were hidden from view – that is, hidden from the conscious mind. And he saw the main purpose of dreams as 'integration' – a word used by Jung to mean the achievement of personal wholeness by reinstating those parts of the personality that have been rejected or neglected.

It was Perls who insisted that whenever you tell the story of a dream you should use the present tense: 'I am at the entrance to a cave. A light is shining from the depths of the cave. I am frightened, but step gingerly inside the cave . . .' In this way you are actually reliving the dream, not merely beholding it as a past event or something external to yourself. Perls believed that every dream refers to and expresses something in your present situation, your present life, your present state of mind. The causes of a present anxiety may lie in the remote past – in infancy, perhaps – but all you need to do is to deal with that anxiety in the here and now. You do not need, as Freud thought, to uncover the starting point of the anxiety; you can find all you need to know about the anxiety by taking a penetrating look at yourself as you are now. And in this your dreams will help you.

As with any other approach to dream interpretation, my advice would be to take from Gestalt whatever you find useful. You needn't suppose that everything in every dream is a part of yourself. Probably many of your dreams will be about real people in your life and your relationship with them. However, many dreams – perhaps many more than we fancy – have a purely inward, internal reference. In these dreams what appears to be a straightforward represention of an external object or person is, in fact, some part of your psyche expressing itself – a fear or a desire, an instinctive drive, or some frustrated and neglected talent.

Note that recurring dreams should nearly always be treated as expressing some more or less long-standing inner conflict or anxiety.

Again, do not suppose that dream interpretation has to be done in a group. If there is a group in your vicinity, by all means avail yourself of its services. However, the techniques developed by Perls can easily be adapted for private use. Having other people act out in front of you the items in your dream can obviously be a powerful aid in understanding what is going on inside you. But, given determination and honesty, and by using such physical ploys as changing chairs for the different 'characters' in the dream, you can apply the Gestalt method to good effect entirely on your own.

In Conclusion

Do not fall into the dogmatism of supposing that only this or that dream theorist (Freud or Jung or any other) has the truth, and the whole truth. Take – from anyone – whatever makes sense for you. If you come to feel that this or that approach does not go far enough for you, move to another one. Use this dictionary carefully – intelligently and honestly – and your dreams will do the rest. The dictionary will tell you what sort of interpretation you might give your dreams; your dreams will tell you what interpretation you should be giving them – if you get it wrong the first time, your unconscious will try again, until you get it right.

Have faith in your unconscious; it knows best. As Jung said: 'The unconscious is nature, and nature never lies.'

DREAM SYMBOLS A–Z

ABANDONMENT FORSAKENNESS

1 If you dream of being abandoned or forsaken, the dream is almost certainly expressing your own (albeit unconscious) feelings. Perhaps you felt uncared for as a child. If so, your dreams will probably include direct or indirect references to your parents. Alternatively, the feeling may be of more recent origin. Whenever the feeling originated, it has to be dealt with now. The first and most important step is to look at the feeling as objectively as possible, as something that is living inside you but is not essential to your being. You can choose to nourish it or wave goodbye to it. What is the point of nourishing it? Self-pity is negative and destructive – though this is not to say that you should be hard and unsympathetic with yourself: you should offer love and understanding and forgiveness to yourself as well as to others.

Realize that you are not identical with your feelings: you can change them at will, and by changing them you change the quality of your life. NB To say you should look objectively at your feeling does not mean that you shouldn't employ the Gestalt tactic of identifying imaginatively with the abandoned one in your dream and thereby reliving the abandonment. Such identifying and reliving, however, are helpful and therapeutic only when they enable you to see the feeling as something you can say yes or no to, as something that is a part of you but does not have to be a part of you (for this Gestalt tactic, see Introduction, pages 58–60).

2 The abandonment may signify a loss of external guidance in your life. Perhaps circumstances have caused a rift between you and your father or mother or some other 'authority figure' from whom you previously took your moral code or other values and attitudes. The authority in question may have been some religious or other ideological set of rules and sanctions that you have now discarded.

Some people throw off one authoritarian code of conduct only to embrace another. However, if you have rejected such externally imposed codes outright, this probably means that you have become aware that you alone are responsible for your life, for any choices or decisions. Ultimately, you are the sole authority in your life: if you let someone or something (pope or guru, or social conventions, or whatever) have authority over you, it is you who choose to give them that authority. This is not to say that it is wrong to allow them that authority, only that it is you who decide whether it is right or wrong. It is no use putting the blame on people or things outside you – the Church, or the government, or some external fate or circumstances. You create yourself, you create your own happiness or misery, success or failure. Of course, there are some things that impinge upon your life that you cannot remove, but although the things themselves are beyond your control, your reaction to them is always within your control: you can succumb or not, become angry and embittered or not. There is perhaps a kind of 'destiny' or life-plan; but it is grounded in the centre of your own being, and fulfilling your destiny simply means being – or, rather, becoming – yourself. And that entails getting rid of anything that has no positive or creative role to play in the unfolding of your true nature, and nourishing and developing those parts of you – feelings, attitudes, aims, desires and so forth – that can and should contribute to a full and rich blossoming of your true self.

3 The feeling of abandonment may be the result of the death of someone you relied on (consciously or unconsciously) for your own feeling of worthwhileness, for a sense of purpose or meaning in life. If so, again – as in **2** above – you should look within yourself for meaning and worthwhileness and strength. (This does not necessarily mean a slide into extreme subjectivism. What I am recommending is a subjective method of finding the meaning of life. This does not mean that what you find by this method is a purely subjective truth, something that has no reality outside your own imagining and is true only for yourself and not for others. There may well be a meaning and a purpose – a destiny – in all things, in the totality of existing universes. However, for all but a few – e.g. advanced physicists – the experiential grounding for such meaning is to be found in themselves, their own destiny and meaning within the great cosmos.)

4 The forsaken one in your dream may represent a neglected part of you, be it an instinctive drive or a desire or ambition, or some unrealized potential. If so, try to identify it and, having identified it, try to find an honourable and appropriate place for it in your conscious life.

'LETTING GO', THROWING OFF INHIBITIONS

If the abandonment in your dream is a state of licentious abandonment, the dream is either expressing feelings or desires that you are conscious of having, or telling you that at the unconscious level of your psyche there is a demand for greater freedom, for throwing away the chains with which you (or, more precisely, your guilt-feelings) have shackled yourself. In other words, you need to let yourself go in order to find yourself.

In most cases such dreams will be referring to your sexual life (or lack of it). Please understand, therefore, that licentious behaviour in a dream is usually an instance of how dreams may use exaggeration or hyperbole as a tool for penetrating the conscious ego and forcing it to give attention to something in the unconscious that is rightfully demanding proper scope for expression in the dreamer's day-to-day life. Obviously, to let oneself go completely and continuously and relinquish all self-control may well lead to the loss of self.

ABATTOIR

Perhaps you are recalling in your dream either an actual visit to a slaughterhouse or a photograph of a slaughterhouse. In that case, it may be that what you saw on your visit or in the photograph (or read in the caption) has preyed on your mind ever since. In any case, to get at the meaning that is pertinent to you, it may be necessary to relive the dream to note your emotional reaction. Generally there are the following possibilities:

1 Raw animal flesh may signify 'raw' emotions or instinctive drives.

2 Carcasses obviously mean death.

3 If your reaction is one of disgust, it may be that you are expressing revulsion at the practice of killing animals in order to eat them. Perhaps your dream is pushing you towards vegetarianism.

Equally, however, it may be that what you find disgusting is raw animality – that is, your own raw nature bereft of its skin, the thin (or thick) veneer formed by social–moral–cultural deposits – in which case we are back at **1** above.

4 If the dream centres on the killing of animals, is it you who are doing the killing? If so, the animals probably represent aspects of your own animal nature (sexuality, pre-eminently); and your unconscious may be warning you against repressing or suppressing some natural urge.

5 Possibly the dream may be suggesting to you that you ought to forsake all fleshly pursuits in favour of 'higher' spiritual pursuits. (This remark should not be taken to imply that spirituality can be pursued only by abandoning sexual and other sensual pleasures; heightened sensuality is fairly typical among mystics, and in some Indian and Oriental mystic-meditative traditions the spiritual is sought in and through the physical.)

6 Animals were at one time – and in some parts of the world still are – slaughtered as a religious sacrifice. See **Sacrifice**.

ABBEY SEE ALSO CHURCH, HOUSE, MONASTERY, MONK, TEMPLE

1 An abbey is a holy place and represents a more profound dimension of reality than most of us are aware of most of the time. It may, therefore, be a symbol of those parts of the psyche that lie below the surface – that is, below the level of consciousness. It may even represent the self – that is, the 'true' or 'essential' you.

2 An abbey is usually an old place and as such may symbolize the older, more basic parts of your psyche. All the mental processes of perceiving, naming and recognizing things, knowing facts, following a train of thought, spinning arguments and so on are, on the evolutionary scale, recent arrivals in the world – or at any rate on the planet Earth. But there is a kind of awareness that is quite independent of these mental processes, is much more ancient and may indeed be as old as evolution itself, and often, in order to get at the truth about ourselves, we need to stop thinking and learn to rely on older modes of knowing.

Other very old, primitive parts of the psyche are the instincts for sex and survival.

ABDOMEN OR LOWER BODY

1 The abdomen may represent sexual feelings.

2 It may also represent the unconscious. Naturally, **2** may include (1), and a dream in which the abdomen or lower part of the trunk plays a significant part may be trying to get you to pay more attention, and give more space in your life, to the instinctive functions.

3 The meaning may be more specific. For example, for a professional woman the message might be that she should allow her body the biological fulfilment of sex and/or motherhood.

4 There may be some purely physiological reason for the abdomen featuring in a dream: perhaps a full bladder or indigestion.

5 If there is, in the dream, a feeling of pain in the stomach, it may represent a psychological indigestion, an inability to accept something. For example, it might be that there is some situation that you are refusing to face up to; or some lesson in life – or some word of wisdom from your unconscious – that you are not assimilating.

ABYSS

1 An abyss may symbolize impending danger, real or imagined. In either case the important thing is that the dream is expressing your anxiety. Look for anything in your present life situation – at home or at work – that may have triggered off anxiety. Otherwise, and especially if this sort of dream is recurring, look inside yourself for the causes of your anxiety.

2 A dark abyss may symbolize the unconscious. The unconscious appears to be bottomless, since no matter how deeply you delve into it there is always more depth to explore. Note the emotional 'feel' of the abyss in the dream. Are you entering it, or just standing fearfully on the brink? The unconscious may well be frightening because you are unfamiliar with it or because you have buried there some morally unacceptable or intolerably painful experience. However, the only way forward is to uncover those buried parts of yourself, face them, give them a proper hearing and, finally, allow them a proper place in your everyday conscious life.

3 The dark abyss may signify death. This may be physical death or some form of psychic death. There are times when the present ego has to be dissolved to make way for the next phase in the unfolding of a fuller, more positive self.

If you are convinced that the message of your dream has to do with physical death (and you should allow yourself to be thus convinced only after you have seriously and thoroughly considered possible metaphorical interpretations of 'death'), do not rush to the conclusion that the dream is foretelling imminent death. Perhaps your dream is reminding you of the fact of death in order to give you a new perspective on your life – which could be liberating. See also **Dead/Death**.

ACCIDENT

The accident may be a car crash, a careless dropping of a brick on someone's head, or just slipping on a banana skin. Whatever it is, you have to ask who is the victim of the accident and (where applicable) who caused it? Usually it will be you, or some aspect of you.

1 If the accident in the dream involves only you – if, for example, it is a repeat of some accident that actually happened to you – then ask yourself: am I accident prone? If you are, the dream may be expressing your worries about this accident proneness. It may also be asking you to do something about it.

Accidents are often less accidental than we think. If there were no unconscious dimension to the human psyche, then we would be justified in speaking of 'pure accidents' – unless we subscribe to the notion of some implacable God or fate that causes them. But if we accept the existence of unconscious drives, unconscious desires and motivations, then what otherwise we might properly call accidents may be seen as misfortunes we have brought upon ourselves. We may, at an unconscious level, be playing the martyr or punishing ourselves for imagined guilt. Does any of this apply to you? If so, try to discover ask your unconscious to reveal the cause of your neurotic self-punishment. The cause will almost certainly turn out to be not so much a fact as a fantasy, and any factual element in it will almost certainly be quite innocuous and innocent. If, for instance, you concluded that the cause of your guilt-feelings and consequent masochism was connected with your father's death, was it really you who killed him? Or if you think the cause is a childhood sexual desire for your mother or father, isn't that a natural part of human development, and therefore blameless?

2 If the dream strikes you powerfully as a premonition, act accordingly. Avoid whatever action might expose you to an accident of the kind depicted in the dream.

3 If the accident happens to someone else in your dream, you have to decide who that person is or, alternatively, what part of yourself is represented by that person.

If the victim is identifiable as someone in real life, then, no matter how close the person is to you and no matter how much you love that person, you should consider the possibility that the dream is expressing an unconscious hostile wish or resentment towards that person. Even if the dream makes you anxious for the safety or well-being of the person, it may be that the anxiety is a cloak for repressed antagonism towards him or her. Feelings and desires are repressed because they are felt to be unacceptable. But, however disgusting or morally reprehensible those feelings or desires may appear to you, it is better to face up to them in the clear light of consciousness than to leave them to brood and breed in the dark cellars of the unconscious. What is repressed does not cease to exist (what is out of sight is *not* out of mind!); nor does it cease to function negatively and destructively.

Siblings, as well as parents and spouse, are likely objects of jealousy and even of uncharitable death-wishes. For siblings, see also **Brother/Sister**; for parents, see also **Father, Mother**.

4 Dream accidents of a rather different kind may be mere reviewings of actual happenings: forgetting your spouse's/parent's/sibling's birthday, or failing to do in a certain situation what you normally do in that situation (e.g. complimenting a person on his or her looks or performance).What may appear to be accidental may, in fact, be the effect of an unconscious cause (see **1** above), and the dream's repetition of the 'absentmindedness' or 'inexplicable lapse of memory' may, in fact, be a prompting from your unconscious to get some inner conflict sorted out.

On the other hand, such dreams may be pure anxiety dreams, representing your fear of making such a slip. Remember, though, that anxiety can cloak unconscious anger, and it is anxiety that causes repression. (Freud began by saying that repression causes anxiety; but he later reversed that formula.) See also **Anxiety**.

ACHE SEE ALSO PAIN

An ache may mean that whatever is associated with the part of the body where the ache is felt, is receiving inadequate expression.

ADVERSARY SEE ENEMY

AEROPLANE SEE ALSO FALLING, FLYING

1 An aeroplane may be a sexual symbol, representing the penis by virtue of its forceful penetrative motion.

2 The symbolism of an aircraft may be the same as that of a bird: liberation, release, transcendence. See **Bird**, sections **2** and **4**.

AGGRESSIVENESS

1 If you behave aggressively in a dream, then either your unconscious is telling you that there is some aggression in you that you have not acknowledged fully or that you need or ought to be in some sense aggressive: more self-assertive, more in conscious control of your life and circumstances, less passive or subservient, less submissive or fatalistic. Do you tend to be unnecessarily or inappropriately aggressive towards people, for example, when the shop assistant ignores you or you find that you have been sold a faulty article? If so, perhaps there is a history of feeling rejected or undervalued. Are you – in your dream – aggressive towards your wife/husband /partner/parent/brother/sister? If so, the dream may be expressing unconscious resentment or jealousy towards that person. Unconscious hostile wishes towards someone closely related are very common.

2 If you are the victim of the aggressiveness in the dream, the message may be that you are in a situation – at home or at work – that is threatening to destroy or diminish you. In that case, you must get yourself physically out of that situation.

Bear in mind, however, the possibility that everything in your dreams represents some part of you. Therefore, look for some part of you that is aggressively disposed towards the rest of you, or towards some other part of you. Perhaps, for instance, there is some guilt-feeling which causes (another part of) you to be angry, either against yourself or against other people. (Anger and guilt often go together, as the two sides of the same coin; anger frequently stems from guilt, and guilt from anger.)

3 If the aggressor in the dream is not yourself, the meaning of the dream may be that there is some part of your psyche – some instinctive urge, perhaps – that has been neglected or repressed and is now getting rebellious. Sympathetic control of instincts is good; keeping them in chains is bad, and can only lead to trouble. Identify and get acquainted with the rebellious element in yourself, and engage in honest and receptive dialogue with it. See also **Fear**.

Freud spoke of an 'aggressive drive' which showed itself everywhere, in sex as well as in war. For Jung's contemporary, Alfred Adler, this aggressive power-drive was the most fundamental force in the psyche. Aggressiveness, however, may be sublimated; it may be tamed and directed into creative channels. I don't know to what extent entrepreneurial enterprise would qualify as creative, but it is certainly an expression of aggressiveness a few degrees less savage than the crudest forms of physical aggression. Less ambiguous examples of sublimated aggressiveness are problem-solving of all kinds, scientific research, artistic work and making love. (Making love is almost invariably to some extent forceful, even when it is also tender or indeed reverential. On the other hand, brutal love-making is a contradiction in terms, and usually results from emotional or sexual repression.)

AIRPORT

1 As a place of departure for foreign lands, an airport may symbolize (a desire or need for) a new departure in your personal or working life, a new venture or, indeed, adventure.

2 The foreign country could represent the unconscious, in which case your dream is probably advising you to explore your psyche more fully in order to establish your true identity and true goals. See also **Alien, Travel**.

AIR-SEA RESCUE SEE ALSO SEA

1 The sea may represent your mother. If you need to assert your independence from your mother, therefore, the dream may mean that rescue is at hand – rescue from the possessive psychological grip of your mother. See also **Mother**.

2 The sea may represent the feminine in general. In this case your dream may be drawing your attention to (the need for) some remedy for an imbalance in your psyche caused, for example, by insufficient assertiveness. See also **Woman**; and see pages 47–51 on anima/animus.

3 The sea may be a symbol of the unconscious. In this case, the aircraft in the dream may symbolize reason rescuing you from a hitherto uncontrolled sea of emotions – uncontrolled because unrecognized and repressed.

NB To be 'rescued from the unconscious' means only to put an end to a situation in which your life is being determined and shaped by forces outside your control (a situation symbolized by drowning). It does not mean that the unconscious is itself a negative, harmful thing. On the contrary, it is your unconscious that is telling you – in the dream – that something has gone wrong in your life and what you must do to put your house in order.

4 For Jung the first stage of the individuation process (see Introduction, pages 45–47) is the establishing of the person's individual ego-identity, and this involves a struggle of consciousness to lift itself out of the all-encompassing darkness of unconscious existence. See also **Drowning**.

ALIEN

1 A person of foreign appearance or encountered in a foreign land may represent some part of the psyche which is unfamiliar to you. You will need to get acquainted with that 'foreign' part of yourself if you are to realize a happiness or satisfaction that has so far eluded you. The first step, of course, is to identify the 'alien': what part of you is it that has been neglected and is now courting your attention?

The foreigner may symbolize the whole of your unconscious psyche, rather than a particular part of it.

2 Journeying to or in a foreign country may represent an inner journey, an exploration of the unconscious, the not yet discovered or integrated realm of your being. No matter how advanced you are in self-exploration, if you are still exploring you are still entering foreign territory (but see also **Travel**).

If the foreign country in the dream is one you have visited in real life, the significance of its appearance in your dream may lie in what you associate with that country or what feelings you have about it. Of course, the same could apply even if the country was one you had never been to, so long as that country had particular associations for you.

3 What is 'alien' in the sense of 'unfamiliar' often carries emotional overtones of 'alien' in the sense of 'enemy'. Getting acquainted with the 'enemy', however, will result in making the (potential or actual) enemy a friend. There is no part of your psyche that will harm you so long as it is not neglected or repressed. If you learn to love yourself – the whole of yourself, all your components – you will have no internal enemies.

The alien may not be an adversary at all, but a helper. It may be that your alter-ego has something of value to offer you, if only you will be courteous and hospitable to this hitherto neglected part of yourself. See also **Fear, Journey, Travel**.

ALONE(-NESS)

1 If your aloneness in the dream is painful, your dream is probably expressing your fear of being alone, or resentment at being shut out from warm human relationships or being out on a limb at work.

2 If the aloneness feels good, the meaning is probably either that you need to 'go it alone' or that you need to be alone (from time to time, at least) in order to achieve greater personal equilibrium. Perhaps the physical setting of the dream will give the crucial clue. For instance, if you are alone in a landscape of mountains and valleys and far horizons, your aloneness is probably a positive factor that you need to cultivate in order to find (new) direction in your life. If, on the contrary, your loneliness is enclosed by four walls (perhaps with a window looking out on to anonymous people in the street), the dream is probably forcing you to take stock of your unhappy situation and to look for causes and cures.

ALTAR

1 An altar, besides being a place of sacrifice, may represent both death and resurrection. What happens at the altar in your dream may give you the clue to its meaning. If you or someone else is being sacrificed on the altar, ask yourself what part of you must 'die' if new life – fuller, happier, more satisfactory life – is to be made possible. See also **Sacrifice**.

2 The altar may symbolize a wedding. Possibly the wedding may be a psychic one: a (needed) union of opposites, of conscious and unconscious, to compensate for a one-sided development of personality. See also **Marriage**.

ANAESTHETIC

1 An anaesthetic may symbolize some kind of death-wish or some longed-for escape from painful circumstances. See also **Dead/Death**, section **4**.

2 Alternatively, the dream may be telling you that you need to get into the habit of letting your consciousness go to sleep occasionally so as to allow the unconscious to have its say.

ANCHOR

1 An anchor may express a desire for security, for someone or something reliable in your life.

2 Possibly, the anchor symbolizes a constraint that prevents you from fulfilling yourself. For example, it may symbolize your mother if you are still 'tied' to her, still dominated by her or too dependent on her, so that you have not been able to find or express your own individuality or some unconscious programming that holds you back from exploring and releasing hidden aspects of yourself. (The sea may symbolize the unconscious, or mother.)

ANGEL

Angels, spirits, demons and the like may feature in dreams either as symbols of blessing or warning or as symbols of parts of yourself which could lead you to greater fulfilment or, if neglected and scorned, could severely damage your chances of happiness.

1 Is the angel in your dream a guardian angel, well disposed towards you and perhaps offering you help or protection? If so, see it as a propitious sign, or as a symbol of something in your (as yet) unconscious psyche that can remove obstacles and advance your progress towards fulfilment and happiness.

2 Is the presence of the angel sinister and disquieting? If so, try seeing it as something within yourself that is going to erupt and cause trouble if you do not pay attention to it and allow it proper expression in your life.

3 It is just possible that your dream is a premonition: that the angel is the angel of death. But, although dreams are frequently clairvoyant in the root sense of the word ('clear-sighted'), and contain intuitive insights, only rarely do they foretell the future in any physical sense. What they frequently do is to give warnings about the likely consequences of persisting in certain habits of behaviour or attitude. It is most likely that the meaning of the angel in your dream is to be found along the lines of **1** or **2** above.

ANGER SEE AGGRESSIVENESS

ANIMAL(S) SEE ALSO ENTRIES FOR PARTICULAR ANIMALS; E.G. BEAR, CAT

1 Parents may appear in dreams in the guise of animals. The animal will then usually be a focus for the dreamer's ambivalent – love–hate – feelings towards the parent. For example, a spider or a cat may signify the threatening aspect of a mother from whose influence you need to liberate yourself.

Two of Freud's most famous patients had animal phobias, as did a patient of Sandor Ferenczi (a member of Freud's inner circle). One dreamed of white wolves in the branches of a walnut tree outside his bedroom window and the other had strong ambivalent feelings (fear and attraction) towards horses; the third was obsessed with poultry. Freud concluded that in all three cases the animals were father surrogates: in each case the person's feelings for his father had been displaced on to animals.

2 Animals may represent other people, besides parents. What you associate with the particular animal – slyness or aggressiveness or whatever – may be a characteristic of the particular person; the way you react to the animal in the dream may express your (perhaps unconscious) feelings towards the person.

3 Animals in dreams may be symbolic of some primitive – 'animal', or even 'beastly' – part of your psyche: some instinctive urge, for example. Thus, if in the dream your emotional response to the animal is one of fear, this would seem to indicate a fear of the instinctive urge (which, because of the fear, has been repressed).

If the animal has a threatening appearance, it may be a symbol of the danger that threatens the peace of the psyche when some part of it is neglected and confined to the 'cellar'– the depths of the unconscious – and not allowed proper expression at the conscious level. This situation may also be symbolized by the figure of a caged or wounded animal: we sometimes control our instincts too tightly or even maltreat them, and, just as animals are never more fierce or dangerous than when wounded, so it is with our 'wounded' instincts.

A view well worth considering is that we cannot – without detriment to ourselves – dispense with our animal nature, any more than with our 'higher' or 'spiritual' nature. The way to achieve peace and happiness is to allow both these sides of our nature to develop and find fulfilment in and through each other, in a symbiosis in which body and spirit, instead of going their separate ways, cooperate with mutual respect, each supplying means for the other's fulfilment.

4 A threatening or ferocious animal may represent aggression or anger buried in the unconscious. If you think this may be so in your case (perhaps because you are prone to irrational, disproportionate outbursts of rage), look for the origins of the aggression. It may go back to early childhood: a child's desire for a parent and its consequent jealousy and resentment towards the other parent may result in feelings of guilt, which in turn give rise to a desire to punish oneself. This aggressiveness directed against oneself (i.e. masochism) may then spill over into aggressiveness or rancour towards other people (i.e. sadism), especially loved ones or people closely related. Typically, an unresolved Oedipus complex (the ambivalent, love-hate feelings of an infant towards a parent) may display itself in later life in a similar ambivalence towards a spouse – an inability to love someone without simultaneously wanting to punish him or her.

Contradictory feelings towards others are a sign of inner conflict, usually a conflict between desire and conscience. And what we call conscience may be a morbid censoring and prohibiting mechanism set in motion by a childhood fear of punishment. This needs to be distinguished from a healthy conscience, which consists of all those moral guidelines we give ourselves by rational reflection. Some compromise between desires and the need to survive and succeed socially is almost inevitable; but a reasonably negotiated compromise is far preferable to the potentially dangerous inner tension that results from submitting to irrational phobias posing as the moral law.

5 A tamed animal, or the act of taming an animal, may symbolize (the need for) that kind of controlled expression of instinct that is appropriate for living as a part of civilized society or for feeling that you are 'king of the castle' – that is, in control of your own actions.

6 The wolf in the Little Red Riding Hood story exemplifies another piece of animal symbolism. The wolf here represents for a sexually inexperienced woman the terrifying aspect of the male, the fear of sexual contact. In its earliest versions the story possibly served as a warning to young girls against socially premature sexual relations with men. Animals in dreams may certainly have a sexual meaning and the wolf is an obvious example of this, if only because the word 'wolf' is itself commonly applied to men whose sexual lust is unbounded and purely 'animal'. See also **Frog, Wolf**.

7 If in your dream you are being chased by an animal, the animal probably represents some (repressed) emotion or instinct. As long as you keep such things buried in your unconscious they will continue to plague and disturb you. Face up to whatever it is, and enter into receptive and patient dialogue with it.

8 The killing of an animal may symbolize either what has been described in **5** above (but now given exaggerated, dramatic expression) or the actual destruction of some essential, because natural, part of your psyche. The second alternative would indicate some fear of your own instinctive nature, some phobic undervaluing of the body, the senses, or sex. You would have to be very honest to work out which of these alternatives – an irrational slaughter (repression) of the natural self (a symbolic castration), or a rational taming of an instinct that is threatening the balance of the psyche – is applicable in your own case.

ANTICLOCKWISE

1 Anticlockwise movement, being contrary to the sun's motion, may signify that you are going against (your) nature, taking a wrong direction, pursuing a wrong path in life.

2 Going towards the left, which you would be doing if you were following an anticlockwise curve, may signify moving over from a cerebral to a more intuitive or instinctive approach to life.

ANTLER

The antler is a symbol of male sexuality, or of (male) aggressiveness.

ANXIETY SEE ALSO FEAR

When anxiety features in a dream it may be just that – straightforward anxiety. On the other hand, it may be a disguise for some repressed aggression or resentment.

Let us say you dream of the death of a loved one, and you wake up in a sweat and frantic with concern about that person (partner, parent or whatever). It may be that the anxiety you felt in the dream and/or on waking from the dream is what Freud called a defence mechanism – that is, a ruse we adopt for protecting ourselves against unbearable, unacceptable feelings. The first time we experience a strong negative feeling against someone near to us, we tend to 'put it out of mind'. In reality, however, what happens to such banished feelings is not they disappear; rather, they remain with us, in the unconscious part of our psyche. Rejection of feelings because they are morally repugnant or terrifying in their possible consequences is what Freud called 'repression' or 'suppression'. (Remember: suppression is a conscious act, repression an unconscious act.) What causes us to suppress or repress a feeling of hatred or jealousy or resentment, or a desire to kill or hurt or perform some other socially proscribed act, is anxiety – anxiety about the consequences. Therefore, whenever anxiety reappears in our dreams we need to look for possible repressed feelings or desires that brought the anxiety about in the first place.

'A dream is a (disguised) fulfilment of a (suppressed or repressed) wish,' said Freud in his epoch-making book ***The Interpretation of Dreams***; and this, he went on, applied even – no, especially – to so-called anxiety dreams. Freud is wrong, of course, in over-generalizing: many anxiety dreams are quite straightforward undisguised expressions of fears for someone or about some situation. However, do not assume that Freud is wrong with regard to any particular dream before you have honestly examined both your dream and yourself with a view to finding (which may mean recollecting) a negative desire that might be lurking behind the dream's cloak of anxiety.

One of the categories of dreams that Freud classified as 'typical' is the death of a person of whom the dreamer is fond. Such dreams, said Freud, always represent the dreamer's wish that the person should die. Between brothers and sisters there is often jealousy, and wicked wishes arising in childhood may be harboured in the unconscious for a very long time – for as long as we care to leave them there. The same applies to the jealousy and hatred a young child may feel towards a parent.

It may be that your dream of a loved one dying is prompted by a recent worry about the loved one. But dreams whose contents are determined by recent experiences may express feelings that have a long history in your life. Indeed, it could be that, if the loved one in the dream is your partner, any jealousy or hatred you may be feeling towards him or her may be the jealousy or hatred you felt as a child towards your parent of the opposite sex, now. transferred to your partner. Repressed hostile feelings have a way of repeating themselves in one situation after another, with one person after another (see Introduction, pages 19–20).

APE SEE MONKEY

ARM(S)

AS LIMBS

1 Arms are what we do things with. They therefore represent our ability or effectiveness, creativity or usefulness.

2 Aches or pains in the arms may symbolize feelings of inadequacy, or a loss of self-esteem.

FIREARMS SEE GUN

ARMOUR

Armour may symbolize efforts to protect ourselves against emotions that fill us with anxiety. Whereas the armour on an animal or a tank protect against external dangers, the armour-plating we construct is a defence against internal threats. Needless to say, such construction is misdirected labour: the 'foes' within must be disarmed, but this can be done only by accepting them, which means, first, acknowledging their existence, and secondly, entering into dialogue with them, giving them a fully sympathetic hearing.

ARROW SEE DAGGER

ARTIST

A painter or other artist may represent the (unfulfilled) creative and/or intuitive side of your nature.

ASCENT SEE ALSO CLIMBING, LADDER, MOUNTAIN

1 Climbing a ladder or steps or a mountain, or going up in a balloon or a lift, may signify simply high achievement; an arduous mountain or rock-face climb may signify the accomplishing of a hard but rewarding task.

2 The significance of the ascent may lie in the wider, more comprehensive (or more god-like) view of things gained by the ascent, signifying a possible transformation of your own life through changing your view of life in general – or by putting a problem in perspective, seeing it in a more detached and less emotional way.

3 High ascent – to the top of a mountain or high in the sky – may symbolize the gaining of (or a desire for) a more spiritual, less worldly perspective or lifestyle.

4 On the other hand, an ascent in the air may represent a state of mind that is too idealistic, or too much in the grip of fantasy. The dream may be telling you that you need to anchor yourself more firmly in reality, that you need to 'come down to earth'. For 'earth' you might need to read 'body': the dream might be telling you that you are in danger of lopsided development through too much emphasis on the head – intellect, thinking – and too little on the senses and instincts. See also **Flying**, section **4**.

5 What is ascending in your dream may represent something that is rising from your unconscious into your conscious mind. This interpretation would be indicated if the thing was rising from a deep place or surfacing from the depths of the ocean. That something is coming up from the unconscious into consciousness is good: it is giving you a chance to become aware of desires and anxieties that you have previously ignored (perhaps deliberately).

NB Anxieties are often associated with repressed desires. Desires are repressed – rejected from the conscious mind – because they gave rise to anxiety (perhaps in the form of guilt-feelings or fear of punishment).

6 A special instance of **4** is where what is rising symbolizes libido or psychic energy. This interpretation would certainly be suggested if what was seen rising was a snake or serpent. (In Hindu thought, the serpent Kundalini –

feminine – lies coiled in the base of the abdomen; from these genital regions she may be induced, by meditation and breath control, to rise through various psychic centres to the crown of the head. This represents the bringing of the sexual–psychic energy into union with consciousness – thought of as masculine. The opposite process may then be induced: the conscious ego descends into the unconscious psychic depths. And so the twofold process may continue, up and down, until there is a complete mixing of the mental–spiritual and psychic–physical factors.)

ASS

1 The ass may signify stupidity – your own! Track it down. In what respect, in which department of your life, are you being a silly-billy?

2 It may be a symbol of animal impulses, not in any aggressive or savage sense, but in the sense of what is pre-rational, non-intellectual – in other words, unconscious, intuitive.

In folklore, animals may have visions and speak with great wisdom. In dreams the humble ass or donkey may be telling you that you need to return to nature and observe the natural law of your being.

3 Tony Crisp (*Dream Dictionary*) mentions the ass as a symbol of 'tine plodding, long-suffering body'. Yes, but also remember that the body may eventually kick out at you if you go on neglecting or maltreating it.

AUTUMN

1 Autumn is the transition from summer and harvest-time to winter, the season of death. It may therefore symbolize the ending of (a particular kind of) achievement; a time to stop getting and concentrate on being; maturity.

Autumn is also a time for tidying the garden and digging in manure for new growth in the following year. So in the process of personal development the message of autumn may be that the cessation of some kinds of activity is a prelude to growth in other areas of one's life; and that accumulated 'rubbish' – non-productive or counter-productive habits and attitudes – must be got rid of, to make way for new growth.

2 The occurrence of autumnal scenes in your dreams may coincide with your own 'autumn years', the second half of life. If so, remember that trees bear fruits in autumn, and autumn has a beauty of its own.

AVALANCHE

1 What is being expressed in an avalanche dream is probably a fear of disaster, or a warning of impending disaster. Identify carefully with the avalanche itself and with the other images in the dream, to identify the object of the fear or warning. Is it, for example, a fear of failure? See also **Failure, Flood.**

2 If the avalanche is of snow or ice, it may symbolize 'frozen' emotions.

AWAKENING

If you dream of waking from sleep, this may be a symbol of a new awareness that is either already dawning in your life or needs to be allowed to dawn.

AXE

1 Does it feel like an executioner's axe? If so, the symbolism is of punishment and judgement. It may be that you are morally anxious about something you have done or intend or desire to do.

2 Alternatively, it may be your job that is being axed. Are you in danger of – or fearful of – losing your job?

3 Is the axe being used to fell a tree? If so, this may be a symbol of the stopping of (old) growth (in favour of potential new growth) – where 'growth' may mean some area of endeavour and achievement.

B

BABY SEE ALSO BIRTH, CHILD

1 A baby commonly appears in the dreams of pregnant women. Usually in such cases no symbolism needs to be looked for.

2 In other women's dreams a baby may express (unconscious) desire for a baby.

3 The baby may represent your own vulnerability, or your need for love. This applies to both men and women. When the 'baby' within you – the hurt, frustrated self – cries out, it is very difficult to look at yourself objectively, but an effort must be made to see this frightened or rejected child as a part of yourself that needs your love. It may be that this self-pitying part of you is crying out for another person's love, but in the first place, at least, the love must be given by you: you (the conscious, decision-making ego) must positively love yourself (the sensitive, hurt 'child' within your psyche). Only that way will the child in you grow up and mature.

4 A baby may symbolize your pure, innocent, true self: what you really are – or were intended to be – as distinct from what various kinds of conditioning and wrong choices have made you.

5 The baby may represent some new development in your personality or in your personal life.

BACK

1 The back parts of anything – a building or a body, for example – may symbolize those parts of your personality that are hidden from view, buried in the unconscious because they are disapproved of and rejected as inferior or disgusting, or because they are frightening, disturbing, threatening. Are these parts of you really inferior or shameful; and what is it that made you feel they were? You must learn to get in touch with your deep emotional needs, and this means communicating with the parts of yourself that have been pushed to the 'back' of the mind.

2 The human back – unless it is bent – may represent moral uprightness and physical or moral strength. A bent back is probably a sign that you are (feeling) overburdened or downcast. What is it that prevents you from holding your head high and opening yourself to life? Is it guilt-feelings, causing you to punish ourself? Is it your parents, your boss, or someone else who won't 'get off your back' and keeps on imposing his or her choices and values on you? If a situation is getting you down, seriously consider getting yourself out of it physically.

BACKWARDS

Moving backwards – on foot or in a train or car – may mean you are getting further away from your (true) goal. Perhaps you are too preoccupied with the past and its associated failures, rejections, guilt-feelings and resentments. As long as your present response to life is conditioned by traumatic events in the past, there is no possibility of either peace or personal fulfilment. Wounds inflicted by past experiences will heal only when you learn to live in the present, neither anxious about the future nor angry about something in the past.

BAG LUGGAGE

Being a receptacle and therefore womb-like or vagina-like, a bag may be a sexual symbol. What may determine for you the meaning of the bag in your dream is your feeling about what is in the bag, or what the bag is for.

BAGGAGE SEE LUGGAGE

BAKING

1 Baking a loaf or cake may be a symbol of pregnancy.

2 Since 'pregnancy' and related words such as 'birth' and 'baby' may be used metaphorically, the baking in your dream may represent the opening of a new phase in your personal development, a new idea, a new perspective on life or new attitude towards (yourself and) life.

BALLOON

1 A hot-air balloon in the sky may symbolize either (a desire for) freedom from the problems associated with your daily existence, or the achieving of an objective, detached or more spiritual view of things.

2 Coloured party balloons may symbolize rejoicing and happiness: something to celebrate.

BANANA

May be a sexual symbol, representing the penis.

BAND SEE ORCHESTRA

BAND SEE ALSO VAULT

As a storehouse of wealth, a bank may symbolize the (stored up, not yet used?) potential of your psyche.

BAPTISM

In the dream it may be the baptism of another person, child or adult, or you may be the one baptized. In either case, though, the meaning refers to you.

Whatever the particular form of the baptism, the principal symbolism is that of death and resurrection/rebirth, the ending of one stage of life and the beginning of another, or the letting go of something in order to take hold of something new and (for you, now) better.

Baptism may be a symbol of self-realization. Through the death of the old and false (because partial) self-image, a new self – the true self – is achieved. (In the religious ritual of baptism the immersion in water represents death and the emergence from the water represents resurrection, new life. The myth of the Flood shows baptismal symbolism on a cosmic scale: water and fire are the great purifiers, making new life-forms possible by destroying the old.) See also **Baby, Drowning, Flood**; and Introduction, page 46.

BARRIER SEE OBSTACLE

BASEMENT SEE CELLAR

BASKET

1 Like other receptacles and hollow things, a basket may be a symbol of the feminine. See also **Woman**.

2 A basket full of fruit or other provisions may symbolize well-being. An empty basket, besides symbolizing the feminine, might represent (unconscious feelings of) personal emptiness.

BAT

NOCTURNAL ANIMAL

1 As a creature of the night and – for many people – frightening, a bat may symbolize something in your unconscious, possibly some part of you that has been repressed because of its association with an early traumatic experience.

2 Alternatively, it might symbolize intuitive wisdom. (The bat seems to navigate without the aid of ordinary vision.)

CRICKET OR BASEBALL BAT

A cricket or baseball bat may symbolize either male sexuality or aggressiveness.

BATH

1 The symbolism may be that of baptism. See **Baptism**.

2 If the imagery of bathing or washing yourself recurs in your dreams, then almost certainly it indicates neurotic guilt-feelings.

3 Otherwise, and particularly if the washing is of the body and not just of the hands, it may symbolize the getting rid of old and negative attitudes/habits/emotional reactions.

BATON SEE CONDUCTOR, OFFICER, STICK

BEAR

1 A bear may symbolize the feminine side of a man's psyche. See also Introduction, pages 47–51; **Brother/Sister**, sections **4–6**.

2 A bear may also symbolize mother, either your actual mother, or the wisdom that is available to you in your unconscious. See also **Mother**.

3 Alternatively, simply take the bear as a symbol of your unconscious and try to work out – from the dream action – what particular aspect of the unconscious is being presented to your attention: for example, the functions of feeling, as distinct from thinking or fantasizing; or an intuitive oneness with Nature.

BEARD

1 Beards may symbolize virility and male sexuality. In a man's dream, therefore, a very hairy man may symbolize the dreamer's own libido or primitive psychic energy. (Yes, in real life beards may sometimes be worn as a substitute for virility, and to compensate for the lack of it, but this only underlines the original association of beards with virility.)

2 A bearded old man in your dreams must be listened to: he probably represents the profound but practical wisdom that resides in the depths of the psyche. (God has sometimes been represented as a bearded old man.) See also **God, Wise Old Man/Woman**.

BEAST SEE ALSO ANIMAL/MONSTER

A beast may symbolize your own 'animal nature'. If so, it probably means that you take a low view of instinctive forces ('the Beast', after all, is a traditional name for the Devil or Antichrist). You – the conscious ego – therefore need to begin to interact creatively with your unconscious (your body and your primal psychic energies) and give it more value and more expression in your conscious life.

BEHEADING

Like any other form of execution, beheading may symbolize punishment. We often punish ourselves, unconsciously, as a result of guilt-feelings connected with some traumatic experience in childhood or early adulthood. The dream, therefore, may be showing you a negative pattern in your life that needs to be dealt with.

2 Alternatively, beheading may signify a need to get free of a too dominating head: you may have been relying too exclusively on intellect – in which case, you need to give more room in your life to instinct.

BIRD SEE ALSO ENTRIES FOR PARTICULAR BIRDS: E.G. EAGLE, FALCON.

1 A bird may represent the sweet directness and simplicity of Nature, unpretentious and contented 'is-ness'. In this case, your dream may be telling you what you need to make room for in your life and in your fundamental attitudes. For example, the bird may be seen (or, indeed, heard) as calling you to an uncomplicated but holistic state of being, in which consciousness and body – spirit and matter – are completely attuned. This call will undoubtedly come if consciousness (brain) has become detached from the more primitive or primal layers of being (body, instinct, Nature).

2 It may be that the bird signifies an entry into, or an invitation to enter, realms of spiritual power (symbolized by the sky). (In religious traditions that focus on a supreme sky-god – as in pre-modern Siberia – there is invariably a shaman, a person who is regarded as maintaining order and well-being in the human community and in the individual by maintaining a proper communication between the human world and the spirit world (see also **Spirit(s)**.) The shaman is said to fly – to make contact with spirits or the sky-god himself – and his emblem is often a bird, sometimes worn in the form of a bird-mask.) See also **Flying, Shaman**.

3 Because of its association with the shaman figure, a bird may symbolize some energy or function within your psyche that can bring you healing or wholeness or balance.

4 If the bird in the dream is taking wing, ask yourself if you, or some part of you, needs to take wing. Perhaps you are beginning to feel shackled by circumstances. Perhaps it is a particular component of your unconscious psyche that needs to be given its freedom – that is, accepted into consciousness and incorporated into your (external) life. (Sky is often a symbol of consciousness, contrasted with earth or sea, which may be symbols of the unconscious.)

5 If the bird is descending from the sky to you, you may need to consider another piece of bird symbolism. In mythology a bird, or a winged god (like the Roman Mercury), may serve as a messenger from the supreme deity. In psychological terms this may mean your dream is letting you know that

your unconscious is offering you some great truth, some recipe for your healing, a solution of your problem(s), or the key to a new and fuller life.

Sometimes such a messenger bird is associated with the sun. The sun is a natural symbol of the source of truth ('light') and of new life.

6 Possibly, a bird may be a sexual symbol. Freud saw it as a symbol of the male penis; and for men who are accustomed to speaking of attractive women as 'birds', a bird in a dream may presumably have sexual meaning.

7 A black bird, in addition to representing in a general way something in your unconscious, may symbolize the feminine in a negative aspect. See also **Woman**.

8 Carrion birds – vultures, crows, ravens and the like – are associated with death. Dreams do sometimes predict an event in the outside world, but such dreams are rare. If death is referred to in a dream it is more likely to express your anxiety about death – your own or someone else's.

Alternatively, the unconscious may be telling you that some phase of your life, some habitual attachment or negative attitude, has gone on long enough, and the time is ripe for a change. In other words, the dream is calling for the death of something within you, to make way for a new development in your life and/or in your personality. See also **Vulture**.

BIRTH

1 If you are a woman, the birth in your dream may refer either to an unfulfilled desire for a child or – if the associated feeling is bad – to an unwanted pregnancy. Otherwise, it will almost certainly represent some possibility of new experience (inner or outer) and new personal growth.

2 Just possibly it is your own birth you are dreaming about. If so, it might mean, especially if you are depressed, that you are asking why you were born. But don't miss the opportunity to relive your dream and note the emotions – positive or negative – associated with the birth. By 'reliving your dream' I mean closing your eyes and taking yourself all the way through the dream again.

'. . . the act of birth is the first experience of anxiety and therefore source and model of the affect of anxiety' (Freud, *The Interpretation of Dreams*). This idea of birth as the prototype of all anxiety, which all later feelings of anguish revive and reinforce, was developed by Otto Rank (*Trauma of Birth*), who singled out the birth trauma as *the* decisive psychological event and the ultimate origin of all neuroses. So, it may be worth asking yourself if the birth image in your dream could possibly be associated with an anxiety, either conscious or repressed. For example, it might be that such an anxiety-associated birth image is telling you to sort out some unfinished business with your mother – by which I mean what your mother symbolized for you as a child or young adolescent, as well as your real relationship with your mother as she actually is or was. (Even when dead your mother may live on in your psyche, perhaps preventing you from being your own person. In such cases some people find it helpful to ask their unconscious to let them meet their deceased mother in dreams, where they can engage in dialogue with her.)

3 For Jung, birth, life, death and rebirth all function as symbols of aspects of what he calls the 'individuation' process, which is the development of the human psyche to full maturation, wholeness and harmony (see Introduction, pages 44–55). In Jungian terms, therefore, birth may symbolize the beginning – actual or potential – of a new phase in your personal development. If you feel some such intimation of a possible new phase in your life (inner or outer – though for Jung the stress is on the inner), you would be well advised to work seriously and purposefully towards its realization, even if this means giving up something: the death of something – an old negative attitude, old anxieties or guilt-feelings, for example – is nearly always a precondition of new life.

4 Birth may represent the waking of the ego – that is, consciousness. This might be the obvious meaning if the image of birth in your dream was in some way associated with light (e.g. the sun). In mythology the sun-god dies – is swallowed by the ocean (which is a common symbol of mother/the feminine/the unconscious) – and is reborn daily. In the same way, the conscious ego must die and be born again, submerge in the unconscious and rise again renewed or transformed. Only thus can one grow inwardly, in wisdom and strength and wholeness (see also **Sun**).

Understood in this way, the birth image may still have connections with mother or mother image (as in **2** above): the ocean commonly symbolizes mother, or simply the feminine. If you are male, the feminine symbolism may refer to either your mother or your anima, the feminine side of your personality (for anima, see **Brother/Sister**, section **6**, and Introduction, pages 47–51).

5 Giving birth in a dream may symbolize the (sometimes painful) process of bringing something new into your life, fashioning a new lifestyle for yourself, achieving a greater degree of maturity, or releasing and expressing in an appropriately creative way some psychic function hitherto repressed. See also **Baby, Child**.

BITING

1 Biting is a symbol of aggressiveness. If you are doing the biting and it feels good, the dream may be expressing anger that arises out of repression. What is the repressed part of you that is craving – and undoubtedly deserves – recognition and expression in your outer life?

2 If you are being bitten, what is 'biting' you? What is bothering you in your life, or what is the inner problem that you need to resolve? Bear in mind that everything in a dream is usually an aspect of yourself. Therefore, both what is biting and what is being bitten need to be both identified and reconciled. In other words, the biting means there is some inner conflict, which will usually be between your conscious ego and something in your unconscious.

BLACK

1 A black hole or dark depths – for example, an unlit cellar or a deep well or oceanic depths – may represent the unconscious. This blackness may be frightening, so long as the unconscious remains alien and unfamiliar. However, black can also he warm and comforting – which is why insomniacs are sometimes advised to close their eyes and imagine themselves wrapped round in black velvet. If you begin to trust your unconscious (which means trusting Nature), each previously horrifying or disgusting part of your unconscious will show itself in a new light, as something you need for personal fulfilment. Putting your consciousness into the unconscious – becoming aware of it – means putting more and more light into the darkness. If a star or other bright light appears in the blackness, this may be seen as a 'light at the end of the tunnel', that is, as a symbol of the 'illumination' – new wisdom or insight – that may be achieved by dwelling a while in the unconscious and making its better acquaintance.

2 Black (particularly for white people) may symbolize evil. If so, bear in mind that, as a general rule, what appears in your dreams is always some part of you, and that the so-called 'evil' (and therefore repressed) parts of you are really evil only if, because of neglect, they become rebellious, or if you let them take control away from your conscious self. These 'evil' things are transformed into good things – creative, and bringing fuller life, happiness and wholeness – when conscious and unconscious interact and establish a harmonious working relationship.

NB It is only Judaism, Christianity and Islam that have a thorough-going dualism of good and evil, and a matching moral dogmatism. In the earliest known forms of religion, and in traditions (such as the Hindu, Buddhist and Taoist traditions) that have not cut themselves off from their early roots, good and evil are opposite but equally necessary components of reality; and in mystical traditions (including Jewish, Christian and Islamic mysticism) even God is described as a coming together of opposites – good and evil, but also masculine and feminine.

3 A person dressed in black may represent your shadow (see Introduction, pages 45–47).

4 A black-skinned person (if you are white-skinned) may represent either the shadow or closeness to Nature.

5 A black animal probably represents some unconscious repressed drive or emotion. If the animal is fierce, this possibly means that something you have repressed is now urgently pressing you to give it your conscious attention and let it have some expression in your waking life.

6 Blackness (as in a black night, etc.) may simply signify diminished visibility, in which case the meaning of the dream may have something to do with a loss of orientation in your life. Do you feel you don't know which way to go; or that you don't have the energy or will to go in any direction? If so, make a pact with our unconscious to the effect that, if it will tell you where you have the potential – and the need – to go, you will respond accordingly in your life. Then pay close attention to the dreams that follow. (If you go the next few nights without dreaming – or, more precisely, without recalling any dreams – this probably means that you are backing out of the pact and setting up a defence against what you tear your unconscious might have to tell you.)

7 Black may symbolize despair or deep depression. If so, follow the advice given in **6** above.

8 In many parts of the world black is associated with death. It is possible, therefore, that this is what the colour signifies in your dream. Bear in mind, however, that death in a dream may refer to something internal: the 'death' – or the giving up – of something within you (for example, some irrational fear, or other negative attitude or emotion). See also **Death**.

BLIND

If a blind person appears in your dreams, the reference will almost certainly be to some blindness – lack of awareness or understanding – within yourself.

1 Ask yourself what you are turning a blind eye to. Is it something external– some problem in your work or in your domestic partnership? Lack of success in one job or in one relationship does not necessarily mean that you are a failure. It may mean only that you are failing or not getting fulfilment in that particular job or relationship. So look for another, more suitable one. On the other hand, what has gone wrong in your external life may be an effect of some repressed material in your unconscious, so see **2** below.

2 Are you refusing to see what is going on inside you? Obviously, what is going on inside you – emotional conflict, for example – may be a result of your present work or domestic situation. It may, however, have a long history – perhaps the conflict, or guilt-feelings and failure-programming, or self-denigration or whatever, started in childhood. Whatever it is, face up to it; stop ignoring or evading it. First, identify it and then try to get back to the time in your life when it first showed itself. It may be difficult to trace repressed material to its origins without the help of a psychotherapist. But make a real effort, asking your unconscious to reveal more of itself, and more clearly, in your dreams (or, for that matter, in meditatioll). The unconscious is not your enemy, it is there to assist and guide you in your quest for happiness and wholeness. It is repressed desires, festering within your unconscious, that are your enemies, and even they are enemies only so long as you continue to ignore and neglect them.

3 Being blind may mean not knowing where you are going and/or a feeling of helplessness. In that case, you need to challenge the 'you' that is making excuses for not taking control of and accepting responsibility for your life. Take this 'you' in hand. You are not blind: you can see very well what is going on in your psyche – if you want to.

BLIND ALLEY SEE CUL-DE-SAC

BLINKERS SEE HORSES, SECTION 4

BLOCK(AGE)

A blockage in a dream – a traffic jam, for example, or a blocked throat preventing you from speaking – almost certainly signifies a blockage in the free flow of your psychic energies. Identify with and be the thing in your dream that is being blocked; and, having in this way made acquaintance with the blocked energy (desire, instinctive drive or whatever), resolve to give it proper scope for expression in your conscious life.

BLOOD

1 Blood may be a symbol of life, or, if shed, of death, and therefore – if on one's hands – of guilt.

2 Blood may also symbolize passion, especially love or anger.

3 Possibly the blood is (displaced) menstrual blood. By 'displaced' I mean that what you are really seeing in your dream may be menstrual blood even though it appears as just a pool of blood on the pavement or a nosebleed. If you are a woman, such a dream may be expressing a sexually related anxiety; if you are a man, it may express your horror – that is, far – of sex and/or women.

4 Drinking blood means receiving (new) life or strength. (In religious ritual, symbolically drinking the blood of a sacrificed human or animal may symbolize participation in the life and power of God.)

BLUE

1 Blue may sometimes symbolize the universal or collective unconscious (as distinct from the individual unconscious). (See Introduction, pages 43–44). Perhaps the dream is asking you to base your life on intuitions that come from a deep source within your psyche.

2 Alternatively, blue may represent the power of the conscious mind, particularly if it is the blue of the sky.

3 Dark blue may be associated with depression – 'the blues'.

4 Blue clothing may symbolize masculinity. Tony Crisp (in his *Dream Dictionary*) observes that women sometimes dream of threatening men dressed in blue – dark blue or navy. Such a dream should motivate the dreamer to get in touch with her animus (the masculine side of her own psyche; see Introduction, pages 47–51) and enter into dialogue with it, with a view to establishing a more positive relationship both with the masculine in herself and also with real men in the extemal world. Perhaps examining her relationship with her father will be the key to understanding her negative attitude towards men and masculinity.

5 The blue sea may symbolize the unconscious or the feminine (anima, mother, or Great Mother). See also **Mother**. For anima, see Introduction, pages 47–51, and for Great Mother, see pages 51–52. See also **6** below.

6 At an advanced level of mystical awareness, I understand blue may represent the primal energy from which the universal life-force comes. (In mythology the primeval ocean is that from which all other things arise; though, strictly speaking, the primeval ocean is not itself a thing: it is without form or shape but contains the potential for all forms and shapes.)

BOAR

1 If the boar in your dream strikes you as ferocious, perhaps it represents some part of you that is struggling for recognition, some buried instinct or desire that is defying your attempts to kill it. Perhaps its defiance is justified: perhaps you need precisely that part of you that now appears so wild and threatening. It is threatening only because it is threatened! Talk to it, and listen to it; then it may reveal itself as a valuable aide in your quest for happiness or fuller self-realization.

2 If you associate fertility with the boar, the symbolism may be straightforwardly sexual. On the other hand, the fertility in question may be of a more metaphorical kind: the giving of life to those repressed parts of yourself that frighten you. (Yes, ferocity symbolism may coexist with sexual or fertility symbolism, just as in real life aggression is often mixed in with our sexuality.) These hidden repressed things may be desires or instinctive drives associated in your life with some traumatic experience.

3 It may be the animality of the boar that strikes you. The animality probably refers to the primitiveness or social unacceptableness of some repressed and buried part of your psyche (see also **Animal**). Animality symbolism, ferocity symbolism and fertility symbolism may all combine in the boar image. That which frightens you by its animality may be precisely what you need if you are to get rid of an inner conflict and find peace or fulfilment.

4 If you associate evil with the boar image, the evilness may be in the eye of the beholder. In other words, if the boar has sexual overtones for you, its evilness may represent your own (irrational, repressed) feelings of abhorrence, disgust, fear or guilt about sex. If so, you might want to dig into your past to discover the roots of those feelings. Ask the unconscious to assist you in the search, and pay special attention to your dreams over the next week or two.

5 The boar may represent an aggression that you have not come to terms with in yourself. Aggressiveness may be a good thing – if tamed and properly employed. If it is 'wild', however, it can seriously damage your relationships with other people. And, strangely enough, aggressiveness is frequently directed against oneself: in fact, sadism usually has its roots in masochism. So do take notice of your dreams, to discover the sources of any aggression you encounter in yourself. Have a dialogue with the boar and find out what he wants. Sometimes aggressiveness may be traced back to an Oedipal conflict. In the case of a male, the infant desire for mother and accompanying jealousy towards father may give rise to guilt-feelings which in turn may generate a compulsion to punish oneself. The masochistic desire to hurt oneself may then spill over into sadistic desires to hurt other people, particularly those close to us. All this may occur at an unconscious level, so that it is only by taking a look at our unconscious (in dreams) that we can unravel the thread of cause and effect.

BOATS

1 Because of their connections with water, boats may symbolize (some aspect of) the feminine, either with a plainly sexual reference or with reference to the unconscious (in the case of a male dreamer, the reference may be specifically to the anima), or with reference to mother or Great Mother (for anima, see Introduction, pages 47–51; for Great Mother, see pages 51–52). See also **Mother**.

2 Leaving one's own shores for a foreign country may symbolize entry into the unconscious insofar as the latter is unknown and frightening – alien, in fact.

3 If the boat is crossing a narrow stretch of water, it may symbolize death or some other transition: for example, moving from one phase of life to another, or making a new start and a clean break from the past. See also **Dead/Death, Ferry.**

4 If in the dream you miss the boat, the meaning would seem to be obvious: you have failed to take advantage of an opportunity that has offered itself – perhaps an opportunity to open new vistas in your life.

BODY

1 If the body is your own and clothed, it almost certainly represents your ego, your conscious self.

2 If it is yours and unclothed, the meaning will usually be determined either by the context, that is, the *situation* in the dream; by what, if anything, you are doing with your body; or by what, in the dream, you are feeling. For example, if you are exposing your private parts to members of the opposite sex, this may signify a desire for sexual relationships; or, if you feel embarrassed at being 'on view', it may signify a fear of the other sex. If there are no sexual connotations, nudity may represent (a feeling of) vulnerability. See also **Nudity.**

3 If it is someone else's body, the chances are that it represents some (hidden) part of yourself. If the body is of the opposite sex from you, it may represent your soul, your anima or animus (see **Brother/Sister**, sections **4–6**, and Introduction, pages 47–51).

4 A dead body may signify either that some part of you is as good as dead, usually because you have suppressed or repressed it (for repression/suppression, see Introduction, pages 19–20), or that you are harbouring (unconscious) hostile feelings towards someone, or that you are anxious about death. See also **Dead/Death.**

5 For parts of the body see particular entries: for example, **Abdomen, Head.** Generally speaking, the lower half of the trunk symbolizes sexuality, instincts or the unconscious. The chest may symbolize emotions; but female breasts may also represent sexuality or motherhood, or mother. The head may represent intellect, rational – as distinct from intuitive – thinking. If only one of these parts of the body appears in a dream, the meaning may be either that you need to give much more attention and much more scope to that part and the functions associated with it, or that you are currently giving attention and scope exclusively to that part, at the expense of other parts of your psyche. For example, if the head appears on its own, the meaning may be that you are too exclusively intellectual and are giving insufficient expression to your deep needs, feelings or instincts.

BOG

1 The symbolism is pretty obvious. You need to ask yourself what you are currently bogged down in.

2 If in the dream you are up to your waist in a bog or marsh, the meaning may be that you need to activate or express some instinct or unconscious desire, some part of your 'lower' nature.

BOMB

1 A bomb may be a symbol of some unconscious emotional force – for example, sexuality, or aggression. Repressed desires or drives are likely to explode eventually, causing perhaps a lot of hurt to yourself and others. Deal with them now by giving them your conscious attention and allotting them some place in your daily life. Don't wait for the explosion – except in the dream itself: in all nightmarish dreams it is a good idea to stay with the dream to the very end, instead of waking up before the frightening conclusion (the explosion; hitting the ground after falling from a height; or whatever it might be). If you wake up from such a dream before it is finished, you are probably shirking some issue in your personality or in your external life.

2 If the bomb is an atom bomb, the dream may represent your anxiety about the way things are going in the world. On the other hand, even anxiety about the atom bomb may be a symbolic representation of deep anxiety about yourself. Some dreams allow both an objective external interpretation and a subjective-internal interpretation.

BOOK

The meaning could be either positive – wisdom or valuable knowledge – or negative – mere opinions, mere theories, superficial learning. The feelings you have about the book in the dream will guide you to the appropriate meaning.

BOSOM/BREAST(S)

1 Possibly the symbolism is straightforward, pointing to a desire for love or sex.

2 It or they may symbolize your mother, who gave you birth and nourishment. But are you too attached to her; does your attachment prevent you from achieving a properly independent individuality?

3 The bosom or breasts may be those of Mother Earth, that is, the source of (new) life. In this case the dream is probably beckoning you to look inside for sources of renewal and growth. Mother Nature dwells within us: not in our consciousness, perhaps, but in our unconscious depths – the source of life, growth and healing.

BOSS

1 If your boss appears in your dreams, the meaning could have something to do with your real-life relationship with him or her.

2 On the other hand – particularly if the boss is a man – he could be an authority figure symbolizing your own super-ego (for super-ego, see Introduction, pages 15–16).

3 If you are the boss in the dream, the one who is behaving in a masterful, bossy way, taking charge of things and giving orders, either the dream may be showing you what you are like in real life, and urging you to relate differently to people, to be more gentle and receptive, more ready to cooperate (rather than command) or even to submit to another's teaching or guidance, or it may be asking you to be more assertive than you are in real life. Provided you are honest with yourself, it should not be difficult to decide which of these alternatives applies to you.

BOTTLE

1 The symbolism may be Freudian: a bottle represents a vagina.

2 If the bottle is not empty, the meaning may be provided by the contents – wine, for example, or poison. See also **Poison, Wine.**

3 If the bottle is empty, it probably represents your own (feeling of) emptiness. Do you feel drained, exhausted? Has all the enjoyment gone out of life? If so, ask your unconscious to put you in touch with appropriate inner resources, then observe your dreams carefully over the next week or so.

BOTTLENECK

This may symbolize something that is obstructing the free flow of energy in your psyche – or, indeed, in your body. (Physical tension, as exponents of acupuncture or acupressure will tell you, commonly has psychological causes.) See also **Block(age).**

BOX

1 For Freud a box, like anything else that is hollow, represents the womb or the vagina and is therefore a feminine and principally sexual symbol.

2 A box may also represent yourself, your own psyche. Opening the box would signify a resolve to get to know yourself. If the box contains something precious, it probably represents your true or essential or deep self, a rich store of energies and powers and wisdom and love.

3 If the box in the dream fills you with fear – like Pandora's box, from which all kinds of pestilential things came – there are at least three possibilities:
(a) It may symbolize your unconscious. The powers, instinctual drives and buried emotions that are kept out of sight in the unconscious layers of the psyche are things that have at some time in the past – possibly in childhood – frightened you or been associated with frightening experiences. The way forward is to cultivate their acquaintance and give them their proper place in your conscious life.
(b) If you are a man, the box may represent the negative aspect of woman (or the feminine) as the feared *femme fatale* luring you to destruction, or the possessive and devouring mother depriving you of your independence. In that case, you need to become acquainted with the feminine side of your own nature (anima) and/or come to terms with and deal with your (buried) feelings towards your mother (for anima, see Introduction, pages 47–51 and **Brother/Sister**). See also **Woman**. (For man, woman is an ambivalent reality, desired and feared. In mythology, Pandora exemplifies this ambivalence – as do most goddesses. 'Pandora' means 'all-giving' or 'all gifts' and was probably originally a name given to the Earth Goddess, giver of all life. It was only later – at a stage of development where male deities were the supreme gods and female deities had been demoted to subservient roles – that Pandora was seen as a symbol of woman as the source of evil.)
(c) It may represent any source of disaster. Is there anything within you or in your home or working environment that is threatening you or making you anxious?

BRAWNY MAN SEE HE-MAN

BREAST(S) SEE BOSOM/BREAST(S)

BRIDAL PAIR SEE MARRIAGE

BRIDE SEE ALSO MARRIAGE

This may be an anima figure, in a man's dream, representing the feminine side of his psyche. It is vitally important for a man to make contact with and integrate his anima, since it is a neglected anima that is mainly responsible for projections, whereby we construct a world out of our own (repressed) fears, etc., thus isolating ourselves more and more from the real world (for anima see **Brother/Sister** sections **4–6**, and Introduction, pages 47–51; for projection, see page 31).

BRIDEGROOM SEE ALSO BRIDE, MARRIAGE

This may symbolize the animus (in a woman's dream), representing the masculine side of her personality (for animus, see **Brother/Sister**, sections **4–6**, and Introduction, pages 47–51).

BRIDGE SEE ALSO CORRIDOR, CROSSING

Freud lists four meanings of the bridge symbol:

1 It may represent the male sexual organ, which 'bridges the gap' between male and female sexual partners

2 It may also symbolize birth – that is, the crossing from 'the other world' to this, or from womb to independent existence.

3 It may represent (something that leads to) death – that is, a return to the womb, or to 'the other world','the other side'.

4 It may symbolize any sort of transition in the dreamer's life. Freud gives the example of a woman who wants to be a man, and consequently dreams of bridges that don't quite reach the other side of the river. However, the symbolized change may be something that can be achieved more easily, but still possibly requiring will and determination; for example, a change of lifestyle, or a passing from middle years into old age.

To Freud's list we may add the following:

5 The bridge is a means of crossing a river, and even perhaps crossing from one country to another – foreign, new, strange – country. It may therefore symbolize a critical juncture in the dreamer's life, a situation that calls for a definitive decision, a decision which may be of such a radical kind that it could well be described figuratively as entering a new country.

6 If the bridge you are crossing seems in danger of collapsing, this may reflect your anxiety about a transition in your life: for example, about whether you are going to be able to go through with a change from living on your own to living with a partner (or the reverse); from one job to another; from one set of values to another.

BROTHER/SISTER

1 If your brother or sister appears in a dream you have to decide whether the dream is saying something about your actual brother or sister and your relationship with him or her, or whether your brother or sister stands in the dream symbolically for something else – some part of yourself. If the former is the case, it may be obvious to you: recent encounters with your brother or sister, or some piece of news about him or her may be recognized as prompting the dream. Always be on the look-out, though, for those dreams where a brother or sister plays a symbolic role. The dream source may choose its materials – its images – from your recent external experiences, but what those dream images represent is nearly always some part of, yourself. So please read on.

2 In early childhood a brother or sister is a natural object of jealousy and hatred. In the eyes of a small child the mother may seem to be favouring his or her sibling. When a second child is born, the firstborn is especially likely to develop hostile feelings towards the new rival for mother's attention and affection. Sometimes we carry such jealous grievances (at an unconscious level) into adult life, where they continue to affect our behaviour and attitudes. It is then imperative that we sort them out, face up to them, acknowledge them for what they are, and so liberate ourselves from their damaging influence (see **3** below, second paragraph, on projections).

3 An elder brother or sister (brother for a male dreamer, sister for a female dreamer) may represent your 'other self' ('alter ego'), that side of your personality that has so far been neglected and undeveloped. Jung called it 'the Shadow'. We start adult life with a self-image that is usually some sort of compromise between what we want to be or do and what parents or society at large seems to require of us. If this self-image corresponds to our actual abilities, all may be well for a while; but a time may come when we need to give attention to other facets of our (potential) self. These other facets – our Shadow – will show themselves to us in dreams; and one form they take in dreams is that of an elder brother or sister.

People often project their shadow on to a sibling of the same sex as themselves; and if it is not projected, it may express itself in all kinds of awkward and embarrassing ways – astonishing rudeness, for example, or other antisocial behaviour. The contrast between your conscious ego and your alter ego may be as startling as that between Jekyll and Hyde. Don't be alarmed, though: remember always that your unconscious is your ally – your best friend – and even the most frightening or appalling things that reveal themselves in dreams as parts of your unconscious are frightening or appalling, first, because of their unfamiliarity and/or secondly, because, having been neglected and locked away in the dark, they tend to behave like a neglected child and may become mutinous (on this phenomenon, see **Demon**). Pay proper attention and proper respect to them, and their threatening features will disappear; they will prove themselves valuable supplements to your personal equipment for coping with life and achieving full satisfaction and wholeness. Introduce them into your consciousness, identify them and their needs, and give them a controlled and appropriate part to play in your waking life.

Incidentally, one test you can apply to check whether you have a neglected shadow-self is to ask yourself if there is some characteristic that you particularly dislike in other people (particularly your partner): a domineering tendency, perhaps, or an over-liberal attitude, or whatever. If there is (and of course you need a lot of honesty to admit this), then that characteristic is likely to belong to your shadow-self. We tend to project on to other people the dark, 'nasty' things that live in our own unconscious. If something is going wrong in our life, we tend to put the blame on to other people, the government, or our parents; we look for some scapegoat to carry the blame. The blame, however, is ours, because we have not put our own house in order: we have not paid due attention to the demands of our unconscious and have not allowed our 'other self' proper scope for expression in our life.

4 When a female dreams of a brother, or a male dreams of a sister, the brother/sister may represent what Jung called the 'soul-image', which is the masculine side of a woman's personality (her animus) or the feminine side of a man's personality (his anima). There would seem to be very basic differences between man and woman arising out of different biological functions (as well as less basic differences that owe their existence to social conditioning,). There are what have traditionally been called feminine qualities and capacities (such as gentleness, a caring disposition, creativeness, cooperativeness and relatedness, intuition) and, similarly, what have been called masculine qualities (such as aggressiveness and competitiveness, rationaliry, and a tendency to analyse and look for differences). However, it is widely accepted nowadays among psychotherapists that the male psyche also contains feminine qualities and the female psyche also contains masculine qualities, albeit often dormant and neglected, or repressed. If you are a man, do you admire the 'masculine' type of woman ? If you do, you may be in need of redressing the balance in your psyche: your feminine side has possibly swamped your masculinity, and you now need to promote the latter. In your case, the anima will be rather masculine. This is just one instance of a general rule: the animus/anima will have the opposite characteristics to the conscious self-image.

Either male or female dreamers may find themselves in a dream in an heroic relationship to an anima/animus figure. A man may, in a dream, rescue a damsel in distress; a woman may waken a dead prince with a kiss. These should be seen as invitations to incorporate your anima/ animus into your conscious functioning, to rescue it from oblivion and neglect: to make Cinderella or the Frog-Prince your partner in life. Personal wholeness cannot be achieved without this. See also **Cinderella, Frog**, section **3, Marriage**.

5 A sister in a man's dream or a brother in a woman's dream may take the dreamer into some frightening abyss, to the bottom of the sea, or into a dark forest. This may represent the man's anima or the woman's animus leading the ego into the unconscious, to discover, for example, the deep emotional causes of a psychosomatic illness; the repressed rage that lies at the bottom of a chronic boredom; or the fount of energy or wisdom that can furnish a more fully satisfying existence. Literary and mythological representations of this can be found in the examples of Beatrice, who led Dante safely into hell and out again, and Ariadne, whose thread enabled Theseus to find his way out of the Cretan labyrinth after slaying the Minotaur. Both hell and labyrinths are symbols of the unconscious. See also **Labyrinth, Monster, Underworld**.

6 Sometimes the anima/animus figure in a dream may appear in some way hostile or threatening. For example, in a man's dream the anima may take the form of an enchantress, a *femme fatale*, seducing men into a lake or ocean. The watery depths may be seen as symbolizing the depths of the unconscious. The meaning of such a dream may be that the dreamer needs to explore his other – unconscious – self, despite (or, more accurately, because of) its frightening and threatening aspect. Water, however, is a symbol of the feminine, too. The meaning of the dream, therefore, might be that the dreamer is too heavily fixated on his mother and needs to liberate himself by asserting his masculinity and independence; in extreme cases the man might be in danger of being 'possessed' or 'swallowed up' by the feminine within his psyche. Such a dream may be, however, not a warning, but an invitation: the unconscious may be urging the man to get on better terms – equal terms – with the feminine side of his psyche. Give your anima/animus equality, and it will cease from its mutinous attempts to take over the whole of your psyche.

In the case of a woman, a dream may contain a male seducer: some Pied Piper animus figure. Again, the dreamer will have to decide whether such a dream is a warning or an invitation: a warning against being carried away by her masculininy (perhaps she has not resolved her early father fixation), or an invitation to discover and utilize her neglected masculinity. Commonsense and, above all, honesty should guide her to the correct understanding of the dream; and in any case, bear in mind what was said above about giving equality to the anima/animus.

7 The unconscious compensates the conscious mind. It contains those qualities and capacities which the conscious mind lacks. In this sense it is the opposite of the conscious mind; hence its otherness, its alien appearance.

It follows, therefore, that the image that represents anima or animus in a dream may be the opposite of the psychological type to which the dreamer belongs. For example, if you are a woman of the intellectual type (i.e. if thinking is your strong point at the conscious level), your animus may be represented in dreams as a sentimental type (a romantic Don Juan, for instance). If you are a sentimental woman (moved at the conscious level mainly by feelings – including moral feelings), your animus may show itself as a bearded professor or other intellectual figure. If you are an intuitive woman (an artist, for instance), your animus may take a muscular he-man form in dreams (the sensational type, functioning most strongly at the sensory level).

8 If brother and sister appear together in a dream, this may symbolize either the tension of opposites, or the union of opposites. The opposites are the conscious and the unconscious contents of the psyche. Their union and interfusion are the means by which the self – the true self that is already within you but waits to be unfolded – is realized.

The appearance of this symbol will usually be an auspicious sign, meaning that, despite all appearances to the contrary, there is within you a latent and attainable order and harmony. But of course you – the conscious ego – must make that latent order real by paying loving attention to the needs of your unconscious opposite (like the prince who wakes the sleeping beauty with an embrace).

BROWN

1 Brown is an earthy colour and may, therefore, symbolize the instinctive or the sensuous.

2 Brown is also an autumnal colour and as such may signify a (feeling of) decline; low spirits or depression.

BRUSH

1 In both senses of the word – undergrowth, as well as the implement with bristles. The brush may be a sexual symbol, representing pubic hair. (In Australia a girl or young woman is sometimes called a brush.)

2 A cleaning brush may be saying something about your attitude towards cleanliness or tidiness. Are you obsessed with these things? If so, what guilt-feelings are you trying to hide?

3 Are you brushing your teeth? If so, perhaps it is saying you need to be careful about how you speak to people; or perhaps you are anxious about getting older. See also **Teeth**.

BUDDHA

A Buddha figure will probably signify either your true self or the wisdom that lies in the unconscious and beyond reach until you resolve to get better acquainted with your psyche, or the healing required for your conflict-ridden psyche. In this case, the Buddha may also symbolize the wholeness which is the end-result of the healing process, bringing all the previously warring forces of the psyche into a harmonious coexistence and cooperation.

NB Here we are concerned with psychological phenomena, but I am not suggesting that the Buddha figure or any other deity figure may not stand for something beyond the individual self of the dreamer. Such figures represent a transcendent Ultimate Reality. However, the experience of that transcendent reality may be an inner experience.

BUILDING SEE HOUSE

BULL

1 In a woman's dream the animus may appear as a bull (for animus, see Introduction, pages 47–51, and **Brother/Sister**, sections **4–6**.

2 The bull may refer to your masculinity (whether you are a man or a woman). If you are a woman, it may refer to the opposite sex – perhaps expressing your (unconscious) feelings about men in general or a particular man.

3 Animality may be symbolized. A man may experience his own sexuality as something bestial, getting in the way of his 'higher' pursuits; an object of disgust or fear.

Similarly, a woman may, consciously or unconsciously, see male sexuality as nasty and brutish; the same may apply to other aspects of masculinity – for example, the fighting, competitive aspect.

If a woman dreams of being chased by a bull, the meaning may be that she is afraid of sexual relations with men. The bull may represent the woman's father – in which case she may need to dissolve her father fixation. In any case, the woman would need to assert her femininity, not repress it: her own confident femininity has power to tame wild male lust and transform it into tender sensual adoration.

4 The taming or tethering of a bull may signify the harmonious integration of your animality, especially your sexuality, or the whole of the hidden, unconscious part of your psyche. See also section **8** below.

5 The sacrifice of a bull may signify a victory (achieved or needed) of spirituality over animality. Sacrifice is the relinquishing or transforming of something in order to attain something more desirable. But the mere killing of a bull might signify the repression of emotion or instinct, or of your masculinity.

6 Is it the proverbial bull in a china shop: the accident-prone blunderer, the person who never seems to have any luck and for whom everything goes wrong?

If so, the image may be seen as a warning that you need to change your self-image – which may entail changing your job or even your domestic situation. It is no good thinking of making a living as a concert pianist if you have fingers missing. Take an honest look at yourself and build your career and your life on your strong points, not your weak ones. Give up your fantasies and take a good look at reality Pay special attention to your dreams: they may now begin to reveal to you your real strengths – buried talents, perhaps, that need to be dug up from your unconscious. (On persona, see Introduction, page 40.)

Resist putting the blame for your 'bad luck' on someone or something else. Perhaps what we call 'bad luck' is actually brought about, not by chance, but by our innermost attitude towards life, which in turn is generated by a negative attitude towards ourselves.

7 The bull may symbolize fertility (as in mythology). Your unconscious has the power to bring about new life if you allow it to penetrate your conscious mind.

8 The bull may represent the self (in the Jungian sense, Introduction, pages 52–53), your true nature. Yes, those depths of the psyche that are despised or feared by the conscious ego may eventually be seen – by dint of constant self-exploration – as your true self.

(There are links here with **4** above. There is a famous series of Zen Buddhist drawings depicting the finding, tethering and taming of an ox, representing the search for one's true nature and its discovery and realization through wrestling with and controlling one's wild and stubborn egoistic self.)

BURDEN

1 What load are you carrying through life with you? Guilt collected from childhood traumas? Whatever it is, drop it. Stop playing the martyr.

2 Is there some person on your back – in real life? If so, tell him or her where to get off!

BURGLAR SEE ALSO ROBBERY

A burglar entering a house or room probably represents something in your psyche that is trying to break into your consciousness. Obviously, you need to converse with the burglar figure, to see what it is that demands your attention, and what can be done to satisfy its legitimate pleas for expression in your life.

BURIAL SEE ALSO DEAD/DEATH

1 Who is being buried? If it is someone close to you – for example, your partner – then some unconscious, buried resentment towards that person may be expressing itself. Don't be alarmed by the discovery that your emotions towards the person are ambivalent: emotions often oscillate between opposite poles. Just ask yourself what it is you resent. If it is something actually in the person, have it out with him or her. But is it something you have projected on to that person – some resentment against life in general, that has perhaps been with you since childhood? (For projection, see Introduction, page 31.)

2 Is it a (recurrent) dream of the actual burial of a real-life person – mother or father, perhaps? If so, you probably need to clear your emotional system of any troublesome feelings attached to that person – guilt, hatred, or whatever. It is all right for the dead to live on inside you; but don't let them disturb your peace. If you love the person, there is no problem. If you hate the person, learn to forgive: he or she probably did the best he or she could. If the feeling is guilt, forgive yourself. Why expect the impossible?

3 Is it you who are being buried in the dream? This may be a symbolic expression of a fear of being overwhelmed by unconscious forces. If so, the first step should be to get (better) acquainted with any repressed emotions that are threatening – or seem to be threatening – to take control of you. This done, the next step would be to establish control over them. But this does not mean simply burying them again.

You may wish to trace the emotions back to their origins, to the experience that first gave rise to them. It may be that an objective appraisal will rob the emotions of their menacing power. Should you feel unable to cope with the emotions, consult a psychotherapist or an understanding friend.

4 If it is you who are being buried it may be that the tomb is a womb. That is to say, the burial may symbolize a mother-attachment that is preventing you from achieving a proper independence and fulfilling your individual 'destiny'.

5 The burial may represent a need for a radical reconstruction – a death and resurrection – of the self: All creation involves destruction: in order to shape the clay into the desired form, the potter must first destroy its existing form. The same applies to personal reconstruction: the old self must die – sometimes painfully – if the new self is to be born.

6 Even if it is someone or something else that is being buried, that person or thing may symbolize some part of yourself that you have rejected and buried in your unconscious (for repression and suppression, see Introduction, pages 19–20.)

BUTTERFLY

This may be a symbol of your real, true self.

C

CAGE

What is in the cage – whether person or animal or bird – almost certainly represents yourself or some part of yourself.

1 The cage may symbolize the (felt) restrictions of your present life situation. But the restrictions may be self-imposed, albeit by means of unconscious processes – for example, internal prohibitions arising out of irrational guilt-feelings.

2 Some part of you may be crying out for liberation. (For repression and suppression, see Introduction, pages 19–20.) Wild and dangerous animals are kept in cages. It is likely, therefore, that what is caged in your dream is a part of you that frightens or disgusts you by its animality. Refusal to accept that you belong to the animal kingdom may result in your living in your head entirely, with the body – primitive energies and drives – locked out of consciousness. But a disembodied head, cut off from Nature's vital energy and Nature's wisdom, can only lead to trouble. Particularly in the West, where for two centuries even religion has rejected Nature (the feminine side of God), we desperately need to get closer to Nature, not remove ourselves even further from it.

3 On the other hand, a bird in a cage may represent frustrated spiritual aspirations. Perhaps you are spending too much time and energy in work that brings you only money. Any contradiction between **2** and **3** is only apparent. You can't climb – even to spiritual heights – without your body, without the primal energy and wisdom of your unconscious. To attain the 'higher', first go 'deeper'. The liberation – uncaging – of our deeper psychic contents so that they become part of our conscious equipment will enable us to transcend the limitations of our past and present.

CANDLE

1 A candle may be a phallic symbol.

2 A lighted candle might symbolize enlightenment, or a search for truth. The darkness illuminated by the candle might be what Jung called the

'Shadow'; in which case the dream would be an invitation to explore the unfamiliar and perhaps frightening regions of your psyche.

3 A burning candle may express your awareness or fear of death or of growing old.

CAR

1 A car in a dream usually represents yourself and, in particular, your effectiveness in controlling your life, attaining your goals, etc. If you are driving the car, this may symbolize taking charge of your own life. (Remember that a dream may be either depicting patterns of behaviour that already exist or recommending to you a new pattern.) If someone else is driving, the dream may be expressing your over-dependence on others.

2 A car may be a sexual symbol, representing the penis – especially if forceful motion is emphasized in the dream, or if the car is travelling through a tunnel. See also **Crash**.

CASKET SEE TREASURE

CASTLE SEE HOUSE

CASTRATION PAGES 28–30

ON CASTRATION AND THE OEDIPUS COMPLEX

1 In a man's dream castration may mean he has lost, or feels he has lost – or might lose – his sexual drive or his manliness. Self-castration is not uncommon. It is a result of fears arising from some traumatic experience of sex, or feelings of guilt or disgust bred by early indoctrination.

2 Occasionally, in a man's dream, castration may express homosexual inclinations, or some kinds of disenchantment with his masculinity (which includes other aspects than sexuality: ambition, drive, aggressiveness, competitiveness, relying on head rather than heart).

CAT

1 The meaning of a dream about a cat may depend on what you associate with cats. If you are afraid of them in real life, they may represent in dreams things you are frightened of in yourself. But remember that a real-life fear of cats may be a symptom indicating a fear of some aspect of the femininity that cats generally symbolize: your mother, your own femininity (whether you are a man or a woman), your unconscious psyche, Nature's energy or wisdom, the ultimate mystery of life and death and rebirth.

2 The feminine in its various aspects may be experienced as both positive and negative. The cat may represent the positive, creative – fertile – aspect of the feminine. (In mythology cats are often associated with fertility goddesses.) The dream might be pointing to the possibility of new growth in your personality through a fuller integration of your anima, perhaps (if you are a man), or through a greater reliance on intuition or dream messages.

However, the cat may also symbolize the negative, 'catty' or destructive aspect of femininity. If feminine characteristics in you are repressed, they will probably present themselves, both in dreams and in waking life, in a negative way. For example, a man whose femininity is not integrated into his conscious life may behave in a destructively catty way towards other people.

3 A black cat may have associations of good luck and prosperity or of evil. (Cats are associated with witches, who – according to how informed your opinion of them is – are either priestesses of the Earth Mother and therefore represent the power and wisdom of Nature, or Satan-worshippers and therefore symbols of all that is bad.) See also **Witch**.

4 Cats' eyes are moon-like, and, like the moon, they may signify either the anima, or the unconscious seen as a fruitful womb – a rich source of (new) life. See also **Moon, Woman**.

CAVE

A cave, being womb-like, may carry feminine symbolism.

1 For Freudians, a cave represents the female genitals.

2 It may also represent your mother; or your anima. if you are a man (for 'anima' see **Brother/Sister** sections **4–6**, and Introduction, pages 47–51).

3 A cave may represent a womb, a place of conception or birth. (It is a hollow place in Mother Earth. A Renaissance painting depicts the conception of Jesus in a cave, with a flash of lightning as the fertilizing agent. Here we see the almost universal symbolism of sky = father, earth = mother.)

The conception or birth represented in your dream may not be a physical one. Metaphorically, a 'pregnant' situation is one that may 'give birth' to something new, a new order of things. So it may be that something new is coming to birth – or trying to come to birth, if only the conscious ego will let it.

4 A cave may symbolize the unconscious. Wordsworth ('Prelude', Book III, lines 246-7) speaks of 'Caverns . . . within my mind which sun/Could never penetrate'. The unconscious lies beyond consciousness (of which the sun is a symbol) and is therefore 'dark' and possibly frightening. But we can allow the light of consciousness to penetrate the unconscious. Rock suggests permanence and antiquity. Similarly, the unconscious is a much more ancient part of the human psyche than intellect, much closer to the source of things.

5 If, in your dream, there is someone in the cave, it may be that he or she is a Wise Old Man/Woman figure see **Wise Old Man/Woman**), a personification of the wisdom contained in the unconscious. Perhaps he or she will let you into the secret of your 'destiny', or uncover for you the causes of whatever is troubling you or spoiling your life.

6 There may be a fierce-looking monster, snake or dragon in the cave. There may be treasure there, too, guarded by the monster. If so, the treasure is yourself – your true self – or the key that will unlock the secret of life for you. First of all, though, you must overcome your fear of the unconscious (the frightening monster). The terrifying thing in your unconscious may be some traumatic childhood experience that, being unbearable, was repressed – banished from consciousness. Like St George, you have to slay the dragon, overcome your fear of the unconscious, learn to trust it and let it serve you (which is what it is there for). See also **Monster, Treasure**.

7 It may be that the cave in your dream represents a hiding-place, a refuge from life's problems. If so, there will be other features of your dream(s) pointing towards this interpretation.

CELLAR

A cellar or basement may symbolize the deepest level of your mind. If you have not explored your unconscious, the 'cellars of your mind' will be the whole of the unconscious mind. If you have begun to explore, the 'cellars' will be the parts or levels of your unconscious that you have not yet explored.

Cellars are sometimes dark places; so are the unemployed layers of the unconscious, since they have not been illumined by the light of consciousness.

Because they are dark, and because they may harbour spiders and other creepy-crawly things, cellars may be frightening places. Similarly, unfamiliar parts of our mind may present a forbidding aspect. There are, in the unconscious, things we are afraid to face: that is why they are in the unconscious – we repressed them, banished them from consciousness, because they frightened or disgusted us or made us feel guilty and ashamed. But these repressed feelings or desires will turn out, on better acquaintance, to be quite innocent products of natural instinctive drives, requiring appropriate expression in our life.

CEMETERY

A cemetery may symbolize death, so the dream will be expressing your feelings about death, or your feelings about some dead person.

CENTAUR

1 A centaur, or any other creature having a human head and an animal body, may represent a (needed) union of head and body, 'spiritual' and 'animal' or sensuous, conscious and unconscious. The dream is probably telling you to set about integrating contents of your unconscious psyche into your conscious life.

2 Alternatively it may represent a (needed) union of the masculine and feminine sides of your psyche (see **Brother/Sister**, section **4**, and Introduction, pages 47–51).

CENTRE SEE ALSO MANDALA

1 In your dream you may be drawn towards the centre of a city or a garden, or labyrinth, or whatever. This probably means your unconscious is beckoning you to move towards your own centre, your true self (what Jung called 'the Self'). This is the centre, not merely of your conscious mind (that is the ego), but of your total psyche. Discovering and beginning to live from the centre of your being involves first bringing together the conscious and unconscious realms of your psyche. In other words, finding your centre is finding your wholeness and harmony: when everything in the psyche revolves around the centre, conflict and chaos have given way to peace and order.

It might be said that this is what all dream-work is about, insofar as the act of looking for the meaning of a dream involves a mutual penetration of conscious and unconscious.

2 Another possible reason for the centre motif in your dream is that something is threatening to take you away from the nucleus of your personality, and therefore from your proper 'destiny'. It would be wise to try to identify what that threatening something is, by entering into dialogue with it.

CHAINS

If, in a dream, you or someone or something else is in chains or in some other way tied up or restrained, the meaning is almost certainly that some part of you needs to be liberated, given (more) freedom of action in your life.

1 If you are chained, the 'you' of the dream is likely to be your conscious ego. Therefore, the restraints represented by the chains should be looked for in the external circumstances of your domestic, social or work life.

2 If what is chained is some sort of animal, the likelihood is that it represents your animal nature or some aspect of it – your sexuality, for instance. Perhaps you are living in too rarefied an atmosphere and need to get your feet firmly on the ground or to put your consciousness – your awareness – not only in your brain but also in your body.

3 If some other person is chained, that person probably represents something in your unconscious. Perhaps it is a desire that has been repressed because of guilt-feelings attached to it. If so, take a fresh – and this time an objective – look at it. See it for what it is: a power that may be used by you to enrich your life, but not one that you *have* to employ. You don't owe any of your emotions a living. But don't neglect them. Don't shut them away in your unconscious, where they could fester. Either use them or dissolve them.

CHALICE

1 This may be a symbol of the self – that is, the total and ordered psyche. The silver or gold of the chalice represents the supreme value of the self (as in the holy grail sought by King Arthur and his knights).

2 Is the wine in the chalice, rather than the chalice itself, given the limelight in your dream? Red wine may be a symbol of life (blood) and fullness of life (water fumed into witle represents an enrichment of lite). Your dream may, then, be trying to get you to attend to something in your unconscious that can enrich your life; or even pointing you towards the source of life within you.

CHAOS

Just as, according to mythology, the cosmos was created out of chaos, so we all, in a sense, have to create ourselves out of chaos – the unordered or disordered mass of instincts, emotions, feelings and ideas that constitute the raw materials from which we may consciously shape ourselves. This is the viewpoint from which you should understand the chaos in your dream: a cluttered, untidy room; a junk-shop with miscellaneous articles piled up higgledy-piggledy; or whatever.

NB Putting yourself in order does not necessarily mean getting rid of the junk. There are two possibilities here. Your dream may be telling you that there is a lot of rubbish that you need to get rid of: negative attitudes and habits, destructive guilt-feelings, or whatever. Alternatively, the 'junk' may be your hidden potential; so clean it up and use it. You just have to decide what role each part of your psyche is to play in your life.

CHASE/CHASED/CHASING

1 If you are being chased in a dream, what is chasing you probably symbolizes something you are afraid of, either in your external life or – more commonly – in your inner self, your unconscious. For example, a woman who dreams of being chased by men is probably afraid of sex. (Freud would add that her dreams present, in disguise, an unconscious, repressed desire for sex.)

2 If you are doing the chasing, the 'you' in your dream is probably your conscious ego and the thing you are chasing is almost certainly some part of yourself that frightens you. Chasing it away means disowning it,banishing it from your conscious life. It might be much better to try to integrate it into your conscious life. At the very least, get to know it and understand it.

CHEST

THE HUMAN CHEST

1 The human chest may symbolize emotions. A tight or aching chest may indicate pent-up emotion, or tension; and this may be so even if one of the causes of that symbol is purely physical – a touch of bronchitis or whatever.

2 Female breasts may represent either mother, or motherhood/ nurturing, or sexual desire.

A WOODEN CHEST OR BOX

A wooden chest/box may symbolize your (true) self. If there is a hint of treasure in the chest, the treasure is all the wonderful potential that lies in the as yet unexplored and unintegrated parts of yourself.

CHILD

1 If the child in your dream is you as a child, the significance of the dream may have to do with a childhood experience. But don't be too ready to understand it this way. See also **Childhood Recollections**.

2 The child may be a symbol of your true self, that which is essentially you and which you are capable of unfolding. The fact that your real self is represented by a child suggests that your true self is a beautiful unspoilt product of Nature; that it is worthy of unreserved love; and that it needs the nourishment of your love if it is to grow and unfold all its loveliness.

3 If the child has some divine aura (e.g. if it is the Christ-child), what is symbolized is as in **2** above. The aura represents the transcendent nature of the self: it is much more than your conscious ego or your present image of yourself; it holds together the opposites that are within you (e.g. conscious and unconscious, 'head' and 'heart', extroversion and introversion, masculine and feminine), and it is your ultimate goal and fulfilment (for self, see Introduction, pages 52–53).

4 The child may represent (the possibility of) a new beginning, a new development in your psyche – a new attitude to life, a new set of values, a new balance of your psychic forces, a new reconciliation of previously conflicting forces. The child in you is the growing-point in you.

5 There is in all of us a child – our emotional self – that often needs reassurance, to be told that all is well and there is no cause for fear, or anger, or guilt, and that love makes all things good and dissolves all pain. At the same time the child sometimes needs to be chided and corrected if it is eventually to – as it should – grow up.

CHILDHOOD RECOLLECTIONS

1 Many dreams repeat or allude to childhood experiences and impressions. Nearly all such dreams have a therapeutic purpose, giving us a clearer view of ourselves, perhaps showing us some attitude or pattern of behaviour that has been with us since childhood, and perhaps even showing us the original cause of it.

Unfulfilled instinctual desires provide the energy for many of our dreams, and the fact that an instinctive desire remains unfulfilled may be connected with a traumatic experience in childhood. That experience has probably been repressed because it was traumatic – causing guilt, anxiety, fear of punishment. (For repression, see Introduction, page 19.) Your dreams may, therefore, be helping you to uncover the source of these blockages which inhibit the free flow of the natural forces within you.

2 Recurring dreams may represent some psychic disturbance or problem that originated in childhood. Here are some examples:

Dreams of being naked may sometimes represent recollections of; and perhaps longing for, the paradise of childhood when one walked around unclothed without embarrassment. (Sometimes these dreams, as Freud said, express a desire for someone of the opposite sex to present himself/herself in the nude, and stem from sexual frustration.)

Dreams of flying or falling may derive from childhood enjoyment of swings and see-saws. They may express straightforward yearnings for the remembered joy of childhood, but they may also reflect one's present state of unhappiness and a futile desire to retreat from one's problematic adult life. A problem is not a thing; rather, it is a relationship – for example, a relationship of conflict either between your external circumstances and your inner wishes (in which case the solution consists in either removing yourself from the circumstances or modifying your wishes) or between one part of your psyche and another (in which case the solution is to integrate the part that has been neglected). See also **Falling, Flying**.

Dreams of failure stem from childhood fears of disapproval from parents. However, the fact that your dreams contain these recollections suggests that you have programmed yourself for anxiety. If so, begin by loving the child that is still within you: reassure it, tell it that everything is all right and that there is no such thing as failure where there is love. See also **Failure**.

3 Dreams which contain recollections of yourself as a free and happy child may indicate a desire to find your true self. The child is then a symbol of the complete and permanent inner freedom and joy which are enjoyed only when you have become acquainted with all the forces within you – both conscious and unconscious – and have established harmonious relationships among them. See also **Child**, sections **4–6**.

4 The child may represent the primitive psyche with which your conscious ego needs to get acquainted if wholeness is to be achieved. This primitive psyche is the mind of humankind in its infancy, before the development of self:consciousness and reasoning. This original awareness is still with us, but buried in unconsciousness.

CHRIST

Religious symbols may appear in the dreams even of those who do not consider themselves religious. There are at least two reasons for this: first, even non-religious people have usually had some exposure to religious teaching, and secondly, religion would seem to have an instinctive basis, originating in what we now have to call (because we have lost touch with it) the unconscious part of the psyche.

One might be tempted to say that the Christ figure means whatever it means for you. That may be true; but you are advised to consider the following possibilities.

1 The Christ figure may represent perfection for you. If so, it may be functioning in your dream as a representation of your own true self. There may be a sense in which the Christ/supreme value is outside and beyond us: we are not yet perfect. However, the Christ in your dream comes from your own unconscious and signifies that what is of supreme value is realizable in yourself: indeed, it is yourself, your not-yet-realized but potential self.

2 If the figure is that of the Christ as a child, the interpretation given above is strengthened. See also **Child**, sections **3** and **4**.

3 If there is any association of homosexuality or bisexuality with the Christ in your dream, this again would tend to confirm the interpretation in **1** above. The hermaphrodite (literally, a fusion of the god Hermes and the goddess Aphrodite) is a recurring figure in religious symbolism – for example, the Hindu representation of Shiva as part man, part woman. It stands for the union of opposites. In psychic terms, such a figure represents the bringing together of conflicting forces such as conscious and unconscious, thought and feeling, 'spirit' and 'body', extroversion and introversion. See also **Marriage**.

4 If the Christ in your dream is the crucified Christ, it may be a symbol of martyrdom. If you identify with this figure, so that you are the wronged sufferer, ask yourself what purpose is being served by adopting this role. Does it make you happy? Well, pain may give pleasure if it helps us to feel 'different' and superior. (And that is often the other side of a martyrdom complex: an inflated view of self – inflated by fantasy.) But to get happiness by making yourself unhappy is self-contradictory.

Your dream is most likely telling you to look at yourself objectively, and to get rid of the fantasy that has taken possession of you. It may help you to do so if you can identify the occasion that first started off this programme of self-punishment, or – failing that – any later occasions that reinforced the programme. The first cause will probably be some childhood feelings of guilt; and almost certainly it will be an imagined guilt, with little or no justification. (For instance, did you have, as a child, erotic desires for your parent of the opposite sex? So did we all.)

Above all, realize that you are not in the grip of some inexorable fate. What we call fate is actually those unconscious self-programinings that begin as attempts to ward off the anxious fears that arise when our desires conflict with (real or imagined) parental or other authoritative disapproval.

5 What is the Christ in your dream doing or saying? Is he healing someone – you? If so, the figure probably represents Nature's power of healing that lies within yourself. The fact that this inner healing power reveals itself in a symbol means that it lies in your unconscious. You need to activate it, and the first step towards this consists of getting to know yourself better – your unconscious self. In particular you need to get to know the opposed positive and negative forces at work in you and that element within you – perhaps long neglected – that is essential for healing. In psychological terms 'healing' means wholeness and harmony (the resolution of all serious inner conflicts). What is it you need in your life to bring about wholeness? What part of you has been neglected?

The fact that the healing Christ has appeared in your dream, however, is a very good sign. It means that your unconscious is offering you its healing power. Don't refuse it.

6 Is the Christ figure pronouncing forgiveness? If so, it may mean either that you have been suffering from guilt-feelings and you have identified these as the symptoms of an inner conflict and are now ready to let go of the guilt and the tension; or that your unconscious is now offering you the means by which those guilt-feelings and the associated paralysing anxiety can be laid to rest once and for all.

In essence, forgiveness is a dissolving of guilt and anxiety (i.e. fear of punishment); and the dissolving agent is objective intelligence which sees through the guilt-feelings to their innocent cause. How can an innocent cause give rise to guilt-feelings? The answer lies in the power of fantasy, which, especially in early childhood (when, according to the psychologist Jean Piaget, no distinction is made between fantasy and reality), makes mortal sins out of natural and unavoidable desires and leads to a belief that the whole world is bent on punishing the 'offender'.

7 Does the Christ figure in your dream suggest submission and selfsurrender, or non-resistance? If so, the dream may be understood to be showing you a pattern in your life that you need to change – a negative pattern of submitting to 'fate' or 'circumstances outside your control'. Alternatively, it could be urging you to practice a positive kind of submission, in which the ego gives way to the greater wisdom of the unconscious, and false ambitions give way to the promptings of the inner true self – which represents your true'destiny' (not to be confused with 'fate': fate is external, destiny comes from within).

8 Is it the risen – resurrected – Christ who appears in the dream? If so, this may be taken as an auspicious sign of potential self-renewal or self-transcendence: the possibility of rising to a new and fuller selfhood, leaving behind all deep internal conflict, anxiety and discontent.

9 Is the Christ in your dream surrounded by four figures (the four evangelists, or their symbols – angel, lion, ox, eagle)? This is a mandala (see **Mandala**), which represents psychic wholeness.

NB It can be dangerous to rely too heavily on a being outside ourselves. For example, to think of our sins as being off-loaded on to an external Christ may be a useful and, indeed, healthy stratagem so long as the idea is not taken literally; so long, that is, as it is seen as a symbolic representation of an internal process in which the sin-dissolving agent is our own intelligent 'I'. Otherwise, we are in danger of relinquishing responsibility for our actions and for our own future.

The Christ figure – like all other figures that occur in your dreams – is thrown up by your unconscious and is a pictorial representation of something in the depths of your psyche.

This does not contradict the religious view of the Christ as a universal reality. It would seem that there is a layer of the individual psyche which is not an individual possession but belongs to Nature as such and manifests itself in every existing being. Psychology and theology meet in the mystical understanding which sees the Christ as the universal 'I', the only subject there is. This is to see all things and all persons as incarnations or embodiments of one and the same reality. This mystical view is found in all the great religious traditions. If this view is true, it provides a basis for an immediate and intimate relation between the individual and God, a relationship which can properly serve as a source of certainty and confidence, a correct self-esteem and immunity to anxiety.

CHURCH

What applies to a church may apply equally to a temple or a circle of stones or any other sacred place.

1 A church may symbolize the self; the totally integrated psyche, with all its elements organized as a harmonious whole centred on whatever, in terms of your individual personality and 'destiny', constitutes the supreme value of truth. (For self, see Introduction, pages 52–53.)

The image may therefore be taken as a sign that your unconscious is urging you to 'centre' yourself, to put an end to the fragmentation which results in your going off in opposite directions; to 'pull yourself together' in the almost literal sense of unifying all the currently conflicting parts of you into a creative and fulfilling collaboration or commingling.

Other buildings – a house, or just a room – may represent your psyche. The fact that your dream presents the psyche in the image of a church means that you are being invited to perceive the self as something sacred – that is, something of supreme value and perhaps in some way transcendent.

2 The church may symbolize, not the total psyche, but some most valuable ('sacred') part of it which holds the meaning of your life – the key to your true destiny.

3 In primitive times a sacred place was regarded as the birthplace of the tribe's original – divine – ancestor(s). In the same way, your dream image of a sacred place may be a reminder that you are not a worthless creature living a meaningless life; that your self is a divine reality, something of supreme value and to be taken with the utmost seriousness; that you are not only to love yourself but also to revere yourself.

4 The church – or what is going on inside it, or how you in the dream are reacting – may represent your feelings about religion or about some institutionalized form of religion.

5 For church crypt see **Cave, Cellar**.

6 Is there someone in the church – a priest or (other) holy person, or someone you love dearly and respect deeply (father or elder brother, for instance)? If so, the figure may represent the self, the part of you that transcends the ego (for self, see Introduction, pages 52–53). See also **Wise Old Man/Woman**.

CIGAR/CIGARETTE

1 Much depends on your reaction to the cigar/cigarette in the dream. For example, if in the dream you feel admonished, the message may be that you ought to give up smoking.

2 Smoking may be a symptom of anxiety, and this may be the point of the dream. Smoking may also be a substitute form of selfgratification – in which case you need to ask which of your basic needs (e.g. love, sex, recognition or fulfilment in work) is not being satisfied, and why.

3 A cigar or cigarette may be a sexual (penis) symbol. (Freud acknowledged that his voracious cigar-smoking was possibly a substitute for masturbation.) (On compensation, see Introduction, page 31.)

CINDERELLA

1 Any dream image that, like Cinderella, depicts a spurned, ill-treated and subjugated being may be taken as a symbol of some part of yourself that you – the conscious ego – have repressed and/or denied adequate expression. (For repression, see Introduction, page 19.)

2 It may be – if you are male – an anima figure (for anima, see **Brother/Sister** sections **4–6**, and Introduction, pages 47–51), but in its neglected aspect, indicating that you need to value the feminine side of your nature more highly and allow it more expression – more 'say'- in your life.

3 If the Cinderella figure is in a cellar, this should be seen as a symbol of the unconscious. Clearly the message here is to get in touch with the unconscious and lift its neglected contents into the light of consciousness with a view to integrating them into your conscious life, letting them add their special energies and enrichments to your enterprises and to your personality.

CIRCLE

1 Anything circular or spherical may be a symbol of wholeness, completeness, perfection, and therefore of your total self. The circle may have an obvious centre. If so, when working on your report of the dream, hold on to the centre – identify with it and converse with it – until it reveals its identity, at least partially. It is the centre of yourself. See also **Circular Movement**, section **1**, **Mandala**.

2 It may be a symbol of the source of life, especially if it resembles sun or moon. In your dream, therefore, it may represent something within you that is potentially a source of new life, new growth, new energy, new wisdom or creativity.

CIRCULAR MOVEMENT

1 If in the dream you are moving round a central object, this may mean you are becoming aware – or are being asked to become aware – of your true self. Plotinus, a third-century mystic and philosopher, wrote: 'The soul will therefore move around the centre, that is, around the principle from which she proceeds; and, tending towards it, she will attach herself to it, as indeed all souls should do.' The centre, for Plotinus, is both self and God, but names do not matter; the main thing is to envisage the centre as holding the secret of your 'destiny' – your personal ground-plan.

2 Going round in circles (without a centre) means not achieving anything. The important thing is to ask yourself why. The answer is almost certainly that you have been 'barking up the wrong tree', and the reason for this is almost certainly that your self-image is not an accurate one and needs correction or amplification.

3 The circle may be a 'vicious circle', signifying that you are (or feel) trapped in a situation that can only get worse. However, this is not true; you can always break the seemingly inevitable chain of cause and effect by introducing a new cause, a new source of energy – derived from the unconscious.

CIRCUMCISION

In the traditional circumcision ceremony a boy was transformed into a proper human being by having his animality symbolically removed. In a dream, circumcision may mean you need to progress from a stage of development where unconscious emotion holds sway to one where consciousness is strong enough to control the unconscious drives.

NB Controlling unconscious drives does not mean repressing and neglecting them; it means giving them an appropriate place in your conscious life. See also **Initiation**.

CITY

1 A city may be a symbol of your self. See also **Mandala**, and Introduction, page 55.

2 Entering a city may symbolize an intention – or need – to explore your unconscious and acquaint yourself with what is going on there.

3 A buried city, or a city at the bottom of the sea, may symbolize a neglected self. This would indicate a need to dip into your unconscious (for self, see Introduction, pages 52–53).

4 If it is busy-ness of the city that is emphasized in your dream, ask yourself what this means in terms of your feelings about everyday life, or about people. Alternatively, what is going on in the city (confused, chaotic movement in opposing directions, for instance) may be symbolic of what is going on in yourself.

5 Are you lost in the city? This probably represents a loss of direction in your life.

CLIFF

To be at the edge of a cliff is to be where earth meets both sky and sea. Sky is a symbol of consciousness/masculinity; sea is the unconscious/ femininity.

1 What is symbolized may be a critical point in your life, a time for decision.

2 The decision may be one concerning the polarity of male and female, the masculine and feminine components in your psyche. If you are a woman, it may be that a decision has to be made concerning the conflicting worlds of career and domesticity. (Sky would then symbolize masculine assertiveness and active participation in the world; sea, feminine attributes such as motherhood and nurturing.)

3 The cliff edge may be 'the end of the road', signifying that you have come as far as you can in a particular endeavour of lifestyle, and that something radically new is called for. Perhaps this new approach to living means entering into a close relationship with Nature (represented by sea and sky) or bringing together the conscious and unconscious parts of your psyche (sky representing consciousness, sea the unconscious).

It may be a question of whether you can find within yourself enough strength and faith to step out into the unknown future; or throw yourself off the cliff- that is, withdraw from life's challenge.

4 The horizon may be the significant thing in the dream. This may mean you are being challenged to take a bigger view of things,to see life and/or yourself on a grander scale, in order to find a new and more satisfying motivation for your life.

CLIMBING ASCENT, HEIGHT, LADDER, MOUNTAIN

1 Climbing may be a symbol of ambition or success. Does the climbing fill you with fear; or do you feel giddy when you reach the top? If so, this may symbolize a fear (unconscious) of 'coming a cropper'. Perhaps you need to sort out an inferiority complex.On the other hand, the dream may be a warning. There is such a thing as climbing too high. 'Pride comes before a fall.'

2 Are you climbing (a tree, for instance) to escape from a fierce animal or to save yourself from a river in flood? This would symbolize an attempt to escape from some emotion, some inner disturbance; or from some external situation – at home or at work.

3 Climbing a mountain may give you a panoramic view. This might mean that you desire – or need – a more detached view of yourself or your situation; that you need to get things in proportion; or that you need to lift yourself above mere material values.

4 On the other hand, climbing a mountain may be a form of escapism, and the mountain an ivory tower where the world and your problems (external or inner) can be left behind. Needless to say, anxiety, resentment, inner conflict can never be left behind; not, at any rate, until you face them and talk things out with them. Otherwise, wherever you are, they are. (For 'talking things out', see Introduction, pages 58–59.)

5 Climbing a wall, particularly if it has jutting-out bricks or stones that you can take hold of, may (Freud would say *must*) represent, for a male dreamer, sexual intercourse. The protuberances are symbols of female buttocks and breasts. On the other hand, it may express (a need for) liberation – for example, from irrational or neurotic constraints; from a habit of selfdenigration; or from a state of morbid withdrawal from life.

CLOCKWISE **SEE ALSO ANTICLOCKWISE, LEFT, RIGHT/LEFT, SPIRAL**

Moving clockwise means going to the right, which symbolizes consciousness; intellect; spirituality; masculinity.

CLOTHES

1 The feelings associated in the dream with the clothes you are wearing may indicate what your feelings are towards yourself, especially in relation to the image you present to the world. For example, if in your dream you feel inadequately clothed, this may mean you feel vulnerable or inadequate, or ashamed (perhaps in certain kinds of situation, which may be shown in the dream).

2 If you are wearing old and worn-out clothes, this may indicate either anxiety about your attractiveness or feelings of inferiority, or that you need to discard some habitual way of meeting life, some set of (negative) attitudes or beliefs.

3 If old and tattered clothes are worn in the dream by someone else, this probably means there is some part of you – some capacity or aspect of your potential self – that you are neglecting or keeping locked away in the cellars of your psyche. If the person wearing the tattered clothes is of the opposite sex, your anima or animus may be in need of attention (for anima/animus, see Introduction, pages 47–51). See also **Brother/Sister**, **Cinderella**.

4 Changing your clothes might indicate a change of lifestyle or of attitude; changing your persona or becoming a new person. (For persona, see Introduction, pages 40–41.)

CLOUD(S)

1 Clouds in dreams may symbolize different moods, bright or dark, optimism or depression.

2 Threatening storm-clouds may be warning you of impending psychic disturbance. Is there some frustrated, neglected part of you that might soon cause trouble if not allowed its proper place in your life?

3 Clouds fertilize the earth. They may therefore symbolize (the need for) growth within yourself.

4 Because of its lack of fixed shape, a cloud may symbolize potential.

5 If the cloud is obscuring the sun, the sun may symbolize your true self. Try to identify with the cloud – get inside it – to find out what it is that is preventing you from perceiving your true identity. Alternatively, this may be a mood dream as in **1** above.

CLUMSINESS SEE BULL, SECTION 6.

COCK

1 A cock may represent aggression. Is there some anger in you (rising from unconscious guilt-feelings?) that needs to be dissolved?

2 A symbol of (male) sexuality.

3 A symbol of fertility. As such, it may signify – particularly for a woman – that it is time to give some hitherto unused part of your psyche an active role in your conscious life.

4 A black cock is traditionally a symbol of evil. Bear in mind that 'evil' aspects of you are potentially creative and are dangerous only if you keep on pushing them aside.

5 A weathercock (e.g. on a church spire) may have something to do with finding a new direction in life. Alternatively, the combination of spire and cock may be a strong sexual symbol – particularly in a woman's dream.

COCKCROW

1 Because of its association with Judgement Day, a cockcrow may signify that now is a time for decision.

2 It may simply mean dawn. See also **Dawn**.

COCOON

1 A cocoon holds potential new life and may therefore symbolize (the possibility of) new psychic life and development.

2 The cocoon is a covering and may therefore symbolize unwillingness to uncover and face up to your true self.

3 Are you in the cocoon? If so, it probably represents a web of fantasies produced by an unconscious neurosis which is cutting you off from reality.

COFFIN SEE BURIAL, DEATH

COLD SEE ALSO ICE

Coldness in a dream may symbolize a cold, hard heart. Have you become emotionally frigid? What traumatic experience has caused this?

COLLISION

If in a dream you are driving a car which collides with another, this may indicate a collision between conscious and unconscious. In other words, there is a conflict going on in your psyche.

COLOUR(S) BLACK, RED, ETC.

COMPASS

Have you been disorientated? The compass probably indicates a need to take fresh bearings; to get your goals sorted out.

COMPOSITE

1 If a dream contains a composite person/figure/image or a merging of what in actual life are distinct persons/things, first look for what its real-life components have in common. (For condensation, see Introduction, page 20.)

2 A composite of opposites – for example, a figure that is half male, half female – symbolizes (the need for) the union or intermingling of opposed forces in the psyche: masculine and feminine, conscious and unconscious, etc. See also **Centaur, Hemaphrodite**.

CONDUCTOR

1 The conductor of an orchestra or choir may symbolize the need for your conscious ego to get all parts of you to work together creatively – 'making music' in your soul.

2 At another level, the conductor may represent what in mystic-meditative traditions is sometimes referred to as the 'inner-self' and is both the real you and God. This is sometimes called the 'inner controller'.

CONFLICT SEE FIGHT(ING)

CONFUSION

If a dream has a sense of confusion, this represents psychic confusion, resulting from a collision between the conscious and unconscious.

CONTEST SEE FIGHT(ING)

CONVERSION SEE INTRODUCTION, PAGE 44

COOPERATION

Any cooperative activity in a dream may be taken as revealing the interrelatedness and potential creative cooperation of the various parts or functions of the psyche. What obstacles, what inner resistances need to be dissolved in order to make the ideal a reality?

CORNER/CORNERED SEE ALSO CUL-DE-SAC

1 If in a dream you are – or feel – cornered, this will symbolize some frustration in yourself, the causes of which may be internal or external. In either case, you are being called on to make a decision. Ultimately the choice is between sliding into a neurosis and taking control of the situation (internal or external).

2 Turning a corner, on the other hand, may signify taking a new direction in life, taking a turn for the better. See also **Left**, **Right/Left**.

CORRIDOR

1 As a passage connecting different rooms, a corridor may symbolize a passing from one phase of your life to another; from one self-image to another, or from self-image or something deeper, and closer to your real self. See also **Bridge**, **Crossing**, **Door**.

2 If, however, the corridor is long and/or dark and you never get to the end of it, the most likely meaning is that you are desperate to get out of some situation, external or internal.

COUPLE

Any couple in a dream may symbolize the need to bring together two different components of your psyche to achieve more balance and fullness. For example:

1 We all have a 'shadow' (see Introduction, pages 45–47) and therefore need to learn to converse and consult with our unconscious.

2 Men have a feminine side to their psyche, women have a masculine side. Usually this contrasexual element is repressed or suppressed as a result of social conditioning. Personal wholeness, however, depends on bringing the two sexual sides of one's nature together. This union may be represented in dreams by a couple, male and female. Sometimes this is a royal couple.

3 A royal couple may also represent your parents. If so, what does the dream reveal in the way of hidden emotions towards your parents, or unconscious parental influences on your attitudes and behaviour patterns?

COW

1 The cow may represent your mother. Please note: this does not mean your mother (or mother-in-law) is either fat or stupid! Rather, the cow is an obvious symbol of motherhood, since it produces an abundant supply of milk from its prominent udders.

2 The cow is also a symbol of fertility, signalling a possible new development in your life, new personal growth.

3 The cow may be an anima figure, representing a man's feminine psychic components (for anima see **Brother/Sister**, sections **4–6**, and Introduction, pages 47–51).

4 A cow may represent a primitive awareness; intuitive knowledge that comes, not from making a detached, objective examination of things, but from an inner oneness with natural things and processes.

5 Cows (and cattle generally) may symbolize dignity, strength, passive endurance.

6 Is the cow chewing the cud? Well, are you ruminating over something? Perhaps your unconscious is telling you not to. What's the point of turning something over and over? Once you have the necessary information, only a decision will change things – change your life – for the better.

On the other hand, your unconscious may be telling you that you need to think things over, and not to be in too much of a hurry. Perhaps you need to take time off from frantic – compulsive – activity to meditate on the meaning of your life with a view to re-orientating yourself, giving yourself new values and more positive goals.

CRASH SEE ALSO COLLISION

1 If in your dream you crash – in a car or train or aeroplane – this probably signifies that you are in a state of anxiety over some undertaking or situation.

2 If you are driving, the crash may symbolize an unconscious desire to punish yourself. What guilt-feelings are you harbouring? Guilt and sado-masochism often go hand in hand. Dissolve the guilt-feelings (which are almost certainly irrational and which, anyway, can contribute nothing of value to life – your own or anyone else's), and the violence will dissolve, too.

3 The crash may express a (hidden) fear of mental breakdown, in which case you ought to seek help.

CROCODILE

1 A crocodile may be a symbol of the 'devouring' aspect of your mother. See also **Mother**.

2 It may symbolize aggressiveness; or the shadowy world of instinct.

CROSS

A cross may have private associations for you. On the other hand, the cross is such an ancient symbol that its meaning in a dream may have come from the collective – not the personal – unconscious (for this distinction, see Introduction, pages 43–44).

1 It may mean simply 'no-go': that something in your life has come to an end; or that it ought to come to an end. Look deeper into yourself for new directions, in both senses of the word.

2 It may be a crossroads sign. See also **Crossroads**.

3 Is the cross in the dream a burden? If so, don't be too ready to accept the notion that crosses have to be borne. Discover what it is in your life or in yourself that constitutes a 'cross', and then remove it – dissolve it with a proper self-love. Burdens prevent you from reaching your full stature as a person.

4 The cross may be a symbol of death. It may be that your present self, or something in you, must 'die' as a necessary prelude to new and fuller life.

5 It may be a symbol of martyrdom. Is the martyrdom something you feel as an oppressive and crippling restraint, or is it self-imposed? These are not absolute alternatives: what is consciously felt as an undeserved punishment may be unconsciously self-inflicted – for some imagined guiltiness.

6 A crucifix (cross with the crucified one fastened to it) will carry the symbolism of crucifixion, which may be either martyrdom (as in **5** above), or severe restraining of 'bodily' or 'earthly' desires. Alternatively, it may represent extreme neglect of some psychic component or function (for repression

and suppression, see Introduction, page 19). Decide whether your unconscious is recommending or protesting against the repression/suppression, and act accordingly.

7 The Greek cross, having all four arms of equal length, may symbolize wholeness: the unified psyche – the unification of conscious and unconscious (The union of opposites is represented by the vertical and horizontal lines of the cross; wholeness is represented by the way the arms reach out to embrace reality in all directions.) See also **Mandala**.

CROSSING

1 Crossing a river may symbolize a decisive change of attitude; making a crucial decision.

2 Crossing the sea, going from one country to another, may symbolize a fundamental personal re-orientation; perhaps leaving conventional values behind in favour of values discovered within oneself.

3 Even crossing the street may have similar significance. Pay attention also to the direction: are you crossing from left to right, or from right to left? See also **Left**, **Right/Left**.

CROSSROADS

1 A crossroads will almost invariably symbolize a crisis, a point in your life where you must make a choice of direction. Usually it will not be difficult to identify the crisis situation, and the choices open to you – though the act of choosing may be extremely difficult and painful.

2 Rarely, a crossroads may represent death. (People were sometimes, in earlier societies, buried at crossroads.) See also **Dead/Death**.

CROW

1 A crow may symbolize death or misfortune. See also **Dead/Death**.

2 Possibly, it may represent something in your psyche that can enrich or renew your life. (Crows sometimes fly high, and have therefore been regarded as messengers of the gods; or as emblems of fertility.) This might be true even if the crow in the dream frightened you: we are often afraid of

those dark parts of our psyche that nevertheless contain all that we need for a fuller life.

CROWD

If a crowd features in your dreams, it is important to register your (the dream ego's) reaction to the crowd and the mood of the crowd itself.

1 The crowd may represent (your feelings towards) people in general. In this case you will probably be seeing a pattern that repeats itself in your everyday life – usually a negative one that you need to liberate yourself from.

2 It may represent the multitude of forces, instincts, interests, etc. that fill your psyche, in which case your unconscious would seem to be urging you to pay attention to what is going on 'down there'.

CRUCIFIXION SEE CROSS, SECTION (6)

CRYPT SEE CAVE, CELLAR

CRYSTAL

1 A crystal may be a symbol of the self (for self, see Introduction, pages 52–53). Dr Marie-Louise von Franz writes in *Man and His Symbols:* 'The mathematically precise arrangement of a crystal evokes in us the intuitive feeling that even in so-called "dead" matter there is a spiritual ordering principle at work. Thus the crystal often symbolically stands for the union of extreme opposites – of matter and spirit.' The self, too (which Christians have called the image of God in the human being), is a union of opposites – conscious and unconscious, masculine and feminine, and so on.

2 A crystal may be a symbol of purity and innocence, openness and receptiveness.

CRYSTAL-GAZING

Crystal-gazing may symbolize its psychological equivalent, namely, turning our attention inwards to explore the psyche and discover our 'destiny'. But don't forget that exploring your psyche entails uncovering your complexes or neuroses, inner conflicts, phobias, compulsions, projections, and so on, and it may take a long time to reach the centre of the crystal ball – that is, the centre of yourself.

CUL-DE-SAC

1 A cul-de-sac may symbolize an unprofitable course of action. Perhaps you need to change your ambitions and draw up a new plan for your life, or, rather, discover the original plan within the depths of your psyche.

2 If in the dream you are being driven into a cul-de-sac, ask yourself what it is (in your unconscious) that is causing you to waste time and energy on fruitless pursuits. There would seem to be something in your unconscious that needs to be integrated into your conscious life.

CUPBOARD

1 Cupboards may symbolize the womb, and therefore represent either your mother or women in general (in a man's dream), or a desire to return to the womb – that is, to escape from life's demands and problems.

2 A cupboard may symbolize yourself. Do you, in the dream, open the cupboard? If so, what do you find there? Whatever it is, it should be seen as some part of yourself, albeit your unconscious – hidden – self. 'Skeletons in cupboards' are parts of yourself to which you have denied a place in your conscious life.

CURRENT SEE ALSO ANTICLOCKWISE, BLOCKAGE, CLOCKWISE, LEFT, RIGHT/LEFT

A current, whether electric, in a river or in the sea, will represent a flow of psychic energy. Therefore, pay attention to the direction of the current (to left or right, clockwise, or anticlockwise) and its strength (weak or violent). It is blocked by something?

CURTAIN(S)

1 The curtains may symbolize your inability or unwillingness to look at the hidden parts of yourself – emotions, attitudes, drives which, because of your fears, you keep shut in your unconscious.

2 Alternatively, what you are shutting out may be some intolerably painful external situation.

In either case, bear in mind that what is shut out of consciousness does not cease to influence your attitudes and behaviour; and that its influence will be detrimental to your personal growth and happiness unless and until you reclaim the banished part of yourself.

3 Opening a curtain, of course, has the opposite symbolism. It means a readiness to look at what has hitherto been hidden.

4 Drawing the curtains will sometimes (and the falling or closing of theatre curtains will invariably) symbolize the end of something – a relationship, for example, or some phase in your life.

5 In a woman's dream the curtain may possibly represent the hymen. In that case, the closed/open curtain will probably refer to fear of/desire for sexual intercourse.

CURVES

Anything that is curved may be a feminine symbol, representing woman; anima (for a man); sexuality (usually for a man); or, at a more fundamental level, life-giving or life-enhancing energy. ('Dragon-lines' – see **Dragon**, section **6** – are always curved, never straight.)

CUT(TING) SEE ALSO KNOT

AS WITH A KNIFE

Cutting hair or a hand or some other part of the body may symbolize (preparation for, or need for) passing from one phase or manner of life to another, from one set of values and goals to another. (Compare traditional initiation rites and rites of passage. For instance, in a boy's initiation to manhood the cutting – of hair, or face or whatever – was a symbolic killing of the boy-ness as a pre-condition for the emergence of man-ness.) NB The second phase is always fuller than the first.

2 Any cutting of a part of the body may symbolize castration. In a man's dream this may express anxiety about his masculinity or sexuality. In a woman's dream the focus may be on her (hidden) masculinity, or her resentment of sexual discrimination in favour of men. See also **Castration**.

3 If something is cut in half, this may symbolize a separation – for example, of those qualities of your psyche that belong to your original individual ground-plan from those that belong to the ego.

RAILWAY CUTTING

4 A railway cutting may be a sexual symbol representing the vagina. A train passing through it would symbolize the sexual act.

CYCLONE SEE WHIRLWIND

CYPRESS

1 A cypress tree symbolizes death and mourning. See also **Dead/Death**.

2 Being evergreen, however, it also symbolizes immortality; the hope of new life on the other side of death. See also **Dead/Death**.

3 Of course, a cypress may have special significance for you: perhaps, for instance, you associate it with a Mediterranean holiday in which you experienced something meaningful.

D

DAFFODIL

As a sign of new life, in your dreams a daffodil means you should look for clues as to the nature and source of potential personal growth, or renewal.

DAGGER SEE ALSO CUTTING, INITIATION, SACRIFICE

1 A dagger may be a sexual symbol, representing the phallus.

2 It may represent aggression or anger. Identify with the dagger, its possessor and its victim with a view to discovering the cause(s) of your (repressed) anger (for repression, see Introduction, page 19).

DAM

A dam in your dreams probably means there is some pent-up (repressed) emotion that needs to be unblocked.

DAMSEL IN DISTRESS

1 In mythology and folklore a hero rescues an imprisoned beautiful young woman, slaying a dragon or other monster that is keeping her a prisoner. If this scenario appears in a man's dreams, they may be calling on him to rescue his anima from its imprisonment in the unconscious, to utilize this previously hidden and abused feminine side of his nature, and so attain a proper balance in his personality. (For anima, see Introduction, pages 47–51.) See also **Dragon**.

2 When Theseus saved Ariadne from the Minotaur, he had to make his way through a labyrinth; Perseus cut off Medusa's head to rescue Andromeda. Both labyrinth and Medusa may be negatively charged symbols of mother. If such an image appears in a hero-rescuing-damsel dream, it may be taken as indicating that the dreamer needs to free himself from an emotional entanglement with – or all-consuming dependence on – his mother. Only then will he be able to let the feminine in himself express itself. (If he doesn't let it express itself, it will still do so – but in destructive emotional outbursts.)

DANCING

1 Dancing may be a sexual symbol, representing sexual intercourse.

2 By virtue of its sexual associations, dancing may represent a coming together – courtship – of the masculine (animus) and feminine (anima) side of one's nature (for anima/animus, see **Brother/Sister**, sections **4–6**, and Introduction, pages 47–51).

3 Joining a dance probably means relating cooperatively with the other person or group. What does that person or group symbolize? It may be some part of you: your hidden self, with its multitude of emotions, instinctive impulses, ideas, ideals, beliefs/prejudices, attitudes, ambitions, etc.

4 Perhaps it is the 'dance of life'. Participating/not participating in the dance would then mean relating harmoniously with Nature (or your unconscious)/being out of step with it. (Dancing clumsily might signify that you were 'out of step'.)

5 If the dance is a frenzied solo performance, it may represent some kind of 'possession', indicating that some psychic element is threatening to take you over. If this is the case, you need to identify the causes of any compulsive behaviour you observe in yourself; and then to come to terms with it – which will usually mean either making space in your life for some hitherto repressed part of you; or getting rid of (repressed) guilt-feelings; or both. (For repression, see Introduction, page 19.)

DANGER

Any sense of danger in a dream means there is some inner conflict – between conscious and unconscious – that needs to be sorted out. In such dreams you should try not to run away from the danger but to stay with it, to get the feel of it and so identify the particular conflict that needs to be resolved.

DARKNESS SEE ALSO BLACK

1 Darkness is a common symbol of the unconscious. If the darkness is frightening, this represents your fear of the unknown forces in your psyche. If the darkness is warm and velvety, you are being invited to regard your unconscious as your friend.

2 Darkness pierced by a light may be a sign that 'light shines in darkness': that the truth you are seeking (about yourself, or about life) is to be found in the unconscious. Darkness represents the unconscious in its unknown aspect; when it has been integrated into one's conscious life, all is light. (On the shadow, see Introduction, pages 45–47.)

3 It may be that, in the dream, you cannot find your way to the light, for example, at the end of a dark tunnel. This may reflect desperate feelings; frustration; depression. See also **Tunnel**.

4 The dark place may be womb-like and represent your own mother or, more likely, your emotional relationship to your mother. The unconscious may be recommending that you liberate yourself from a dominating mother (or mother image) and become your own person.

It may represent, not your own mother, but mother in a vaguer and profounder sense: 'Mother Nature', physiological, natural, instinctive functions; the unconscious. See also **1** above and **5** below.

5 Darkness may represent death. (The womb, too, may be a symbol of death: the desire to return to the womb is a desire to escape from life's pains and problems.) See also **Dead/Death**.

DART

A dart may be a sexual symbol, representing the penis or sexual penetration.

DAWN

1 The dawn may symbolize a fresh start, opening to a promise-filled future.

2 As night is a symbol of the unconscious, so dawn may symbolize the raising of unconscious contents into consciousness – a prerequisite of personal growth.

3 It may symbolize illumination; 'seeing the light'.

DEAD (PERSON/ANIMAL)/DEATH

1 Does the dream contain a dead person you actually knew? If so, the dream may mean you should take notice of what he or she said or did, or of what happened to him or her. The dead person is 'coming back', not to haunt but to advise and help you.

There's really nothing 'spooky' about meeting dead people in dreams. Such encounters may help you to fulfil a long-desired deep relationship, or to put something right. For example, you may learn to forgive the person and as a consequence get peace and healing for yourself.

2 If a deceased partner or parent appears in dreams, **1** above may apply. Bear in mind also that the dead do live on – inside us; and that it is important to realize when this is a healthy and life-enhancing thing and when it is purely negative, stunting our own personal development. If it is the latter, resolve to have it out with the person the next time he or she appears in a dream.

3 If the dead person in the dream is actually a living person – and especially if that person is your partner or parent or sibling – the dream may be expressing unconscious resentment towards that person, or a desire to be independent. Feelings towards someone close are often ambivalent: love or respect mixed with fear or hatred or resentment or jealousy.

The usual conscious response to such a dream will be anxiety, and you may even feel anxiety in the dream itself. However, Freud was convinced that in such cases anxiety was a cloak for unconscious – because repressed – hostility. (On the Oedipus complex, see Introduction, pages 28–30.) See also **Murder**.

4 The dead person may be you (and could stand for you even if in the dream he is distinct from the dream ego). In that case, consider the following possibilities:

a What is being expressed in the dream may be your own anxiety about dying. Death is inevitable, and facing up to that fact may bring great rewards: self-acceptance; new values; a broadening of one's personality, compensating for past omissions or lopsidedness and utilizing hitherto neglected personal resources. This would be specially applicable if you were in the second half of life.

b The message may be that your old self needs to be left behind. This may mean that you must stop carrying around with you the crippling burden of your past (irrational guilt-feelings and martyrdom complex, or any other negative self-programming); and, instead, you must open yourself to what the present moment is offering. Alternatively, the 'old self' may be old attachments, habits, ambitions, values, goals; in which case the dream is telling you that the only way forward for you lies through giving these up and looking deeper within yourself for better values, etc. (where 'better' means more in tune with your real self).

(Primitive rites of passage, which mark transitional stages in a person's life – birth, initiation into adulthood, marriage, death – all contain death-and-rebirth symbolism and express a recognition that the dissolving – 'death' – of past attitudes is a necessary prelude to the development of new attitudes more appropriate to one's new stage in life. The symbolic death of the initiate in these rites may also be seen as a descent of the conscious ego into the unconscious: it is the unconscious that provides the means for new growth – 'rebirth'. See also **Sacrifice**.)

c It is just possible that, if your own death features repeatedly in dreams, it is an expression of an unconscious wish for death. Freud speculated in *Beyond the Pleasure Principle* that there might be, in everyone, just two contending basic drives: one towards life and love and pleasure ('Eros'), the other towards death ('Thanatos'). This is highly controversial, but it is indisputable that many people display a strong masochistic tendency.

Are you compelled to repeat a painful experience? Do you tend to interpret what other people say as a criticism of yourself? If so, you may be suffering from repressed guilt-feelings and an unconscious urge to punish yourself – which may sometimes take the form of a fate-neurosis and/or a wish (unconscious) to see yourself dead. If you feel this applies to you, talk to a friend about it or consult a psychotherapist. See also **Suicide**.

A wish for death may be a retreat from life's problems and pains, or a response to (a sense of) failure. If this applies to you, bear in mind, first, that a very sensitive person may also be burdened with an over-severe conscience (the product, perhaps, of having a stern father or a sin-and-guilt religious upbringing). In that case, see the previous paragraph. Secondly, what makes a thing a problem is usually one's attitude towards it. For example, suppose you have been made redundant. If your reaction is to see this as a punishment, see the previous paragraph. If you see it as failure, try to change your attitude or perspective by asking what creative purpose may be being served by your redundancy: perhaps, for instance, the demolishing of an inadequate or false selfimage in order to make way for the construction of one that corresponds more closely to your individual ground-plan or 'destiny'.

5 If the gender of the dead person is stressed, the meaning may be that your masculinity/femininity or your animus/anima needs reviving.

6 A dead animal in a dream almost certainly refers to some part of you – an instinctive force, perhaps – and the dream will be telling you either that this part of you (e.g. guilt-feelings or inferiority complex) ought to die, because its effects are wholly negative; or that it is a valuable but repressed part of yourself that you must now bring to life, to rectify an imbalance in your personality.

DEAD-END SEE CUL-DE-SAC

DEBAUCHERY

A scene of debauchery in a dream should be taken as a strong expression of a normal desire for sexual satisfaction.

DECAPITATION SEE BEHEADING, HEAD

DEER SEE HUNTING

DEMONS SEE ALSO DEVIL, EVIL

Demons in dreams probably represent parts of your unconscious mind that have been repressed and neglected and are now threatening to disrupt or mutilate the psyche. They should be approached lovingly, given attention and integrated into your conscious life. This will bring about their 'conversion': they will cease to threaten and will contribute their vital energies to the enhancement of the self.

Self-knowledge – knowing what we are carrying around with us in our unconscious – is the only sure defence against what in ancient times was called demonic possession, which in psychological terms means the conscious ego being taken over by unconscious forces (obsessive fear or anger, or whatever).

DEPTHS

Depths of any kind – a deep place in the earth, a deep well, the depths of the sea, a cellar – may represent the unconscious. If you want to 'get to the bottom of' something in your personality that is causing problems, you must be prepared to descend into your unconscious to uncover wishes or fears that you have buried there.

DESCENT SEE ALSO DEPTHS DOWNHILL

The meaning of a descent may be determined largely by what you are descending into. Descending into a deep well or other dark place may symbolize the 'descent' of the conscious ego into the unconscious.

DESERT SEE OASIS, WILDERNESS

DESERTED SEE ABANDONMENT

DEVIL

1 The Satan of Jewish–Christian–Islamic tradition was originally a horned fertility god, a personification of the fertilizing power of Nature. In psychological terms, a fertilizing agent is something within the psyche that can inaugurate a new phase in the individual's development.

2 The evil connotations of the devil figure may reflect the dreamer's fear of those repressed contents of the unconscious that are, in fact, the very forces that – if mobilized and utilized – could bestow new and fuller life. What we repress is invariably something that had great value for us but on some occasion in the past gave rise to guilt-feelings or a fear of punishment. It is our fears that invest the unconscious with the fearsome characteristics of a dark underworld inhabited by evil monsters. In reality, the unconscious contains all the energy and wisdom we need for healing and wholeness.

It might be said that our fundamental human task is the conversion of the devil within ourselves, that is, converting negatively charged (dissident, destructive) psychic forces into positively charged (life-enhancing and unifying) powers. But you won't convert the devil with brute force, only with love. The negatively charged psychic forces are the ones you neglect and despise or fear. They become positively charged when you acknowledge them and integrate them into your conscious life.

If we do not recognize the 'devil' within ourselves, we shall project him on to others and thereby give more scope for hatred and destruction (the real devil!) in the world. See also **Evil**.

3 In certain contexts – if, for example, he has homs or is sexually involved with naked women – the devil may be a sexual symbol. If sexuality is represented in such a guise in a woman's dream, it is possibly because she has a fear of sexual relations. In a man's dream the indication might be that he has a guilt-ridden attitude towards his own sexuality (which Freud might trace back to anxiety arising out of the normal male infant's erotic feelings for his mother).

DIAMOND SEE CRYSTAL

A diamond may be a symbol of the self; of the Absolute/God; or of eternity.

DIGGING

This may mean digging for treasure – that is, your true self; 'digging' into the unconscious. Pay attention to whatever is dug up in the dream: it will symbolize something (within yourself) that your unconscious is wanting to draw your attention to for your own good.

DIRT(Y)

1 Dirt is a common symbol for something you regard as (morally) prohibited or disgusting. The thing will almost certainly be something – an instinctive drive or desire – within you. Your dream is expressing your emotional reaction to the thing. You now need to take a detached look, which means detaching the instinct or desire from the traumatic experience that triggered off your repulsion.

2 If you are dirty in the dream, this probably signifies that you cannot accept yourself – because of guilt-feelings that possibly stem from childhood. A depressive person is likely to feel that way. Such a person is programmed to run himself down, deny himself enjoyment, turn down opportunities for bettering himself, and generally punish himself for some imagined sin. For example, a very young child whose father dies may thereafter be plagued by guilt and self-hatred, which may attach themselves to actions or desires in later life that have no real connection with the imagined action – killing the father – that first gave rise to them.

DISC SEE ALSO MANDALA, SUN

Perhaps the particular disc has particular associations for you. However, a disc may symbolize your (true) self; personal wholeness or completeness; what Jung called 'the Self', as distinct from 'egg' or 'persona'.

DISEASE

1 If someone close to you features in a dream as suffering from some disease which in reality he or she does not have, then it is possible that your dream expresses either genuine anxiety for the person or a hidden hostile wish. See also **Dead/Death**, section (3).

2 If the diseased person in the dream is you, the dream may be referring to an actual physical illness, or to some psychological disease or inner conflict.

DISGUST SEE DIRT(Y), SECTION 1

DISORDER SEE CHAOS

DIVIDING/DIVISION SEE CUTTING, SECTION 3

DIVINE SEE CHILD, SECTION 3, GOD(DESS)

DIVING

1 Diving may be a sexual symbol, representing male penetration. Water often symbolizes the feminine.

2 (Deep) water sometimes symbolizes the unconscious; so diving may symbolize descent into the unconscious. If this is the case, it will usually be a sign that your dream is recommending you to get in touch with your unconscious. Perhaps there are unconscious motivations – desires or fears – that are causing you to function inefficiently; some neglected or undervalued part of you that you need to learn to respect and utilize if you are to achieve (fuller) satisfaction or happiness.

3 There are myths of divers who plunge to the depths of the sea and bring up treasure. In psychological terms this represents either what is described in **2** above or the ego descending into the unconscious and finding the self (see Introduction, page 46).

DIVORCE

1 A dream in which you and your spouse are divorced may express a (hidden) desire for an end to the relationship, or a feeling of frustration in the relationship.

2 Divorce may be a symbol of a split within your psyche: perhaps between conscious and unconscious; the masculine and feminine halves of your personality; intellect and feelings.

DOG

1 A dog may symbolize your 'animal' nature, particularly if you haven't yet accepted that you have an animal nature!

2 It the dog is frothing with rage, this might indicate some repressed part of you is now 'at the end of its tether' and will cause a lot of trouble if not given attention and allowed its proper place in your life.

3 If the dog is paired with, say, a wolf, then it is the wolf that will symbolize your animal nature, and the dog (if its emotional 'feel' is contrasted in the dream with that of the wolf) will represent some 'higher' part of your nature.

4 The dog may stand for some person you know, in which case the dream will be telling you something about the person's character or expressing what you feel about the person (that he or she is a 'dog' or a 'bitch'). See also **Animal, Wolf.**

DOLPHIN

A dolphin thrusting itself out of the water (and diving in again) may symbolize communication between unconscious (sea, water) and conscious (sky). More particularly, it might symbolize some specific unconscious content that is speaking – or trying to speak – to you.

DOME

1 A dome may symbolize intellect, or the conscious ego.

2 It may symbolize the self, the total/true self, your potential perfection. See also **Mandala.**

3 It might be a sexual symbol, representing the female breast. On a mosque there may be both domes and minarets. The latter may be phallic.

DONKEY SEE ASS

DOOR

1 A door may represent an opening to a new phase of life or a possible new development – either in your external circumstances or in yourself.

2 It may symbolize an invitation to enter the not-yet-explored parts of your psyche, with a view to bringing these under conscious control.

3 If someone/something is on the other side of the door, this probably means you need to let something come out of your unconscious into your conscious mind.

4 The symbolism may be that which Christians apply to the Christ: the way to 'salvation' – that is, healing and wholeness. (Compare St John's Gospel 10:9: 'I am the door. By me, if anyone enters in, he shall be saved'.)

5 A closed door may symbolize A 'no-go' situation. You need to determine whether the impasse is unavoidable and therefore to be accepted (because, for instance, you have been pursuing a path that is out of keeping with your deepest values or needs) or one that you have artificially made for yourself (as a consequence of irrational guiltfeelings and anxiety, for instance) and can therefore remove by an act of will – though it may require a lot of preparatory work by way of investigating the (partly) unconscious psychic processes that have constructed the obstacle.

DOVE

1 A dove is a well-known symbol of peace.

2 It may also symbolize love, including sexual love. (Doves were sacred to goddesses of love – Astarte, Aphrodite, Venus – and appear today on Valentine cards.)

3 If the dove speaks, take this as a word of advice or warning from your unconscious. (In ancient times doves were regarded as having oracular

powers, bringing messages from the spirit-world. In psychological terms the 'spirit-world' is 'the unconscious'.)

DOWNHILL SEE ALSO DESCENT

Be guided by the emotional 'feel' of the downhill motion.

1 It may be a symbol of decline, or it may be expressing your fear of 'going downhill'. Such fears are common in people approaching middle age or old age.

2 On the other hand, going downhill can mean letting go, relaxing, leaving stress behind.

DRAGON

1 Is the dragon guarding treasure, or a cave which might contain treasure? If so, the cave probably represents your unconscious, the treasure represents your self, and the dragon that stands between you and your true self represents the fearsomeness of the unconscious for one who is still afraid of what may be lurking there. (For self, see Introduction, pages 52–53.)

2 For Jung, the first stage of the individuation process is the conscious ego's heroic struggle to lift itself out of the original all-encompassing unconsciousness and to establish its control of unconscious forces. This finds symbolic representation in the legendary dragon-slayer, St George (St George = the ego; the dragon = the unconscious).

3 The dragon may represent the devouring aspect of (your relationship with) your mother. 'Slaying the dragon' may therefore mean putting an end to whatever in your attachment to your mother is detrimental to the process of finding your own psychic individuality. Once the individual has achieved liberation from the 'dragon', the feminine side of the man's psyche and the masculine side of the woman's psyche will no longer appear in threatening form, but as an indispensable companion and guide in the further stages of selfdiscovery.

(In some male initiation rites in which boys are given adult status, the boys withdraw from the community and live in huts shaped like a dragon or crocodile. This may be seen as a symbol of a young person's victorious struggle with the devouring mother or all-encompassing unconsciousness: descending into the unconscious realm, acknow- ledging its powers, and transforming any negative functioning of those powers into positive ones.)

4 A dragon may represent the generative power of (Mother) Nature; the unconscious, felt as a womb pregnant with new possibilities of life.

5 A winged dragon may symbolize some kind of transcendence, some passing from a 'lower' to a 'higher' level of personal maturity. The fact that it is a dragon that does the flying suggests that the energy for further personal development must be looked for in your unconscious, perhaps in something you have been hitherto afraid even to look at. A winged creature may symbolize spirituality. But a winged dragon is a symbolic reminder that spiritual heights may not be attained by abandoning our 'lower' nature, but by letting it serve us as a vehicle. For example, sexuality can be bogged down in fantasizing lust and unedifying topdog/underdog games; it can also be something that releases and activates the power of love within us, a form of self- expression in which sensuous pleasure fuses with the joy of worship; indeed, it can be an experience of the mystical oneness of all things.

6 A dragon may be a symbol of your sexuality, particularly if it – your sexuality – frightens you. Is your fear irrational; or does sexuality threaten to rule your life? In either case, don't kill the 'dragon'; if necessary, tame it.

(In China 'chi' is good, life-giving energy and the channels it runs along are called 'dragon-lines', which are said to follow the flow of underground water and underground magnetic fields.)

DRAWER/CHEST OF DRAWERS

1 You go to a drawer for something you want or need. It may, therefore, symbolize a source of wisdom, a place – within yourself – where you will find the answer to your problem, the cure for your disease.

2 A chest of drawers may represent your psyche. The top drawer will then be your conscious ego, the bottom drawer or lower drawers the unconscious layers of your psyche.

DRINK(ING)

If you are drinking usually this will mean your unconscious is offering you something which, if accepted, will improve the quality of your life. If you do not, in the dream, accept the drink, make sure you do on the next occasion; or relive the dream, only this time taking the drink and swallowing it. In this way you may come to identify what it is that is being offered.

DROWNING SEE ALSO AIR-SEA RESCUE

1 If there is some area of your life where you are – or feel – unable to 'keep your head above water', this is probably what the dream is about. Dreams that follow may tell you what to do about the situation. You can either change the situation or change yourself, so that you react differently, or remove yourself (physically) from the situation.

2 Water may be a symbol of the unconscious, so drowning may express a threat or fear of being swallowed up or taken over – overwhelmed – by unconscious forces. If there is such a threat, it will be from repressed and neglected contents of the unconscious. What have you been bottling up? Consult a friend or, if need be, a psychotherapist. See also **Flood**.

3 Since water may represent the feminine, your dream may be asking you to do something about a mother-attachment that is stunting your development as an individual in your own right. A man's failure to free himself from such an attachment (which may be largely unconscious) may have disastrous results in his relations with women – in whom he will always seek his mother. A woman, unlike a man, doesn't usually have to cope with the effects of an infantile incestuous fixation of her libido on her mother; but both Freud and Rank stressed the crucial influence of the mother on both male and female children: for all infants, male and female, the earliest deep attachment is to the mother, the source of nourishment. Moreover, for the achievement of normal development the female child must – according to Freud – perform the additional task of transferring her libidinal attachment from mother to father. Jung, too, regarded the liberating of oneself from psychological bondage to one's mother as the first great step in the process of self-realization. (For self-realization, see Introduction, pages 44–55.) See also **Mother.**

4 Drowning may simply mean death; or may be a symbol of death-and-rebirth. See also **Baptism, Death.**

DRUID SEE ALSO WISE OLD MAN/WOMAN

DUEL

A duel will almost certainly signify an inner conflict, or a warring relationship with another person. If it is the latter, you already know the antagonists; if it is the former, you must try to identify them by being each of them in turn, in imagination. Get a dialogue going between the two, letting each present his case. Then allot to each of them an appropriate role in your conscious life.

The conflict will almost certainly be between your conscious ego and your unconscious, which means that usually you will only have one antagonist to identify.

DUNGEON SEE CELLAR, PRISON

DUST

1 Something covered with dust is something that hasn't been touched or used for a long time. Is there some shut-away and forgotten part of your personality that you ought to start using, to compensate for some lopsidedness, or to forestall mutiny on the part of the neglected component of your psyche?

2 A person covered with dust will probably be you, in which case you need rejuvenating. Perhaps you are too much under the sway of the past and need to dissolve old resentments and turn receptively to the future (or, rather, to the present) and to your inner self, to see what each of them is offering you.

3 Dust may be a symbol of death or mortality. But it may be that you feel dead, in which case, see **2** above. See also **Dead/Death.**

DUTY

If some course of action presents itself in a dream as a duty, be careful how to react.

1 It may be a true inner voice telling you what you must do in order to stay in tune – or to get in tune – with your 'destiny' (what Indians call '*dharma*', a word which means both 'destiny' and' duty').

2 It may be a pontification from an over-developed super-ego, reflecting either irrational fears or guilt-feelings stemming from traumatic childhood experiences, or conventional notions of right and wrong instilled into you by parents or accepted from other people unconsciously or in an anxious effort to conform. In the former case there will invariably be something compulsive in your behaviour, something that will indicate that what is controlling your life is not reason but (unconscious) emotion. In the latter case consider: no one and nothing has any authority over you unless you give them it; you alone are responsible for your decisions and values; and your essential duty is to your inner self.

DWARF

1 A dwarf, being below normal size, may symbolize a stunted personality – in which case you need to utilize hitherto neglected/ repressed parts of yourself.

2 A dwarf may sometimes symbolize the true self, not yet (fully) manifest. Pay attention to subsequent dreams for further signals concerning the way to move closer to yourself (your self). (On self, see Introduction, pages 52–53.)

(In some primitive societies dwarfs were regarded with awe, as having extraordinary divine powers).

DYNAMITE SEE BOMB, EXPLOSION

E

EAGLE

1 The eagle may be an animus figure (for animus, see **Brother/Sister**, sections **4–6,** and Introduction, pages 47–51).

2 Eagles live in high places and have been associated in primitive societies with the Sun God. An eagle may therefore appear in a dream as a messenger from a helpful source in your unconscious. Does it 'say' anything to you? If so, take it seriously and act accordingly. (Sun may symbolize your true self.) See also **Sun**.

3 An eagle has strong wings and may, therefore, symbolize something within you that can lift you – perhaps out of depression, towards the 'light'.

4 The sun may be a symbol of consciousness, and so the eagle may signify a need to extend your conscious awareness. Perhaps you need to get better acquainted with the contents of your unconscious and integrate them into your conscious active life. See also **Sun**.

5 Eagles have sometimes been associated with fertility. Psychologically speaking, fertility means bringing to life latent powers in the psyche.

6 Is the eagle paired in some way with a snake – holding a snake in its talons, for example? In mythology, eagle and snake represent the conflict of opposites. In psychological terms the opposites may be conscious/unconscious; thought/instinct; 'spiritual'/'animal'; masculine/ feminine. The dream may be pointing out an area of inner conflict that needs your conscious attention. If so, bear in mind that a lasting resolution of conflict is never achieved by denying the right of one of the conflicting parties. Some balance of forces in the psyche is called for, so that every psychic component gets its proper share of attention and expression without threatening the rights of other components. Eagle and lion (or some other animal) may have the same symbolism.

EAR

1 An ear may be a warning from your unconscious to 'give ear' to what it is trying to tell you. This may mean giving your culturally conditioned brain and conscience a rest, in order to concentrate on listening to the inner self.

2 It may be a sexual symbol, representing the vagina.

EARTH

1 Contrasted with the sky, earth may symbolize a need to 'keep your feet on the ground' or pay attention to 'earthy' or libidinal aspects of your being.

2 It may be '*Mother Earth*', symbolizing your own mother. Bear in mind that earth, as well as giving birth to things, also swallows them up again (when they die). Similarly, your mother – or your attachment to her – may have a 'devouring' aspect: one that hinders your individual development.

Mother Earth may also represent your unconscious. LIfe-giving energy comes from the unconscious region. This is the 'womb' that contains potential for further development. Again, this may present a negative aspect: the unconscious may seem to be threatening the conscious ego's attempts to maintain order in your life. However, the menacing appearance of the unconscious is a sign that such 'order' is precarious, having been achieved at the expense of neglecting important parts of your psyche. Wholeness is what counts.

Alternatively, Mother Earth may symbolize a need to supplement your reliance on reason or intellectual cleverness with a trust in the wisdom of the unconscious/instinct/body.

3 The planet Earth seen as a sphere floating in space could be a symbol of your true self, as yet unrealized (i.e. not yet translated from idea or ideal into act and fact); wholeness, integration; or a weightless, relaxed 'floating' with the life-giving currents that will carry you to the fulfilment of your individual 'destiny'.

EARTHQUAKE

1 What is quaking, or in danger of falling apart, may be you or your life. Is your marriage breaking up, or your business? Or do you need to look below the surface of yourself, into the depths of your unconscious, to see what is threatening to explode? Violence is usually caused by frustration. What part of you have you buried in the unconscious and robbed of its right to a place in your life.

2 Since earth may represent mother, an earthquake could mean the breaking-up of your mother-attachment; or possibly the death of your mother.

3 Since earth may symbolize the unconscious, an earthquake may represent your fear of being swallowed up by your mother or mother-attachment, or some other unconscious complex.

EAST

1 East is where the sun rises and may therefore signify some kind of 'rebirth': perhaps a radical re-orientation of yourself so that you face and receive all that is good and life-enhancing. 'The star in the east' guided the Wise Men to the Christ; and Christ, psychologically speaking, is a symbol of the true self.

2 Is it eastern countries/culture/values/spirituality that is making a deep appeal to you? This may mean you should go there/do some reading/start meditating. Alternatively, it may simply mean that you need to look somewhere – ultimately, in your inner self- for more real and relevant goals and values than those that have been dominating your life so far.

EATING

1 Eating can be a substitute form of self-gratification and may therefore represent the basic need that has been displaced – for example, sex, love, fulfilment in work.

2 If something or someone is threatening to eat you, the meaning is probably that there is something in your unconscious – a complex, phobia, fixation or whatever – which, if not attended to, may take over your whole life.

3 Perhaps there is something that you need to 'digest inwardly'; some positive idea or attitude that you need to assimilate into your being.

ECLIPSE

1 Do you feel that you are in eclipse, in decline? Look within for the never-ending source of life.

2 The sun may symbolize self/light/consciousness. Its eclipse may therefore represent an obscuring of your true self; a fear that unconscious forces may overpower the conscious ego; or a needed compensation of reason by intuition or instinct.

3 The moon is a symbol of mother or the feminine. Its eclipse may therefore mean getting rid of the sort of attachment to mother that is detrimental to your development as an individual in your own right; or the obscuring of your femininity (your anima, if you are a man). (For anima, see Introduction, pages 47–51.)

EGG

An egg represents (the possibility of) something new in your life, a new beginning: even the emergence of your true self. Something is about to break out of its shell; and the shell is probably your unconscious.

EIGHT

1 Eight has the same significance as four, of which it is a multiple: wholeness; the completely integrated human psyche. See also **Four**.

2 It also symbolizes infinity or eternity; or the endless cycle of death and rebirth.

3 Of course, the number eight may have special meaning for you – a particular date, or a house number, or whatever.

ELEPHANT

1 According to Jung, an elephant may be a symbol of the self (for self, see Introduction, pages 52–53).

2 Particularly for anyone acquainted with Indian religious ideas or iconography, an elephant may represent some power, available within you, to clear away whatever prevents you from achieving your goal. (Ganesha, the Hindu elephant god, is the great 'obstacle remover'.)

EMOTION(S) SEE ALSO FEELINGS

Emotions in dreams are not symbolic; they are just themselves. However, you need to be aware that emotions come from the unconscious, from what Jung calls 'the Shadow' – the 'inferior', undeveloped functions of your psyche. They may therefore be very disturbing, and often you will not acknowledge them as your own: instead, you may project them on to someone else. Therefore you need to be open to the possibility – or even the probability – that other people (or animals) in dreams represent parts of yourself, and that any emotion that is driving them in the dream is driving you in real life. (For inferior functions, shadow and projection, see Introduction, pages 40, 45–47 and 31 respectively).

EMPTINESS/EMPTY

1 An empty container may be a sexual symbol, representing the womb, or woman.

2 What is empty in the dream may be something that symbolizes the self-a room, for example, or house. In that case, it may represent your own (feeling of) emptiness. According to Freud, when a person suppresses or represses something, it often happens that nothing else comes to take the place of what has been suppressed/repressed, and the consequence is that the person's life becomes empty. (For suppression/ repression, see Introduction, page 19.)

3 Emptiness, an empty landscape or an empty container, may be a symbol of potentiality: where there is nothing, there is room for anything. The unconscious is sometimes visualized as an empty container, but – again – as containing the potential for all future personal growth.

ENCOUNTER SEE RELATIONSHIPS

ENEMY

1 An enemy could be a real-life enemy. If so, look for some way of coming to terms with the situation, either by removing yourself from it or by mending the situation – which may involve 'having it out' with the other person.

2 The enemy may be something within yourself. Is there some inner conflict that needs resolving? See also **Alien**, section **3**, **Fight(ing)**.

The enemy in your dream may be those qualities or parts of your psyche that have been neglected: what Jung calls 'the shadow'. This appears as the conscious ego's antagonist because it is struggling to assert its right to participate in your conscious life. Only by letting it do so can you attain personal wholeness.

ENERGY

Any manifestation of energy in a dream – electricity, atomic explosion, etc. – may be a symbol of psychic energy, which may be creative or destructive: creative if integrated into consciousness, destructive if left in a neglected state in the unconscious.

According to both the modern physicists' view and that of mystics, matter is nothing more than a manifestation of energy. The same view underlies the practice of homeopathy, which acts on the psychic energy, not on the maternal level; and acupuncture and acupressure. Get your energies working in a harmonious and positive way, and you will have a healthy body (though, of course, muscles won't develop without exercise). (The earliest known 'concept' of the Ultimate Reality/God is represented by the Melanesian word *mana*, which means energy or power.)

ENGINE SEE LOCOMOTIVE

1 If you are driving the engine, it probably represents your conscious ego.

2 An engine makes something move. It may therefore symbolize things that drive you: instinctive drives, or emotion.

3 It could symbolize your heart, the physical organ.

ENTRANCE SEE DOOR

ESCAPE

1 An escape may symbolize a way of liberating yourself from either an external situation or an inner attitude that has been severely restricting you.

2 On the other hand, it may mean you are evading a problem or its causes.

EVENING

1 Evening may symbolize middle age or old age. How did you feel in the dream?

2 It may symbolize either death or restfulness and peace. Compare the words in the evening service of Compline: 'the busy world is hushed' and 'the fever of life is over' (*The Book of Common Prayer*).

EVIL SEE ALSO DEVIL

Evil manifestations in dreams will nearly always represent something in yourself. Don't be offended: there is evil in everyone. What needs to be understood is that the same psychic forces may be good or evil – that is, they may work constructively or destructively.

Evil (destructiveness) rises up from the unconscious, where we bury the parts of ourselves that have at some time frightened us or caused guilt-feelings. We mostly project these repressed psychic drives or qualities on to other people, and this may be what your dream is saying you are doing.

Anger, hatred, and all other destructive tendencies can be dealt with only in oneself. The key to success in dealing with this evil within ourselves is to realize that what is evil is potentially good. Accept the neglected and feared things in yourself, let them assume their proper destined role in your life, and they will then be a power for good. Evil may reside even in what we call our 'conscience'. Conscience may be of two kinds: a repository for socially accepted norms of behaviour, including notions of right and wrong picked up from parents in our early years; and a medium by which the conscious ego can receive promptings and warnings from the centre of your being. The latter may sometimes conflict with the former – what your 'destiny' calls for may be at odds with what society demands – and courage may be needed to remain true to your inner self. Since we are all in process of evolution, we cannot properly expect perfection in ourselves or others. An unbending perfectionism is a neurotic condition. The essential thing is to be aware of the evil in ourselves. Only thus can we control it; otherwise, it will control us. Beware of the person who thinks he or she is perfect! Self-knowledge is the first step towards solving the problem of evil.

EXAMINATION

Dreams in which one is anxious about an examination or test are very common, and usually express a fear of failure.

EXCREMENT

1 Excrement may stand for something you need to get rid of; something from your past that has been poisoning your psyche. It is almost certainly something you have repressed (pushed down from the conscious mind into the unconscious). We repress what we can't cope with, but the anxiety or guilt-feelings that caused us to resort to repression do not leave us: they linger and fester in the unconscious and, if not given conscious attention, will have destructive consequences. Don't let yourself be constipated psychologically. Get rid of that store of negative emotion – resentments or whatever.

Anxieties and guilt-feelings often have irrational beginnings in early childhood, though they may remain dominant until some later experience wakens them. An emotionally detached appraisal of the situation that first gave rise to them may dissolve them. If not, seek help. Alternatively, adopt a Gestalt approach: don't bother about the origins of the negative feeling; just see what it is doing to you – and others – in the present, and deal with it, expel it like faeces, here and now.

2 Excrement may be a symbol of something you disapprove of or despise – perhaps mistakenly. Take a good look at the excrement to discover precisely what it represents in yourself.

3 According to Freud, faeces may be substitutes for either the penis or a baby. This is more applicable to a women's dream than to a man's.

4 Excrement may symbolize money – 'filthy lucre' ('He's rolling in it'; 'She's stinking rich').

EXECUTION SEE BEHEADING, KILLING, SACRIFICE

EXHUMATION

Digging something out of the ground – particularly a body – may be a symbol of bringing into consciousness what has been buried in the unconscious. If so, the dream is probably recommending that you do this.

EXIT SEE ALSO ESCAPE

An exit may symbolize death (literal or figurative). See also **Dead/ Death.**

EXPLOSION SEE BOMB, VOLCANO

EXTERIOR

An exterior view of something – for example, the facades of a building – may symbolize the persona, the self-image you present to the world (and to some extent to yourself), as distinct from your inner self, or true self.

EYE(S)

1 The eye may be a symbol of wisdom; knowledge, perceptiveness. If someone in your dream has a third eye, or just one eye, in the centre of the forehead, he or she may be taken as a guru figure representing an inner source of wisdom or (self-) knowledge.

2 It may represent the super-ego, an internal censor passing judgement on your thoughts and desires and actions. This understanding might be indicated if the eye in the dream seems to be the eye of God (but see **3** below). (For ego, id and super-ego, see Introduction, page 15.)

3 It may be the eye of God, not as censor, but as a symbol of your true self, the self that it is your destiny to attain or, rather, develop.

4 The eye may symbolize your way of looking at things, yourself and others. Is it a jaundiced eye, a sad eye, etc.? In this way your eyes represent yourself; in this sense all eyes are 'soul-ful' – through them you can see your inner self.

5 The shape of the eye may be a significant factor. Being shaped like a fish, the eye may carry some of the symbolism of the fish: for instance, fertility (i.e. potential for growth and new life); femininity; or the unconscious, especially with regard to the powers of renewal and creative change that reside there. See also **Fish**.

F

FAÇADE SEE EXTERIOR

FACTORY SEE MILL

FAILURE

Dreams of tailing are common recurring dreams: failing an examination, getting your words wrong when making a speech in public, missing a train, etc.

Such dreams may stem from childhood fears of punishment/ withdrawal of love and reflect a continuing self-programming for failure-anxiety. If so, you need to distinguish two kinds of perfectionism: first, the sort that causes constant striving for unrealistic goals – this is a neurotic form of perfectionism; and secondly, aiming at being true to yourself, with a readiness to respond positively to inner promptings towards a fuller embodiment of your ideal self, but also with a readiness to accept and love yourself as you are. Your standards, like your clothes, should fit you.

Above all, do not allow yourself to be overwhelmed and crippled by past failures. Instead, stay in the present, and don't accept a continual reiteration of 'can't' from yourself: 'can't' usually means 'won't', and 'won't' comes from something in your unconscious that needs to be brought into your consciousness (see **Childhood Recollections,** sections **1** and **2**).

FAIRY

1 In a man's dream the fairy may symbolize his anima – the feminine side of his personality – as something capable of bringing good fortune through the achievement of a better psychic balance (for anima, see **Brother/Sister**, sections **4–6**, and Introduction, pages 47–51).

2 In a woman's dream the fairy may symbolize her mother, her own femininity, or some part of herself which, if allowed to participate in the conscious organization of her life, would bring enrichment.

FALCON SEE EAGLE

FALLING

1 If the falling is a result of climbing or flying, the symbolism is probably straightforward: having 'got above yourself', you are now paying the price; or the dream may be warning you of possible future disastrous consequences of present behaviour or ambitions – as in the proverbial 'Pride before a fall' – in which case your present ambitions are out of tune with your real self, your real capacities.

It is not necessarily a case of conscious self-aggrandizement; indeed, usually one is not conscious of it at all. Hence the need for the dream! Self-inflation may be of two kinds: where the ego is 'possessed' by some unconscious factor; or where the ego will not deign to pay attention to the unconscious; or both. If you are prone to accidents, these may be symptomatic of an ego that is too much under the control of (unintegrated) unconscious forces.

2 The fear of falling felt in a dream may be symbolic of your real-life fear of letting go. Perhaps the dream is urging you to stop resisting an impulse from the unconscious.

The anxiety expressing itself in a dream of falling may best be dealt with by letting yourself go with the fall, with a view to both finding out what it is that you are frightened of and finding a way of transforming the anxiety-response into a more positive and creative response. Strephon Kaplan-Williams recommends that you stay with the falling in the dream itself (having prepared yourself to do so beforehand), not wake up before the end of the dream. As a way of preparing yourself to do that, you might try writing out the dream again – or re-living it in imagination – only this time letting the fall complete itself. You may learn a lot from this. See also **Flying**, section **4** and Introduction, pages 18–10 and 40–41.

FAMOUS PEOPLE

1 If some public figure or celebrity appears in a dream, the person may be there to express something about you or someone close to you.

2 The famous person may represent what you would like to be. This may correspond to your shadow-self, the other side of your personality that is still buried in your unconscious. If so, it means you could incorporate into your conscious life those desired qualities that you see in the famous person, because they are already present – latent – in you.

3 Alternatively, what the famous person represents may be a part of your personality or behaviour patterns that you have refused to acknowledge – for example, aggressiveness or a will to dominate.

FATHER

The presence of your father in a dream may not be symbolic at all, but a straightforward representation of him, or of the way you see/remember him (which may owe more to your subjective distortions than to what your father actually is or was). In any case, the reason for your father appearing in the dream will be shown by the part he plays in the dream story.

1 Specially for men, father may be a conscience figure. If this is the case, bear in mind that your father's prohibitions and commands will probably represent either conventional moral opinions which may have no relevance to your true nature or 'destiny', or irrational fears and feelings of guilt that began to take shape in you in early childhood. (On Oedipus complex, see Introduction, pages 28–30.)

2 For a woman, father may figure in a dream as one who generates affection (see Introduction, page 29–30).

3 If father features in the dream as a protector, it may be that you need to 'grow up' and rely on your own resources. After all, life can hurt you only if you let it, only if you identify with your emotional self instead of with that deep layer of yourself that is immune to life's pains and perils.

4 If you dream of your father dying, this may be a wish-fulfilling dream. Feelings of hostility towards parents are common, stemming from childhood feelings of resentment or envy. See also **Dead/Death**, section **3**.

5 Frequent appearances of either parent, or both, in dreams may be a sign that you have not thrown off an infantile over-dependence on them (see **3** above). Jung cites a young man's dream in which the man's father appeared as a drunken driver, smashing his car into a wall. This was the exact opposite of the real father, who was a most respectable person, rightly – but too much – respected by the son. What the unconscious was doing through the dream was dethroning the father in order to enable the son to achieve a proper sense of himself as a person in his own right, with his own unique destiny and value.

6 Father may be an animus figure, representing a woman's (unconscious) masculine qualities. In this case, the dream may be suggesting that she should cultivate this contrasexual side of her nature. (For animus, see **Brother/Sister**, section **4**, and Introduction, pages 47–51.)

7 Father may, if highly respected (and properly so), appear in a dream as a Wise Old Man figure. See also **Wise Old Man**, and Introduction, pages 51–52.

8 For father represented by an animal, see **Animal(s)**.

FEAR SEE ALSO ANXIETY, ESCAPE, FLIGHT (= FLEEING)

Fear is a common theme in dreams and is the essence of what are called nightmares. Its significance may partly depend on what, in the dream, is the object of your fear, but this will nearly always represent something within you – for example, some repressed emotion or instinctive drive.

1 What is frightening in a dream may represent (your encounter with) the unconscious in general, to the extent that it is still unexplored. Since – according to Jung – the unconscious compensates for the conscious mind and therefore contains qualities opposed to those of the conscious mind, you may well be frightened by it. However, those opposite qualities are there to round out your personality as you go through life, till you achieve wholeness; so, overcome your fear and get acquainted with what your unconscious contains. The unconscious may be represented in dreams by anything deep and/or dark (cellar, well, sea, black sky, etc.) or by a mother figure or brother/sister. (On the shadow, see Introduction, pages 45–47.) See also **Mother**; **Brother/Sister**.

2 The frightening thing may represent some particular content of the unconscious, usually something you have repressed – guilt feelings and fears of punishment, sexuality, anger, etc. Sexuality and anger are sometimes represented in dreams by wild animals. (On repression, see Introduction, pages 19–20.) See also **Animal(s)**.

3 A father figure or other authority figure may feature in a dream that expresses fear or guilt. This is because self-condemnation and anxiety often derive from childhood fears of father's (real or imagined) disapproval, prohibitions or expectations. According to Freud, all other fears of punishment get their energy from the fear of castration, which, for a male child, forms part of the Oedipus complex. In a dream castration may be represented by the cutting off of any part of the body. (For Oedipus complex, see Introduction, pages 28–30.) See also **Castration**.

4 Fear of mother may appear in dreams, where mother as an object of fear may be represented by a spider, or water, or crocodile, or dragon. Are you in danger of being overwhelmed by your mother or your mother-attachment?

5 Fear of castration does not appear in women, but its place is taken by fear of losing mother's love; and for both sexes mother is the first object of love, and so any fear of loss of love in later life (e.g. that of a spouse) may evoke that earliest fear associated with mother.

6 Something representing a man's anima or a woman's animus may be the frightening thing in the dream. This would suggest that you have repressed or neglected your anima/animus, probably because you find it difficult to acknowledge that the human psyche is bisexual, the woman's unconscious having strong male characteristics (centring round the use of reason, competitiveness, etc.) and the man's having strong female characteristics (centring on feeling, relatedness, etc.). If you are a woman with a tendency to be bossy or argumentative, you have not brought your animus into consciousness – which is why it sometimes erupts. If you are a man given to emotional outbursts, you need to give your anima a proper place in your conscious life; then it will cease to behave in an embarrassing way and will instead complement your masculinity in a creative cooperation. (For anima/animus, see **Brother/Sister**, sections **4–6**, and Introduction, pages 47–51.)

7 Does the frightening thing seem evil? If so, it will probably represent some part of you that is destroying or threatens to destroy your inner peace or outward efficiency. Bear in mind that nearly everything in your unconscious has two aspects: a threatening or disgusting aspect, when it is shut away and neglected; and a positive, creative aspect, when it is acknowledged and given an appropriate place in your conscious life. See also **Demons, Devil, Evil**.

8 According to Freud, anxiety dreams are invariably disguised wishfulfilments. For example, a dream in which you are anxious about a person's health may reveal an unconscious resentment or hatred of the person. Take this possibility seriously: repressed negative emotions are very common. See also **Anxiety**.

9 Fear of falling is a common dream theme. See **Falling**.

10 Does the fear felt in the dream bring the dream to a premature end? See the advice given under **Falling**, section **2**.

FEELINGS

What you feel in a dream, and the feeling tone of particular items or the environment in a dream are extremely important.

1 Feelings in dreams are not symbolic: they represent nothing but themselves. They are feelings you really do have, even if you have shut them out of your consciousness.

2 Feelings and moods in dreams are more often negative than positive: grey rather than sunny, violent rather than peaceful. This is because dreams express feelings you have repressed out of fear. Dreams have a therapeutic purpose, and that is why they bring to your attention those parts of you that are painful.

3 Occasionally, however, a dream may express a beautiful positive feeling: glorious erotic fulfilment; blissful oneness with life; love, even for people who have hurt you. Such a dream may usually be understood as indicating the direction in which you should be moving.

FENCE SEE ALSO CLIMBING

1 A fence may represent a barrier of some sort, which may or may not be self-imposed: social class distinction, some inner complex restricting your self-expression or the expression of some basic desire, etc.

2 Perhaps it is a set of prohibitions which you have adopted consciously or unconsciously but which are depriving you of normal satisfactions.

3 Your domestic or work situation may be the fence: perhaps it is too restricting and you want or need to break out.

4 Of course, if you are just sitting on the fence, it's make-your-mind-up time.

FENCING SEE FIGHT(ING)

FERMENTING

Something within you is coming up to the boil.

FERRY SEE ALSO BOAT

1 This may symbolize moving from one phase of your life to another; or a resolve to leave the past behind for a new and better future.

2 If the crossing is to a foreign land, the 'journey' symbolized may be that of the ego into the unconscious parts of the psyche.

3 Going across a river or other narrow stretch of water in a ferryboat may symbolize death. (This symbolism occurs in Greek, Egyptian and other mythology.) See also **Dead/Death**, for literal and figurative understandings.

FIELD(S)

1 A dream in which you are out in open fields may express a desire or need to get closer to Nature: perhaps to throw off social conventions or neurotic self-imposed taboos arising from an overdeveloped super-ego (for super-ego, see Introduction, pages 15–18).

2 Fertility may be symbolized: (the possibility of) personal growth; new life.

3 Perhaps the feeling is of earth in general, which may symbolize either the unconscious or instinctive levels of your being; or mother (See also **Mother**).

FIGHT(ING)

1 A fight may represent conflict in a real-life domestic or work situation.

2 The conflict may be within you, between opposed forces in the psyche. An obvious candidate is a clash between what you want to do and what you feel you ought to do. In this case, bear in mind that conscience is usually socially constructed and consists of the prohibitions and ideals that were imprinted in your psyche in your early years. Conflict between society's moral demands and the individual's wants or natural needs is probably at least as old as human history, and perhaps there is no complete solution: some degree of compromise may be inevitable. Do not assume, however, that social norms are always right. It may be that your conscience (super-ego) is an unreasonably severe one, perhaps the product of severe restraints in early childhood or a repressive religious upbringing. In any case, the conflict needs to be sorted out, and quite often this means allowing natural drives a little more expression. (For super-ego see Introduction, pages 15–18.)

3 The conflict may be between what we are in fact and what we are potentially. Jung sees conscience as the voice of an inner wisdom that will lead us to our true selfhood. Seen in this way, conscience keeps conflict alive in the psyche, not only between social morals and inner wisdom, but also between the actual conscious ego and the fully developed and integrated self. It would seem that the only satisfactory way out of these conflicts is to accept your 'destiny' – by which I mean, not some fate over which you have no control, but Nature's plan for you, reflected in your fundamental individual constitution and offering the greatest possible self-fulfilment if you will only go along with it.

4 If the conflict symbolized is between conscious ego and unconscious, the aggressor in the dream fight will probably represent the part of you that is demanding release from the dungeons of the unconscious. It will not hurt you unless you deny it expression. Identify it, and then welcome it as a talent or energy that can contribute to your well-being. Change the conflict into a dialogue, a respectful exchange between your conscious mind and your unconscious.

NB Where there is an unresolved inner conflict, there is a tendency to project the unconscious protagonist on to other people, often with dire consequences in personal relationships.

5 More specific inner conflicts are those between opposite psychic qualities or forces, such as masculinity and femininity, thinking and feeling. (On 'superior' and 'inferior' functions, see Introduction, pages 38–40.) See also **Brother/Sister**, section **4**.

FINGER

1 A finger may be a phallic symbol.

2 Is it the finger of blame being pointed at you? It may be your father or some other authority figure who does the pointing. However, these usually symbolize internal mechanisms of your psyche, and the blaming they represent is self-blaming. What imagined crime are you punishing yourself for?

3 A pointing finger may be showing which way you should go for further self-fulfilment or for the solution of a particular problem.

FIRE

1 Fire may symbolize libido, passion. Poking a fire may therefore mean arousing passion, and may be a symbol of the sexual act.

2 It may symbolize a fever, and the dream may actually have been caused by a feverish bodily condition.

3 If the fire is destroying or threatening to destroy a house, the house will almost certainly represent yourself (or, in the case of **2**, above, your body). The dream will usually mean there is some (repressed) emotion that is liable to burst out destructively if it is not given your conscious attention. The same would apply if the fire was a conflagration – for example, a forest fire – threatening you.

4 Fire – which can change liquids and even some minerals into air – may symbolize purification and transformation. (The Hindu custom of burning the dead is a symbolic purging.) If, therefore, what is being burned in the dream can be seen as a symbol of yourself, the message will be about getting rid of whatever has been blocking the way to a fuller realization of your true self.

What we think we are is usually all those habitual responses that have been conditioned by past events and experiences. What we really are is eternal – that is, not conditioned by the past. So, to find our true self we have to 'burn' the past. Fire, like floods, is a fertilizer, making new things possible by destroying the old.

5 In some contexts fire may be equivalent to light and may symbolize spirituality, truth, (self-)knowledge. (This is the opposite of hell-fire, which has been described as burning without giving any light. For the fires of purgatory see **4** above.)

FISH

1 A fish is a common symbol of fertility, which in psychological terms means (a promise of) personal growth.

2 If the fish are in the sea, the sea may symbolize the unconscious, the fish unconscious urges.

3 According to Jung, fish, being cold-blooded and primitive creatures, may symbolize a deep level of unconsciousness.

4 'Fishes and snakes are favourite symbols for describing psychic happenings or experiences that suddenly dart out of the unconscious and have a frightening or redeeming effect' (Jung).

5 They may also, says Jung, represent libido or greed.

6 A fish is a symbol of Christ and may therefore function psychologically as a symbol of your true self.

FISHING

1 This may symbolize bringing up contents of the unconscious into consciousness.

2 Are you the fish being caught in a fisherman's net? This may mean a promise of 'salvation'; that there is some energy source working for your good. (In Western Christendom the font was called the 'piscina' – fish-pond; those baptized in it were fishes caught in Christ's net.)

3 Are you trying to catch a small round fish? Jung would say this means you have begun to look for your true self.

FLAME SEE ALSO FIRE

This may symbolize libido: some consuming emotion.

FLIGHT (= FLEEING)

If in a dream you are running away from something or someone, this means you are frightened of and trying to get away from something in real life. It may be something outside you or something inside you. If it is outside you, look within yourself to find a perspective that will dissolve the fear: even fear of death will dissolve if you experience the immortal life within you; fear of 'failure' can exist only as long as you consider 'success' important. If the frightening thing is within you, look it in the face; get to know it and what it wants; and give it a proper place in your life. For **Flight (=Flying)**, see **Flying**.

FLOATING

1 Floating may be a symbol of liberation; the letting go of burdens, problems, restrictions, or ambitions; just being.

2 Water may be a symbol of the feminine in its positive aspect, in which case your floating will mean relying on/being supported by 'woman', which in turn may mean an actual woman or women (if you are a man); mother; or the feminine side of your own psyche. (The male psyche has a feminine dimension (anima), just as the female psyche has a masculine dimension (animus). See **Brother/Sister**, section **4**, and Introduction, pages 47–51.) The dream is probably recommending that you put more trust in (your own) femininity.

3 The feminine represented by the water may be Mother Nature; and the floating will then signify identifying with or going along with Nature, or your true inner self, as distinct from being pushed about in the man-made world of economic and moral and emotional pressures.

FLOOD

1 Water may symbolize the unconscious, and being swept away by a flood may mean your conscious ego feels threatened by something in your unconscious. Identify the source of the threat and make some sort of pact with it whereby its demands for expression can be met in a way that will increase the well-being of the total psyche.

2 Water may be a feminine symbol, and the threatening flood may be your mother or your attachment to mother, who/which may be hampering your individual development. See also **Mother**.

3 Flood–water is destructive but also fertilizes and makes new growth possible. (Myths of a flood are universal; and they always represent a purging that prepares the way for something better.) The flood in your dream, therefore, may signify both a need for personal reconstruction and that the only way your new and true self can come into existence is through the 'death' of the old self – or, rather, of those things (negative attitudes, lopsidedness or whatever) that have been hindering the unfolding of your true self. Flood-water may be compared with the waters of baptism. See also **Baptism**, and Introduction, page 46.

FLOOR (UPPER, LOWER) SEE STOREY

FLOWER SEE ALSO MANDALA; ENTRIES FOR PARTICULAR FLOWERS: E.G. ROSE, ETC.

1 A flower may symbolize what Jung called 'the Self': the true self; the fundamental order and beauty of the psyche. (For 'Self', see Introduction, pages 52–55.) (In Easterm mystic-meditative traditions, particularly the Taoist and Zen Buddhist, meditation on a flower is recommended as a means of promoting inner healing.)

2 An asymmetrical flower – for example, with one petal much larger than the others, or in which what should be the centre of the flower is actually off-centre – may indicate a lack of balance in your psyche: some part/function has been developed at the expense of others; or it may be that you have lost your 'centre' altogether – that is, have become disorientated. If so, you may need to put aside externally or intellectually imposed values and rediscover your inner centre, where you will find the values that are right for you. (This does not mean an out-and-out relativity of values. The values that correspond to your individual 'destiny' will be seen to centre on love, which means awareness of the oneness of all life and ensures respect for other people.)

3 The flower in your dream may be a reminder of the beauty and stillness of Nature, and of the need to get back to that beauty and stillness in yourself; a reminder that just being, and letting the groundplan of your life unfold itself, is more important than (external) achieving.

FLUTE

A flute may symbolize sexuality, or seduction. A flute-player (like the Pied Piper) in a woman's dream may symbolize a benevolent animus, ready to assist her in putting her psychic house in order (for animus, see **Brother/Sister**, section **4**, and Introduction, pages 47–51).

FLYING

1 Dreams of flying may derive from childhood enjoyment of swings and see-saws and represent a longing for the freedom and joy associated with (a happy) childhood.

2 Flying may symbolize liberation – for example, getting rid of (self-imposed) shackles or irrational taboos stemming from childhood experiences.

3 Flying may symbolize over-reaching yourself. In this case, your dream is probably warning you against projects that are too grandiose or not in accord with your fundamental constitution. This may mean that, in entertaining wild fantasies, you have actually overlooked your real capacities and gifts (remember Icarus!). See also **Falling**, section **1**.

4 Sky may symbolize consciousness, intellect, spirituality. A dream of flying may therefore mean either that you should extend the range of your consciousness (e.g. by bringing up unconscious contents into your conscious mind, or taking a less wordly view of life) or that you should give your previously neglected instinctual, intuitional or feeling functions a fuller role in your conscious life. The latter would be more likely to apply if you are an intellectual and if the dream includes some fear of falling.

5 Are you looking at the world below in a detached, uninvolved, unemotional way, so that your problems dissolve, or your values undergo radical transformation? If so, the message is clear.

6 Since sky is an age-old symbol of God or transcendence, flying may be a symbol of coming closer to your authentic or true self, or to the meaning of (your) life. See also **God(dess)**.

7 If you dream of flying fish, or a dolphin shooting out of the water, the meaning is probably that something in your unconscious wants to penetrate your conscious mind and/or to be allowed its proper place in your conscious life. If you dream of a pig (or an elephant, say) flying, this may mean some despised and rejected 'animal' part of you is now – or, much more likely, needs to be – integrated into your conscious life.

8 For flying saucers, see **UFOs;** or, if the saucers are flying in the kitchen, see **Fight(ing)**.

FOE SEE ENEMY

FOG

1 The fog may represent your unconscious. Therefore, examine as carefully as possible anything that, in the dream, looms out of the fog. It is almost certainly something you need in your conscious life or something you must come to terms with.

2 If you are lost in the fog, this means you are 'lost' in your waking life: not knowing where you are going; disorientated; needing a (new) sense of direction, new values.

FONT SEE BAPTISM, FISHING, SECTION 2

FOOT/FEET

1 In asking you to look at your feet, your dream may be asking you to take a fresh look at the direction of your life, or its lack of direction.

2 Feet moving backwards may mean that, in real life, you are not making progress – not growing as a person – but are (in danger of) regressing to an earlier stage. For feet moving to right or left, or clockwise or anticlockwise, see **Anticlockwise**, **Clockwise**, **Left**, **Right/Left**.

3 Feet may symbolize what your life is based on. Perhaps the dream is urging you to take a critical look at your fundamental attitudes and values.

4 Feet may symbolize contact with Nature, including instinctual drives and instinctive wisdom. Feet are at the opposite ends of the body to the head, which symbolizes intellectuality and fantasizing. Intellectuals typically have difficulty in assimilating the instinctive wisdom of their unconscious, but desperately need what the unconscious has to offer: without it they are lopsided (or top-heavy, if you will). Keep your feet on the ground and your head in the air? No, that means a split in the psyche. Rather, keep your head in your feet!

5 A foot or feet may symbolize male or female genitals. (Freud says that the foot resembles genitalia in having a strong smell and, although in adult life we may find such pungent body smells disagreeable, in childhood they fascinated us.)

FOREIGN(ER) SEE ALIEN

FOREST

1 The forest may be a sexual symbol, representing female pubic hair. (Arguably it could be male pubic hair, but there is a strong unconscious – mythological – connection between earth and Earth Mother.)

2 The forest may, especially if it is very dark, be a symbol of the unconscious. If there are animals in the forest, they probably represent (repressed) contents of the unconscious: instinctive drives; emotions.

FORSAKEN SEE ABANDONMENT

FORT/FORTRESS SEE ALSO MANDALAS

A fort or fortress may be a symbol of your self, your total psyche, wholeness.

FOUNTAIN

1 A fountain is a symbol of refreshment and (new) life and may represent life-giving powers in your unconscious.

2 Anything from which water flows may represent the penis and be a sexual symbol.

FOUR SEE ALSO MANDALAS

Four is an ancient symbol of completeness; wholeness. (The four corners of the earth, the four cardinal points, the four winds all, in primitive traditions, represent the whole of reality. So does a four-sided figure. The cross, too, extending in all four directions, is an ancient – pre-Christian – symbol of totality. Such figures, along with a four- petalled flower or four-lobed leaf, are mandalas, representing wholeness.)

According to Jung, consciousness has four functions: thinking, intuition, feeling and sensation. Usually, however, at least one of these and possibly three are undeveloped and are therefore still totally or partially unconscious. Personal fullness can be achieved only by lifting these functions out of unconsciousness and integrating them into consciousness (see Introduction, pages 38–40).

Multiples of four – eight, sixteen and so on – may have the same symbolic meaning as four. To see such a symbol in your dream does not mean you have achieved personal wholeness; rather, your dream may be pointing out, by contrast, your lack of wholeness.

FRIEND/COMPANION

1 If in your dream you have a friend or companion of the same sex as yourself, he or she may symbolize your alter ego or shadow, which consists of those aspects of your personality that you have so far neglected or repressed. (Even in real life we may project on to other people some of the contents of our own unconscious – repressed sadism, for instance, or an inferiority complex.)

The conscious ego, says Jung, cannot safely explore the deeper regions of the psyche without the shadow. In other words, there is little chance of re-rooting oneself in the true centre of one's being without first acknowledging that there are aspects of one's personality other than those that one has allowed into one's conscious life. (On shadow, see Introduction, pages 45–47).

2 If the friend/companion in the dream is of the opposite sex, he or she may represent the animus/anima. The anima is the feminine side of a male psyche, the animus the masculine side of a female psyche. Acknowledgement of this contrasexual element in the psyche, and its assistance in tackling life's tasks, are essential for personal wholeness (for anima/animus, see **Brother/Sister,** section **4**, and Introduction, pages 47–51).

FRIGHT SEE FEAR

FROG

1 This may be a sexual symbol, representing male genitals. As such it would appear in a woman's dreams and might express fear of sex, or an ambivalent fear-fascination feeling towards it.

2 The frog may symbolize the unconscious, or some part or function of the psyche that still lies buried in your unconscious, perhaps something you find horrifying or disgusting because of some traumatic experiences that gave rise to anxiety and/or guilt-feelings.

3 Perhaps the frog in your dream comes from the story of the Frog Prince. In the story a young woman is visited in her bed by a frog. At first, the girl is horrified and pushes the frog away. On the third night, however, she relents, and in the ensuing embrace the frog is transformed into a handsome prince.

Ernest Jones, a follower and biographer of Freud, says this is a story of a virgin overcoming her sexual fear.

For Joseph Campbell, an authority on mythology and a Jungian, the frog in the story symbolizes the unconscious, which at first sight is frightening but, when assimilated by the conscious ego, reveals itself for what it is – the total psyche, beautiful and true.

One might add that in both these interpretations what brings about the psychic transformation is a sexual embrace, but in the second interpretation it is an inner embrace, an intermingling and mutual penetration of the masculine and feminine sides of your psyche. (For anima/animus, see **Brother/Sister**, section **4**, and Introduction, pages 47–51.) in the second.

FRONT SEE EXTERIOR

FROST/FROZEN SEE COLD, ICE

FRUIT

1 Fruit may symbolize something that is offering you refreshment or new life, new kinds of fulfilment.

2 As the product of a process of development, fruit may symbolize your true self, the product of a process of integrating into your consciousness more and more of the contents of your unconscious. In the dream, are you reaching out for this fruit?

3 Some fruits, by virtue of their shape or juiciness, may symbolize male or female genitals – for example, a fig (male or female genitals) or banana (penis). Eating such fruits may symbolize sexual pleasure. See also **Eating,** section **1**.

FUNERAL BURIAL

Your own funeral may appear in dreams because you are anxious about your health or for some reason preoccupied with thoughts of approaching death.

If so, probably no good will come from trying to put death out of your mind. Death is something that needs to be taken into consideration in finding a meaning and a direction for your life. Such thinking may bring about a change of values; greater tranquillity; a nearer approach to your true self.

G

GANGSTER

1 A gangster may, particularly in the dream of an intellectual or idealistic person, represent an unconscious desire to achieve one's aims by force.

2 The gangster may symbolize something unruly and potentially violent and destructive in your unconscious.

GARDEN

1 A garden may be a symbol of your true self, particularly if the garden is symmetrical: square or rectangular or circular, and with a central point. See also **Mandala**.

2 Lush growth in the garden may symbolize (a promise of) personal growth.

3 A pool or fountain in the garden may symbolize a source of (new) life in your psyche; or the pure uncontaminated life of the person who is true to himself or herself, who has not exchanged the truth of himself or herself for a false persona (for persona, see Introduction, pages 40–41). See also **Fountain, Water**.

4 Any disorder in the garden will probably represent your own disordered psyche – weeds instead of flowers, decay instead of growth. Have you been pursuing wrong aims to the neglect of your true self, your 'destiny'?

GATE(WAY) SEE ALSO DOOR

1 Freud says a gate may symbolize the vagina; opening the gate, male penetration of the vagina.

2 A locked gate (a recurring image in Freud's dreams) may symbolize a problem to which you have not yet found the key; or it may mean you have not penetrated your unconscious. What is preventing you? It is you – or some part of you – that has locked the gate. Alternatively, it may symbolize something you should not attempt to do.

3 The narrow gate is a Christian symbol of the way to 'life' or 'salvation'. Psychologically, it may symbolize the way to healing and wholeness; the fulfilling of your 'destiny'; where you should be concentrating your attention and effort.

GHOST SEE ALSO SPIRITS

For Freud a ghost was a symbol of mother.

GNOME(S) SEE ALSO GOBLIN, SPIRITS

In folklore, gnomes are subterranean spirits who guard the earth's treasures. In psychological terms they symbolize whatever is keeping you from your task of entering and getting to know your unconscious (= earth) so as to discover your inner, true self (= treasure).

GOAT

A goat may be a symbol of male sexuality.

GOBLET SEE CHALICE

GOBLIN SEE ALSO GNOME, SPIRITS

1 In folklore, goblins are mischievous, destructive spirits. In dreams, they should be understood as unconscious forces; emotions or instinctive drives that have been repressed and are either rebelling against their neglect or forcing you – the conscious ego – to take notice of them. Listen to their story (of when and why they were repressed), consider their demands, and allocate them a useful role in your life.

2 The troll/goblin in the story of the Three Billy Goats Gruff guards a bridge leading to a lush meadow and threatens whoever tries to cross. The goblin figure in your dream may symbolize whatever is preventing you from being happy, or fulfilling yourself. See also **Bridge**.

GOD(DESS)

1 A god or goddess figure may represent a source of meaning/wisdom/energy. Look for that source in yourself, where it is usually covered by layers of emotion.

2 Male god figures may represent the animus in a woman's dreams, and goddess figures may represent the anima in a man's dreams. They may lead you deeper into your psyche. (For anima/animus, see **Brother/Sister**, section **4**, and Introduction, pages 47–51.)

3 Sometimes god/goddess may represent father/mother, functioning as a part of your own (unconscious) psyche. In such cases it is likely – though not invariable – that your feelings towards the parent are ambivalent, with fear or awe as well as affection. A stern Old Testament-type God may symbolize your super-ego, whose origins often lie in irrational prohibitions imposed on oneself in childhood as a reaction to real or imagined threats of punishment.

4 God(dess) may represent your true self, your potential wholeness. (See Introduction, pages 52–55.)

5 The god figure in your dream may be – God! Don't be surprised if your unconscious comes up with god images from a more ancient tradition than the ones you were brought up in: the unconscious seems to have a memory that reaches back to humankind's remotest past, and even beyond. (On 'collective unconscious' see Introduction, pages 43–44.) At a certain level of your psyche you may go beyond everything that is merely individual and experience oneness with life itself: an experience that may cause you to live authentically – for inner wisdom/ values – instead of merely role playing.

GOLD/GOLDEN

1 Symbolically, the colour gold has connections with the sun and may represent new life, self-renewal; some new development in your psyche. See also **Sun**.

2 Gold, as something valuable, may symbolize either your true self, as distinct from your conscious ego, or some faculty in your psyche which, if accepted and activated, could bring you closer to your real self.

3 Gold fruit (like the golden fleece) features in mythology as a hero's prize for overcoming monsters or other evils. This symbolizes the rewards of facing up to the contents of the unconscious, taming those that – through neglect – have become wild or aggressive, and integrating them into your conscious life.

GRANDFATHER

1 If your grandfather appears in your dream he may symbolize wisdom.

2 In a man's dream it may be a Wise Old Man figure. See also **Wise Old Man/Woman**, **Grandmother**, and Introduction, pages 51–52.

GRANDMOTHER

A grandmother in a woman's dream may represent what Jung called the Great Mother who, like her male counterpart, Wise Old Man, represents wisdom – and power – in the 'collective unconscious', the part of the unconscious that is much older than the individual. Sometimes the conscious ego may have to struggle to prevent these archetypes from swallowing him or her up. See also **Mother**, **Wise Old Woman** and Introduction, pages 51–52.

GRAVE SEE ALSO BURIAL, DEAD/DEATH, TOMB

1 A grave may represent death.

2 A grave is a hole in which you rejoin the earth from which you came, and where the decaying body acts as a fertilizer for new life. Therefore, look within yourself to discover what has died in you, or what should die; and what new personal growth is – or ought to be – taking place.

GREEN

1 Green commonly symbolizes the fertility of Nature (as in the Green Man, the spirit of fecundity). In your dreams, therefore, it may indicate personal growth, some new development in your personality.

2 An evergreen is a traditional symbol of immortality. In psychological terms it may symbolize new life or that level of your being where your individuality is united with life as such.

3 In modern life green may mean 'go', 'proceed'. In a dream, therefore, green may signal that all is well; the way is clear for you to go ahead – that is, make personal progress.

4 Green may signify corruption, as in pus or gangrenous flesh. Is there something going rotten in your unconscious? If so, attend to it; bring it into the daylight of your conscious life.

GREY

1 The colour grey may represent old age, death, depression.

2 As intermediate between black and white, and as the colour of mist, grey may symbolize an unclear state of mind where distinctions are blurred, or where you have difficulty in seeing where you are going or have lost all sense of direction.

3 It may – as in grey fog – represent the unconscious. See also **Fog**.

GROTTO SEE CAVE

GUIDE

1 If in your dream someone is guiding you, it probably means your unconscious is offering assistance to your conscious mind in its quest for self-knowledge.

2 If the guide is of the opposite sex, he or she is possibly an image of your animus/anima, whose positive function is to help the ego in its exploration of the unconscious. (For anima/animus, see **Brother/Sister**, section **4**, and Introduction, pages 47–51.)

3 If the guide is of the same sex, and especially if he or she is old and wise, you may have made contact with a deep source of wisdom and power in your unconscious, or – more accurately, perhaps – it has made contact with you. Pay attention to what it 'says', either in the dream itself or when, in reviewing the dream, you identify with or converse with the guide. (For identifying/conversing, see Introduction, pages 57–60; for Great Mother and Wise Old Man, see Introduction, pages 51–52.) See also **Mother**, **Wise Old Man/Woman**.

GUILLOTINE SEE BEHEADING

GUILT

Expressions of guilt are common in dreams. The cause of the guilt-feelings may be indicated in the dream, or in a later one.

1 Normal guilt-feelings are the psyche's way of telling us we are not on the right road for personal happiness.

2 Neurotic guilt-feelings are irrational. For instance, if the father of a five-year-old boy dies, the boy may feel responsible for the death; and the feeling of guilt and a desire to punish himself may linger on into adulthood, not at the conscious level but in the unconscious. (For Oedipus complex, see Introduction, pages 28–30.)

3 Guilt-feelings may arise out of a conflict between inner impulses and conventional – social or religious – morality. Here we have two kinds of duty: duty to society and duty to ourselves, which is a duty to fulfil our 'destiny' – that is, the potential that is contained in the basic structure of our individual psyche.

GUN

1 A gun may be a sexual symbol, representing the penis.

2 It may be a symbol of aggressiveness. If there is any uncontrolled aggression in your behaviour, what is the cause? Are you harbouring guilt-feelings that cause you to be angry with yourself; and does the anger spill over on to other people?

3 Do you kill someone or some animal with the gun? If it is a parent or partner or sibling, the killing may be a symbol of (unconscious) hostility or resentment. Otherwise, it might be some part of yourself that is symbolized by the victim; in which case you need to remember that every part and function of your psyche – including those that you have repressed – is valuable and has a contribution to make to your attainment of personal wholeness.

GURU SEE ALSO WISE OLD MAN/WOMAN

A guru may represent the wisdom within you. Pay heed to what he or she says. (Spiritual traditions in which gurus figure invariably speak of an inner guru.) So far as personal growth or healing is concerned, the unconscious will often take the lead. The ego often obstructs this creative process by clinging to its old way or refusing to acknowledge that the unconscious might know best.

GYPSY

1 'Gypsy' may conjure up ideas of occult psychic powers such as clairvoyance, but perhaps the gypsy in your dream is only asking you to look to the future and pointing to potential areas of growth in your psyche that depend more on instincts or intuition than on intellect or social conventions.

2 A gypsy of the same sex may symbolize your 'shadow', the as yet undiscovered parts of your personality (for shadow, see Introduction, pages 45–47).

3 A gypsy of the opposite sex may be an animus or anima figure, representing the masculine side of a woman's nature or the feminine side of a man's, particularly in the role of beguiling seducer leading you astray – that is, away from the truth of yourself. See also **Brother/Sister**, especially section **6**.

HAIR

1 Abundant hair may signify virility or male sexuality.

2 Long matted hair or a (long white) beard may symbolize wisdom – available in your unconscious depths. See also **Guru**, **Wise Old Man/ Woman**.

3 Cutting hair may symbolize loss of virility, or castration. See also **Castration**.

4 Pubic hair and (in a woman's dream) hair in armpits or on legs may symbolize sexuality.

5 Loss of hair/baldness may express (fears of) getting old and/or unwanted.

HALL

1 A hall, particularly if large and symmetrical, may symbolize the self.

2 If the hall is a mere antechamber (like a doctor's waiting-room) it may mean a large part of your psyche still remains unexplored.

HALO

A figure surrounded by halo or aureole probably symbolizes either your own 'divine' – true and whole – self (a halo is a mandala) or an inner source of wisdom and power. See also **Guru**, **Mandala**, **Saint**.

HAMMER

1 A hammer may symbolize male sexuality. Hammering a nail may symbolize the sexual act.

2 If used as a weapon, it represents aggression. See also **Aggressiveness**.

HAND(S)

1 Hands may symbolize ability, particularly – but not exclusively – practical and social.

2 What is the hand doing: striking, stroking, blessing, healing? Is it a male or female hand? Left or right? See also **Left**, **Right/Left**.

3 Are your hands tied? What is it in your situation or in your attitudes that prevents you from functioning at your full potential, or from doing what you know you should be doing?

4 Washing your hands? What do you think you are guilty of?

HARBOUR

1 Coming into harbour may mean finding/wanting a refuge (from life or some particular problem); reaching your goal; or (because a harbour might represent the vagina/womb) a strong mother-attachment.

2 Putting to sea may symbolize making a start on exploring your unconscious; or a need to liberate yourself from a strong mother-attachment.

HARE SEE ALSO RABBIT

1 A hare may be a symbol of the feminine (your own femininity, or your mother) or fertility (new personal growth).

2 Possibly the hare represents some personal characteristic – intellectual superficial cleverness, rashness.

HAT

1 A hat may be a sexual symbol, representing male or female genitals.

2 According to what sort of hat it is, it may represent a particular quality, role or lifestyle. Changing hats may therefore denote a (needed) change of attitude or direction or values; throwing your hat away may mean a decision to concentrate less on 'worldly' performance and more on self-knowledge and personal wholeness.

HAWK SEE ALSO EAGLE

1 A hawk may symbolize aggression, rapaciousness, ferocity.

2 It may carry a message from the deep centre of yourself. (The hawk is an ancient symbol of the spirit and is associated with the sun.) See also **Sun**.

HEAD

1 A head may be a symbol of intellect: rational as distina from intuitive thought.

2 It may symbolize the conscious ego as distinct from the unconscious (which might be represented by the abdomen or solar plexus).

3 It may be a symbol of masculinity.

4 A monstrous, horrifying head probably represents negative – because repressed – drives or processes in your unconscious. Try to follow Perseus' example. The Gorgons' eyes turned to stone anyone they looked at; but when Perseus succeeded in cutting off Medusa's head, the winged horse Pegasus sprang from her body. This may be seen as symbolizing the psychic or spiritual development that results from facing up to whatever is fearsome in one's unconscious.

5 A two-headed creature may symbolize either duality, antagonistic opposites in your psyche or the (needed) union, or bringing together, of opposing psychic qualities/funaions/forces – for example, masculine and feminine; conscious and unconscious. See also **Beheading**.

HEALING/HEALER

Any act of healing in a dream will usually refer to the healing of your psyche; and the healer in your dream will be or symbolize something you desperately need in your life in order to move towards greater wholeness.

HEAVEN SEE HELL, SECTION 2, PARADISE.

HEAVY BURDEN SEE BURDEN, CROSS, SECTON 3.

HEIGHT SEE ALSO ASCENT, CLIMBING, HILLS, LADDER, MOUNTAINS

1 Height may symbolize level of achievement.

2 The greater the height, the more panoramic the view. Are you getting your personal problem(s) in perspective; taking a more detached, less emotional view of things?

3 The symbolism may be that of 'ascension' or 'resurrection' – that is, transcending your present or former self towards a new and richer state of being.

4 Are you afraid – in your dream – of falling? This probably represents either fear of failure; or a warning that 'pride comes before a fall', and that you should not strive for what is beyond your reach, because it is not appropriate to your real nature. Concentrate instead on self-discovery, so that your endeavours will be in tune with the fundamental structure of your individual psyche.

HELL SEE ALSO ABYSS

1 Images of hell may be seen as depicting the fearsomeness of the unconscious. The fires of hell are those forces of the unconscious that seem to be threatening you. Hell as a place of imprisonment is the unconscious as the receptacle for repressed instinas and emotions (for repression, see Introduction, pages 19–20). Achievement of personal maturity and wholeness requires facing up to those repressed contents of the unconscious and taming them – that is, transforming their negative energy into a positive one. See also **Fire**.

2 Hell as the opposite of heaven may symbolize the mental chaos or even the total loss of self that is always a lurking possibility, whereas heaven represents the achievement of personal wholeness and harmony.

HE-MAN

A he-man figure in a woman's dream may be an animus figure, representing the masculine side of her (probably strongly artistic or intuitive) nature. (For animus, see **Brother/Sister**, section **4**, and Introduction, pages 47–51).

HEN

A hen may symbolize motherhood; female sexuality.

HERMAPHRODITE (A PARTLY MALE, PARTLY FEMALE FIGURE)

1 A hermaphrodite may denote the 'marriage' of conscious and unconscious components of the psyche. The 'marriage' may be total or partial, depending on how much of your unconscious you have integrated into your conscious attitudes and actions.

2 It may symbolize (the need for) perfect balance between the masculine and feminine sides of your nature (for anima/animus, see **Brother/Sister**, section **4**, and Introduction, pages 47–51). Every man has feminine components in his psyche, every woman has masculine components in hers. These contrasexual components are usually suppressed by social convention. However, neglect of the contrasexual side of your nature results in a lopsided development.

Dogmatism in a woman comes from an unintegrated animus. Similarly, a man who has not brought his masculine and feminine sides into harmony may be fickle, moody, and prone to emotional outbursts. See also **Couple**, section **2**, **Marriage**.

HERO

1 For a woman, a male heroic figure may represent her animus (see **Brother/Sister**, section **4**, and Introduction, pages 47–51); or it may be a (romantic) sexual symbol.

2 The hero may symbolize your conscious ego. Just as in myth the hero ventures into strange lands and wrestles with monsters to take possession of some great treasure, so the conscious ego must venture into the unknown realms of the psyche and face up to, tame and use creatively the forces that lie in the unconscious.

3 If the hero rescues a maiden, the meaning – for a male dreamer – will probably be that he needs to bring the feminine side of his nature into active collaboration with his masculine side. See also **Brother/Sister**, section **4**.

4 If in a man's dream the hero is assisted by a young woman, the hero may symbolize the conscious ego and the young woman the anima. The lesson will be as in **3** above.

5 If the hero is accompanied by an older person (or friendly strong animal), that person/animal may represent innate wisdom and power in your unconscious: that which, from within your own psyche, can supply all that your conscious ego needs. See also **Wise Old Man/Woman**.

HIDDEN

Hidden things in dreams should be sought, caught and identified. They almost certainly represent something your conscious ego needs – probably some repressed function or quality. (For repression, see Introduction, pages 19–20).

HILL(S) SEE ALSO MOUNTAINS

1 Rounded hills may be sexual symbols, owing to their resemblance to female breasts.

2 The breasts represented may be those of your mother. Are you still too much under her sway; not yet a person in your own right?

3 The breasts may be Mother Earth's – that is, for a female dreamer, the hills may symbolize innate strength and wisdom available in her unconscious.

NB The hills don't have to be a pair: Earth Mothers are frequently many-breasted (see Introduction, pages 51–52).

HOBGOBLIN SEE ALSO GOBLIN

HOLE

1 A hole may be a sexual symbol, representing vagina or womb.

2 A deep dark hole in the earth, or one that feels like the bottomless pit may symbolize the unconscious, under the fearsome aspect it presents when we have not familiarized ourselves with it.

HOLLOW

A hollow place or object (box, bag, etc.) may represent vagina or womb and symbolize either sexuality; or your mother; or (if very deep/dark) your unconscious.

HOLY/HOLINESS

1 A holy person in a dream probably represents the (spiritual) wisdom and power residing in your unconscious; the deep core of your psyche. What is the holy person saying? (On '***mana*** personalities', see Introduction, pages 51–52.)

2 A holy place may symbolize the deep core of your psyche (as in **1** above). See also **Church**.

3 Holiness may signify some inviolable principle or infallible authority. But beware: this may be the work of an over-developed conscience (super-ego) arising out of an introjected father image (on super-ego, see Introduction, pages 15–18).

HONEY

1 Honey may symbolize sweetness, nutrition – that is, something within you offering you happiness or personal growth.

2 It may symbolize the power of life or the force of nature within you. (In mythology, honey – like milk or the Hindu soma – is the lifegiving fluid in all things: sap in trees, milk in mothers' breasts, blood, etc.)

3 Mythologically, honey is the food of gods. Eating it in a dream may therefore mean participating in divine consciousness – which in psychological terms means that total awareness that results from assimilating the unconscious; the total psyche's (or self) awareness. (For Jung on 'the Self', see Introduction, pages 52–55.)

HORN(S)

1 Animals with horns are often symbolic of male sexuality, virility, aggression.

2 Horns may symbolize fertility – that is, the power of growth within your psyche.

3 Horned animals may represent evil, which in psychological terms would mean destructive/threatening forces in the unconscious. (Fertility gods were symbolically represented as horned animals. The Hebrew notion of God – adopted by Christianity and Islam – as outside and above nature led to fertility gods being identified with Satan.) See also **Devil**, **Evil.** But see also **Unicorn**, section **2**.

HORSE

1 A horse – particularly a stallion – may be a symbol of sexuality. Mounting a horse may symbolize the sexual act.

2 A horse may symbolize animality; instinctive dynamism that may 'carry you away'.

3 A galloping horse, because it appears hardly to touch the ground, may symbolize ecstasy; or a need not to get bogged down in sensuality/material ambitions; being in 'the world' but not of it.

4 Is the horse blinkered? Are you too set in your ways? Open your eyes to new possibilities, wider horizons.

5 A tethered horse may mean that something at the instinctual level needs to be given more freedom to express itself; or that you need to liberate yourself from guilt-feelings or anything else that is stopping you enjoying what life is offering you.

6 Horse(s) may symbolize emotion(s). If the horses are rampaging, either your emotions are threatening riot if you do not seriously attend to their requests or you are allowing your emotions to rule you. Tightly reined or tethered horses probably mean your emotions are too much repressed.

7 The horse may symbolize your unconscious or your whole psyche. In myths and folktales, horses sometimes speak. If the horse in your dream speaks, it is either the voice of your unconscious, or some part of it, or the voice of your true self, your inner centre. (On self, see Introduction, pages 52–55.)

8 If the horse is threatening, look into your unconscious to see what is threatening you there. Is it the whole (idea of the) unconscious that frightens you; or your sexuality, or some (other) repressed desire? Threat is dissolved when fear is dissolved by love that can embrace even horrific things.

9 If a horse or horses are pulling you in a carriage, they are your emotions. Are you in control or are they?

10 Black horses are associated with funerals. What part of you is dead or dying? Should it be allowed to die? Or what should be dead in you – for example, something from the past that prevents you from living freely in the present?

11 A horse's hoof may symbolize fertility or sexuality. Fertility is, psychologically speaking, the power to expand as a person.

HORSESHOE

A horseshoe is a symbol of good luck, well-being, good prospects for personal growth.

HOUSE

1 A house or other building may be a symbol of yourself. Going upstairs may mean going into the 'head' – that is, the layer of mind where (rational) thinking takes place. Cellars may represent the unconscious. Different parts of the house may be of different ages, the modern representing the conscious ego, the oldest the deep layers of the unconscious – what Jung called the 'collective unconscious' (see Introduction, pages 43–44).

If the house feels cramped, this might indicate frustration. Is some part of you not yet developed, not yet integrated into consciousness? What is keeping this or that instinct or emotion repressed?

If the house is cracked or crumbling, this could indicate either anxiety concerning your life, or the breaking down of an old image of yourself, to give way to a more accurate or larger view of your potential.

2 A house may represent your self-image: how you see yourself, or how you want to be seen by the world, or what you want from life.

3 If the house is your parental home, what you feel in the dream may say a lot about your childhood feelings – about your parents, for instance.

HUNGER/HUNGRY

1 The meaning of hunger in a dream may be non-symbolic: you just feel hungry.

2 If the hunger is symbolic, it will usually stand for emotional or sexual craving; but it may also represent a pining for meaning, or personal achievement, or personal development. Are you bored? Is life unfulfilling? This may be what caused the 'hunger' expressed in the dream.

3 If it is someone or something else that is hungry in the dream, perhaps some (repressed) part of you is being starved of attention or deprived of proper expression in your conscious life. See also **Cinderella**.

HUNTING

1 A dream of hunting may be recollecting something recently seen or read about. However, a dream whose contents are taken from recent experience may still have symbolic meaning.

2 Try to identify with or 'talk' with both the hunter and the hunted. Usually they will be parts of yourself. Is the hunter your conscious ego? What part of you are you – unsuccessfully – trying to kill? An instinct? Your anima/animus? (For anima/animus, see **Brother/Sister**, sections **4–6**, and Introduction, pages 47–51.)

3 In a man's dream a deer may represent a (young) woman; the hunting may be a symbol of sexual pursuit, and sexual 'conquest'. If so, what is the dream saying about your relations with women and, by implication, with your own anima?

HURTING

1 Physical hurt in a dream may symbolize hurt feelings. But dreams will often be specific – if, for example, the dream wants to draw your attention to humiliation, humiliation will be felt in the dream.

2 Try to identify with and 'converse' with both the person/animal that is hurt and the one who inflicts the hurt, and also with the hurt itself or the hurt part of the person/animal. In this way you will eventually unpack the meaning of the dream.

HUSBAND

1 If there is no symbolism, the dream will probably be telling you something about your relationship with your husband or your (unconscious) feelings about him.

2 In the dream, does your husband resemble your father in some way; or does your feeling towards him in the dream repeat what you feel/felt towards your father in real life? In this case, you would seem to be projecting your (image of) father on to your husband; and this in turn probably means you need to liberate yourself from a strong attachment to father that is preventing you from being your own person.

3 The husband in the dream may symbolize your animus – that is, the masculine side of your nature. The animus (and, in men, the anima) is a great projector. (For anima/animus, see **Brother/Sister**, section **4**, and Introduction, pages 47–51.)

HYBRID

1 A hybrid form (of plant or animal) may symbolize either two opposing forces within your psyche (e.g. conscious/unconscious; masculine/feminine sides of your nature; (rigorous) reasoning/ (uncontrolled) emotions) or the (needed) union of those opposing forces. See also **Centaur**.

2 For composite words in dreams, see Introduction, page 20–21. A form such as 'shehe' ('she' and 'he') would naturally be understood as in **1** above.

I

The 'I' in dreams is invariably your conscious ego. Other people, animals and objects in your dreams are usually parts of yourself that your conscious self needs to relate to and cooperate with.

ICE SEE ALSO COLD

1 As water may symbolize emotion, so ice may symbolize 'frozen' emotion, emotion paralysed by fear or guilt.

2 Ice may be a symbol of sexual frigidity.
In either case, melt the ice by warmly embracing the repressed feelings.

ICEBERG SEE ALSO ICE

An iceberg may be a symbol of your self, the tip representing your unconscious mind.

ICE-CREAM

Eating ice-cream may symbolize enjoyment of the free flow of previously 'frozen' psychic energy or emotion.

ICICLE SEE ALSO ICE

May be a symbol of the penis.

ILLNESS SEE DISEASE

IMMORAL SEE EVIL

IMPOSTOR

What the impostor is pretending to be is probably what you in real life are pretending to be: your persona or self-image. (For persona, see pages 40–41.)

IMPRISON SEE PRISON

The likely meaning is that what is (being) imprisoned is some repressed emotion or instinctive drive.

INCEST

The act of incest in the dream may of course be a real-life one that you witnessed or were involved in. If so, have you talked about it to a good friend or psychotherapist? If not, why not do so? Where there is symbolism, it will probably be as follows:

1 For a man, a dream of incest with your daughter will usually express fear of the erotic element in your feelings towards your daughter in real life; but could be a straightforward expression of desire.

2 For a man, in a dream of incest with your sister, the sister may be an anima figure, representing the feminine side of your nature. If the positive aspect of the anima is represented – as a source of wisdom and all-embracing love – the unconscious is inviting you to accept and integrate these good things into your conscious life. If the anima figure displays a negative – possessive and moody – aspect, the dream is telling you that love (in this case, proper respect for the feminine components of your psyche) can change a negative into a positive. (On anima, see **Brother/Sister**, sections **4–6**, and Introduction pages 47–51.)

3 For a man, a dream of incest with your mother may express the desire you felt for her as a small boy. This desire, though repressed, may occasionally surface. Try to accept it as natural and innocent (on the Oedipus complex, see Introduction, pages 28–30). Your mother may sometimes symbolize your anima. See also **2** above, and **7** below.

4 For a woman, if you dream of incest with your father, it may be an expression of your (repressed) childhood desire for your father. You need to see the innocence of such feelings.

5 For a woman an act of incest with your brother may be telling you something about your animus, the masculine side of your nature. If the animus figure is a positive one, it represents the source of all you need for wholeness, if only your feminine and masculine psychic components unite fully at the conscious level. If the animus figure is a negative one – obstinate, opinionated – you have repressed and neglected your masculine qualities so

that they express themselves in uncontrolled and threatening ways; and only love – full respect for them, and allowing them a proper place in your conscious life – can transform negative to positive.

6 Again for a woman, a dreamed act of incest with your son, or incestuous desires, are probably expressing your anxiety concerning your – natural – sensuous pleasure in the sight and touch of him.

7 A man's dreamed or fantasized incest with mother may represent a death-wish, a desire to return into the womb. This means your mother has the properties of the Earth Mother in her negative, devouring aspect; and you really do need to make every effort to throw off an attachment to mother that is preventing the unfolding of your own individual self. (See Introduction, pages 49–50.)

Alternatively, incest with mother in a dream could express a desire for new life: a descent, as it were, into the Earth Mother's womb for rebirth.

INITIATION

Initiation rites help a person to make the transition from one stage/status to a higher, more advanced one – for example, from childhood to adulthood, or from a 'worldly' work-and-family orientated existence to an 'otherworldly' God-centred life. Their symbolism is always that of death and resurrection (or rebirth), represented by such features as the following:

- a dagger pointing at your heart, or being used to kill you;
- being laid on an altar for sacrifice;
- sweating profusely in a heated hut or tent – for purging body and psyche of accumulated impurities and for generating spiritual 'treat' or energy;
- circumcision – to turn you into an adult, or to put you among God's chosen ones;
- being given a new name – to mark your new status, to show you are no longer the person you were. What does the new name mean or suggest to you?
- being tattooed – for the same purpose as **5**, above. Does the tattoo suggest anything to you?
- going into a state of ecstasy – signifying a new level of consciousness;
- some esoteric teaching given you by a priest or holy person – new directions for your life. NB This feature, on its own, might count as a pseudo-initiation: substitution of ideas for actual experience.

If any of these items occur in a dream, it may be that you are being called upon to leave your present stage of life/stage of personal development/set of attitudes, beliefs, values and goals for a new one. Who or what is doing the calling? God? Your unconscious? The name is less important than the fact.

INQUISITOR

This is probably your super-ego (see Introduction, pages 15–18).

INSECT(S) SEE ALSO SPIDER

1 If seen as mindless automata, insects may symbolize either (your attitude towards) your instinctive drives or unconscious forces that seem to constitute a threat to the rule of reason. In either case, you probably need to overcome – or at least examine – your repulsion.

2 If it is a solitary insect, it may be bringing a message from your inner self. That your inner self should appear in such a paradoxical guise or employ such a despicable and unlikely ambassador is a reflection of your (very unwise) contempt for your inner self, as shown perhaps in the way you exclude it from your conscious life. (Remember the cricket in Pinocchio's adventures?)

INVALID

The invalid may represent either you or some part of you. (The latter may apply even if in the dream it is you who are pushing the invalid in his chair.) If it is you, what has robbed you of your energy or ability or confidence? Outward circumstances, or some internal mechanism (failure-programming or the like)? If it is some part of you, what part have you condemned to an unproductive existence in the locked cellars of your unconscious?

INVASION

If in a dream you or some symbol of yourself (e.g. a house or a piece of ground) is invaded (e.g. by an angry crowd or an army of insets), the meaning is probably that you are (in danger of being) 'possessed' – that is, taken over by unconscious contents. What is repressed festers and may eventually take over the whole psyche. Take a look at the desires/intuitive drives you have repressed, and give them proper respect and a proper place in your life.

IRON

1 Iron may sometimes signify imperfection, inferiority – as contrasted with gold.

2 It may be a symbol of strength, but often with overtones of inflexibility and ruthlessness ('ruling with a rod of iron', 'the Iron Duke', 'the Iron Lady').

ISLAND

1 An island may be a symbol of the conscious ego's relation to the unconscious (symbolized by the sea).

2 It may symbolize your relations with your mother (represented by the sea). Is the sea threatening to engulf the island (too strong a mother-attachment) ?

J

JADE

In Chinese tradition, jade contains the mysterious cosmic energy in concentrated form. It therefore symbolizes power, life, fecundity, immortality. Perhaps the jade in your dream carries some of this symbolism – even if only because we usually think of green in connection with jade. See also **Green**.

JAVELIN SEE SPEAR

JESUS SEE CHRIST, GURU

JEWEL(S)

A jewel is a symbol of your true self. If the jewel is in a casket (= the unconscious), this means your real self is still something to be discovered and assimilated into your consciousness.

JOCKEY SEE HORSE

JOKE

If a joke is told in a dream, or if the dream story itself seems like a joke, this may be the unconscious trying to get your attention; or to get its message past your internal censor. Concentrate on the symbolism even of minor items in the dream, since these may bear an emotionally weighty message – by displacement (on displacement, see Introduction, page 20).

JOURNEY SEE TRAVEL

1 A journey may express a need or desire to escape from your present situation: external constraints or inner conflict. But dream journeys usually have a destination (see **2** and **3** below).

2 Is it a journey to a sacred place? Psychologically speaking, this may mean either that you are now aware of your true self, as something not yet achieved but to be kept in mind always as the overriding goal; or, if the place is a sacred well or place of healing, that you now feel the need for psychic healing and wholeness.

3 Is the destination not reached? Can't you find the place although you've been before? The dream may be telling you that, although you may have caught fleeting glimpses of your true self, you have not let it become what it ought to be.

4 A voyage of discovery to unknown – previously unvisited – lands probably means your unconscious is inviting you to make its acquaintance. The sea is a common symbol of the unconscious.

5 Journeying with a companion (if of the same sex, your alter ego; if of the opposite sex, your anima/animus) or without one in unfamiliar territory and with feelings of terror and unpredictableness is an allegory of your own progress towards the fulfilling of your 'destiny', coming to terms with your own unconscious 'shadow', healing inner conflicts and expanding towards wholeness. Bits of that allegorical journey probably appear in most of your dreams, and will go on doing so.

6 The journey in the dream may tell you what is actually happening in your life at present, or – less often – how you ought to live. For example, if the journey is a spiral climb and, near the summit, you get confused by the sign-posts, so that you never reach your destination, this is probably a reflection of a recurring pattem in your life. In such a case, you might find it helpful to relive the dream, only this time looking out for different options you might take at this or that juncture in the dream story. This could help build up a more positive and effective pattern of behaviour in your life.

JUDGE

1 A judge may personify your super-ego – that is, the conventional morality assimilated from parents and society, and functioning as an internal censor, prohibitor, inhibitor and standard-setter. Some of its commands/prohibitions/expectations may be irrational and arise from a childhood trauma – that is, an emotional 'wound' that produced anxiety and repression which have become permanent features of your life. (On repression, see Introduction, pages 19–20.)

2 The judge may represent a different sort of conscience, an inner guide that tells you what you should be doing to fulfil your individual 'destiny'.

How do you tell the difference between these two kinds of judge? In **2** the judge in the dream might be awe-inspiring, in **1** merely authoritative.

JUDGEMENT

1 A Last Judgement sort of condemnation may be a symbolic expression of your neurotic desire to punish yourself for some imagined guilt. The content of the judgement will tend to be that if you continue as you are, you must pay the penalty. Its tone will be angry or vindictive.

2 It may be a wise warning from your inner centre: if you allow old habits and attitudes to continue, you will bring unhappiness and suffering on yourself (and others). The judgement will be filled with love.

JUGGERNAUT

1 A huge lorry or other heavy and fast-moving object coming in your direction may symbolize some external catastrophe that you see looming over you constantly. In this case, you may have a guilt complex, arising (perhaps in early childhood) out of some imagined crime, and causing you to conjure up pictures of a future punishment – which may, unfortunately, be a self-fulfilling prophecy.

2 It may symbolize internal, unconscious forces that threaten to destroy the conscious ego – which would mean loss of control, psychic chaos.

In all nightmares you should stay with the dream to the end, and not wake before – in this case – the juggernaut runs over you. In this way you may see more clearly the two aspects of yourself represented respectively by the juggernaut and the 'I' in the dream. If you really can't do this, try living through the dream again in your imagination, this time waiting for the end. Perhaps a friend could help you to do this, or a psychotherapist.

JUMBLE

This is probably a reflection of the disorderly state of your mind; conflict in your psyche. See also **Junk**.

JUNGLE

A jungle is a symbol of the unconscious. Its wild inhabitants are probably neglected, disorderly, possibly mutinous 'animal' or instinctual drives, and repressed guilt-feelings and fears.

JUNK

Discarded rubbish symbolizes the suppressed or repressed contents of the unconscious. You should give it a thorough turning-over. You will find extremely valuable items – aspects of yourself – that you need to rehabilitate. (On repression/suppression, see Introduction, pages 19–20.)

JURY SEE JUDGE

KALEIDOSCOPIC IMAGE

Seeing a jumbled miscellany of fragments come together to form a symmetrical and beautiful image may be a symbol of the order that can come to your psyche when all its components are 'centred' – that is, function as servants or instruments or expressions of your true, inner self.

KEY SEE ALSO LOCK

1 What will the key open? A box? A door? In any case, it is a sign either that your unconscious is offering you access to your true self or, more modestly, a solution to a problem, or that life is offering you an opportunity to fulfil yourself or to exercise some hitherto unused talent.

2 An old man with keys may symbolize a deep inner source of wisdom. Follow him, and all secrets – your 'destiny'/your real self – will be revealed.

KILLING SEE ALSO SACRIFICE

1 Murder in a dream may express your hatred or envy towards the person. There is often enmity or rivalry between siblings, or (unconscious) hostility towards a parent or partner. (For Oedipus complex, see Introduction, pages 28–30.)

2 Killing a person or animal may symbolize repression/suppression of some aspect of yourself – for example, some instinct or desire. Repressed contents of the unconscious need to be integrated into your conscious life. Alternatively it may represent putting an end to negative self-programming arising out of, for example, irrational guilt-feelings and associated fears. The dream is probably recommending that you should do this. See also **Sacrifice**.

3 If the victim is clearly of the opposite sex, he or she or it may symbolize your partner – in which case see **1** above – or your anima/animus. Are you depriving the contrasexual qualities of your personality, not allowing them an equal role in your life? (On anima/animus, see **Brother/Sister**, sections **4–6**, and Introduction, pages 47–51.)

KING (AND QUEEN)

1 A king may symbolize your father – or your subjective image of your father.

2 King may be a symbol of the self. So may king and queen together, representing a union of opposites in the psyche – for example, conscious and unconscious, masculine and feminine qualities, etc. See also **Couple**.

3 If the king and queen are chess pieces, and the king is under threat from the queen, this may symbolize (in a man's dream) a motherattachment that is threatening to smother his individuality and independence; or a threatening – because repressed and neglected – anima; or (in a woman's dream) the repression of the animus. (On anima/animus, see **Brother/Sister**, sections **4–6**, and Introduction, pages 47–51.)

KISS

1 In a dream a kiss is nearly always a kiss of life, symbolizing bringing to life the neglected side – masculine or feminine – of your personality, or other hitherto unemployed parts of your psyche.

2 However, it could be (just) sexual.

KNIFE SEE ALSO CUTTING, DAGGER, INITIATION, SACRIFICE

A knife may symbolize a (repressed) deep-seated destructive wish.

KNOB

A knob may be a sexual symbol, representing the penis.

KNOT

1 A knot may symbolize a problem, external or internal.

2 It may be joining things together – in which case you are being asked to end an inner conflict by reconciling the opposed forces (conscious and unconscious; intellect and instina or intuition; masculine and feminine components of your psyche), and letting them both make their contributions to your personal wholeness. See also **Couple**.

L

LABYRINTH

1 A labyrinth is a symbol of the unconscious. Is there a frightening monster guarding something valuable at the centre of the labyrinth? You must come to terms with the frightening contents of your unconscious if you are to uncover your true self. (See Introduction, pages 47–48.)

2 It may be a symbol of mother. Getting out of the labyrinth means liberation from a smothering mother-attachment.

3 Jung described the 'individuation' process as a 'labyrinth' path, meaning that progress towards self-discovery and self-fulfilment does not follow a straight line, but involves periodic returns to earlier starting-points (for individuation, see Introduction, pages 44–55).

LADDER SEE ALSO ASCENT

1 (Climbing) a ladder may symbolize progress: improving your status; achieving or moving towards a goal.

2 Climbing a ladder to heaven is a recurring mythological motif. It may be seen as a symbol of achieving personal wholeness (Jung's 'Self').

3 Sometimes the ladder – like Jacob's in the Book of Genesis – is used by angels descending and ascending: a symbol of communication between the spiritual and physical aspects of the self, or between the true self and the ego. (On self, see Introduction, pages 52–55.)

4 Descending a ladder to escape from an upper storey of a burning house might symbolize (a need to) escape from your emotional self.

5 Descending a ladder into a deep pit or well might symbolize a resolve – or need – to explore your unconscious depths. Climbing a ladder to get out of the pit or well might symbolize the need to escape from something that threatens to engulf you – a mother-attachment, perhaps, or other unconscious contents.

LAKE

1 A lake may symbolize the unconscious, particularly if it is set in the deep, dark hollow of high mountains.

2 It may be a symbol of self. The stillness (and clearness) may suggest the deep self that lies beneath the turbulent emotional self.

LAMB

1 A lamb may symbolize vulnerability and dependence – the child in you, that needs your love. See also **Child**, sections **2** and **5**.

2 It may symbolize innocence – the beauty of yourself as you originally were, before the innocent joy of being gave way to the perplexing complications of doing, getting and achieving. See also **Child**, section (2).

3 Is it a lamb for the slaughter; a sacrificial lamb (the Lamb of God that takes away the sins of the world)? This probably reflects a longing to be rid of guilt-feelings, but it may also signify that sins can be dissolved – if we learn to forgive both ourselves and others. See also **Sheep**.

LAMP **LIGHT**

LANCE **SPEAR**

LANDING

1 Landing (as of an aeroplane) may symbolize (a need for) grounding yourself, either in reality (instead of fantasizing) or experience (instead of mere intellectual playing with ideas) or in your body, or instincts, or intuition, or Nature.

2 Landing (as going ashore from a boat) may symbolize escaping from a stunting mother-attachment or from other unconscious contents. The sea may symbolize either mother or the unconscious. Liberating yourself from negative emotional ties to your mother is always good: it represents a great leap towards taking responsibility for your life and being your own person. Escaping from other unconscious contents is good for you in the sense of freeing yourself from the threats of the unconscious, and this can be achieved only by becoming better acquainted with what is going on in your unconscious.

LEADING

1 Bearing in mind that the 'I' in dreams is almost invariably your conscious ego, you may be fairly sure that leading others (people or animals) in a dream means you are – or that you should be – in control of your unconscious forces; of your emotions; or of your life-situation.

2 If in the dream you are being led, who or what is leading you?

If it is a person of the opposite sex, it may be your anima/animus. If so, you must distinguish between leading and controlling: that your anima/animus should take you by the hand and show you things you had never deigned to look at – in yourself – before, is good; but an anima/animus that wants to take over the whole psyche is overcompensating for having been neglected – so now is the time to stop neglecting it and denying it a place in your conscious life (for anima/animus, see **Brother/Sister**, sections **4–6**, and Introduction, pages 47–51).

Alternatively, he, she or it could represent some (unconscious) attitude or instinctive drive. Where are you being led: towards your true self or astray?

3 Is the leader an authority figure? If so, he or she may represent either some actual person (father, for instance) or some belief-system (a dogmatic religious or other institution) that is influencing you, perhaps to the extent of moulding you. The dream may be telling you that your life should be ruled from within, not from outside.

LEFT SEE ALSO ANTICLOCKWISE

The left side of the body represents heart, emotions, unconscious factors, intuition. Movement from right to left, or anticlockwise, symbolizes moving over from reason to intuition, from conscious to unconscious, etc. (Movement to the left is contrary to the way of the sun, which is a symbol of consciousness.)

LEGS SEE ALSO FOOT/FEET, SECTIONS 1–4

1 Having strong legs may symbolize being strongly supported, confident.

2 Weak, unsteady legs may suggest a lack of grounding or firm foundation, a lack of centredness.

3 For the symbolism of direction of movement, see **Left, Right/Left**.

LENS

The image of a lens in your dream would probably mean you are being asked to focus your attention on something.

LIFT

1 The symbolism of a lift may be that of things coming up from the unconscious (in which case your unconscious obviously wants you to look at them); or of the conscious ego descending into the unconscious to take a look around.

2 Going up in a lift may symbolize attaining a more elevated or spiritual, or simply more detached, standpoint; or becoming more imaginative; or more 'heady' – that is, more rationalistic but less in touch with instinct and intuition.

LIGHT SEE ALSO DARKNESS

1 Light, particularly sunlight, is a common symbol of consciousness. Moonlight, on the other hand, might represent the unconscious, the intuitive, the feminine.

2 Light at the end of a dark tunnel may symbolize hope, life after death, or the meaning of (your) life.

LIGHTHOUSE

1 Sea is a symbol of the unconscious; light symbolizes consciousness. As a lighthouse helps mariners to navigate safely, so you will avoid disaster when exploring the unconscious so long as you keep consciousness awake.

2 The symbolism of the lighthouse could be phallic (and sea may also symbolize the feminine).

LIGHTNING

1 Lightning may be a sexual symbol. Compare the mythological image of the sky-god impregnating the earth-goddess with a flash of lightning. On the other hand, lightning striking the earth may represent consciousness penetrating the unconscious – in which case your dream is probably urging you to explore the hidden parts of yourself.

2 It may symbolize a'flash' of insight or inspiration.

3 It may symbolize punishment: 'the wrath of the gods'. If so, you may have a guilt-complex that needs sorting out. However, not all guilt-feelings are neurotic; your dream may be telling you you have done something wrong. If lightning strikes you, or something that may symbolize you (e.g. a house), the dream message may be either that you need to demolish your current self-image in favour of one that corresponds more closely to your true self or that your current lifestyle or pattern of behaviour is threatening your true self.

LILY SEE ALSO DEAD/DEATH, WATER-LILY

A lily may be a symbol of new life; life after death (which is why white lilies are associated with funerals).

LION

1 A lion may symbolize your 'animal' nature; or aggressiveness; or power.

2 In a woman's dream it may symbolize the animus (for animus, see **Brother/Sister**, sections **4–6**, and Introduction, pages 47–51).

LIPS

May be a sexual symbol, representing the vagina.

LIZARD

1 May represent something in your unconscious that you don't wish to take notice of.

2 Because it is cold-blooded and primitive, the lizard may represent some part of – or some message from – the collective unconscious (for collective unconscious, see Introduction, pages 43–44).

LOCK/LOCKED

AS IN LOCK AND KEY

Locks symbolize inaccessibility. Perhaps you can't get what you want; or perhaps you have denied parts of yourself access to your conscious mind. In a healthy psyche nothing should be locked.

CANAL LOCK

A canal lock may symbolize a block in the flow of psychic energy. There may be repressed materials that need to be brought up from the unconscious; some neglected function/capacity/instinct may need to be activated.

LOCOMOTIVE

1 A locomotive may symbolize power, energy, instinctive drive.

2 It may be a sexual symbol, representing the penis. A locomotive going into a tunnel might represent the sexual act.

LORRY SEE JUGGERNAUT

LOTUS SEE WATER-LILY

LUGGAGE

1 Luggage may symbolize what you need to get rid of: old habits and attitudes, old conditioning.

2 It may symbolize a desire to – or a need to – get out of some present situation; or fear of having to do so. Perhaps your unconscious is hinting that it is time you 'packed your bags'. See also **Bag**.

MAGIC

Magic may symbolize a power stronger than your ego: some (good or bad) unconscious force.

MAGICIAN

A magician may be a symbol of the Wise Old Man (see **Wise Old Man/ Woman**, and Introduction, pages 51–52).

MAGNET

A magnet may represent something that can bring your true self closer, or draw things out of your unconscious.

MAIDEN SEE DAMSEL IN DISTRESS

MAN SEE ALSO GURU, WISE OLD MAN/WOMAN

1 A male figure may be a symbol of your self; wholeness, completeness; the inner self that represents the ground-plan of your individual psyche. (For Jung on 'the Self', see Introduction, pages 52–55).

2 On the other hand, it may stand for one half of the whole, woman symbolizing the other half of human wholeness, which is a union of opposites. The male half of the psyche comprises consciousness, reflection, rational intellect, 'head' rather than 'heart', competitiveness and aggressiveness, analysis and discrimination, purposive activity (rather than passivity or receptiveness), ambition, getting and achieving.

If, however, the figure is in a meditative posture, like a Buddha or Shiva figure, it represents passivity and detachment. (In Hindu tradition the god's Shakti – female partner – represents activity, all the energy and process of Nature; the god represents the still centre of the turning wheel.) See also **Hermaphrodite, Woman**.

3 In a woman's dream, a male figure may represent her animus or her father. In a man's dream the figure may represent his alter-ego or shadow-self; or the Wise Old Man. (For animus, see **Brother/Sister**, sections **4–6**; for shadow, see Introduction, pages 45–47.) See also **Wise Old Man/Woman**.

MANDALAS

Mandalas are symmetrical figures, usually square or circular and with a central point. Some are purely geometrical, others are not – for example, a flower (as in rose windows in Christian churches or the lotus in Indian tradition). Psychologically they may function as symbols of the self – that is, the complete, whole self; human fullness; the fundamental order of the psyche; the union of opposite psychic qualities or forces.

1 A mandala in a dream is a reminder that order is possible – because already latent – in the psyche. 'Remove' the disturbing elements – that is, bring them into harmony with the other parts of the psyche – and order will be restored.

2 If a disarranged mandala appears in a dream, this will indicate that the healing – whole-making – power of the (unconscious) psyche is temporarily out of action. Some destructive attitude – a guilt-and-anger or inferiority complex, or whatever – is blocking the flow of the natural healing powers.

MARRIAGE

Marriage may symbolize the union of opposite forces in your psyche, and the consequent achievement of wholeness. (For the male/female symbolism of opposing forces, see **Couple, Hermaphrodite, Man, Woman.**) The most obvious example is the bringing together of the masculine and feminine sides of your personality. See also Introduction, pages 51, 54.

MARSH SEE BOG

MASK

1 A mask may represent the persona, the image you present to the world. Perhaps the dream is asking you to take a fresh look at that image and also to look behind it. It may have served you and supported your ego in the past, but possibly you are now beginning – or being urged – to see yourself in a new way. On persona, see also Introduction, pages 40–41.

2 An animal or other strange mask may symbolize something in your unconscious that demands attention. Associated feelings of frenzy might suggest that what is depicted by the mask is threatening to take over control from the conscious ego. To be on the safe side, you could consult a psychotherapist.

MAZE SEE LABYRINTH

MEADOW

Lush green growth may symbolize the need for and possibility of personal growth. A parched meadow would mean you are being deprived of psychic nourishment. What has dried you up – external events, or internal negativity?

MEAN (= HALFWAY BETWEEN EXTREMES)

This probably represents balance in your psyche, perhaps between a particular pair of opposites – for example, conscious and unconscious, masculine and feminine.

MEAN(NESS)

If in a dream you are mean to someone, this person probably represents some part of yourself that you are not allowing adequate expression in your life.

MELODY SEE MUSIC

MELTING

1 Melting snow or ice probably means that repressed emotions should/can be allowed freedom of expression in your life. The only thing that can do the melting is love: total acceptance, encouragement and (where necessary) forgiveness of all the contents of your unconscious.

2 Is metal melting in fire? It may symbolize the transforming – from base to noble or spiritual – of some (despised? 'animal'/physical?) part of yourself. See also **Fire**, section **4**.

MERMAID

1 For a woman, it might express doubts about her femininity, or fears of (sexual) frigidity. In such a case, it may be that your partner is not right for you.

2 In a man's dream it might represent an idealized image of women (which may inhibit relations with actual women). Are you frightened of sex?

3 For a man, it might represent the siren, which might actually symbolize the anima as the part of the psyche that will take you – safely – into the depths of your unconscious, and thereby heighten your self-knowledge.

4 It may also, for a man, express fears of being 'drowned' by the feminine or by the unconscious. See also **Seduction**, and Introduction, page 51.

MERMAN

1 In a man's dream it may symbolize doubts about his masculinity, or fear of impotence. If you have a partner, perhaps she is not the right one for you.

2 In a woman's dream it might represent a romanticized image of men. Is your sexuality inhibited?

3 For a woman, it might symbolize your fear that your masculinity might take control of your psyche at the expense of your feminine characteristics.

4 Alternatively, it may symbolize the union of masculine and feminine sides of the psyche – in man or woman.

MESSAGE/MESSENGER

Any message in a dream may be understood as coming from your unconscious. The same applies to messengers.

METAL MELTING, SECTION 2, GOLD, ETC.

METEORITE

Examine the meteorite closely. It may bring an important message from your inner centre. (In ancient times meteorites were regarded as being sent by God.) It may be offering you greater self-knowledge, or an enrichment of life.

MILK

1 Milk may symbolize mother-love, or your nurturing as a child.

2 It may symbolize nourishment for your psyche, enabling personal expansion.

3 Drinking milk may symbolize sharing in divine life or consciousness; or awareness of the one source of all life, one life-force. Religious traditions speak of a fluid or drink that came from God – as sap in trees, blood, etc. – and was variously named: milk, ambrosia, honey/mead, nectar, etc. Psychologically, 'God'/'divine life' may be experienced/understood as your true self, living in tune with your 'destiny' or fundamental psychic structure.

MILL

A mill may represent the unconscious; the machinery will then represent unconscious processes.

MINE

A mine is a symbol of your unconscious, which contains precious and useful things.

MIRACLE SEE ALSO MAGIC

MIRROR (IMAGE)

1 What you see in the mirror will probably be yourself, but as seen by your unconscious. For that reason it may startle you; but take it seriously if you want self-knowledge.

2 It may represent the way you see yourself; or the way you want others to see you; or the role-playing you do in life. Sooner or later, even in a business context, you may want to base your life – attitudes, beliefs, values, relationships and behaviour – on something more substantial, on the real centre of your being, which means finding your true self and fulfilling your 'destiny'.

Perhaps that is what you are doing in the mirror in the dream – looking for yourself. (On persona, see Introduction, pages 40–41.)

MIST SEE FOG

MONEY SEE TREASURE

Money may sometimes represent faeces. See also **Excrement**.

MONK

In a man's dream, a monk may symbolize the true self; personal wholeness.

MONKEYS

1 Monkeys seem to spend a lot of time playing, and may therefore symbolize not taking life too seriously; letting yourself go (along with Nature).

2 Monkeys are associated with mischief and may therefore symbolize unconscious forces that are 'up to no good' – because you have deprived them of their proper place in your conscious life.

3 They may symbolize sexuality – your own. So, why does sexuality disgust you ?

MONSTER

Monsters represent the fearsomeness of the unconscious insofar as it is still unexplored. If you overcome your fear, you will find in your unconscious all you need to complement your conscious ego. (In legends monsters guard treasure sought by a hero; in religious myths they guard *mana*-filled things – sacred objects/places. Psychologically speaking, you are the hero, seeking your self; the sacred place is your inner core; 'slaying' the monster is bestowing love on a feared and repressed desire/drive/emotion, and so transforming it into a creative factor in your conscious life.) All that is now unconscious is destined to become conscious. That is why you have to 'wrestle' with the 'monsters'.

MOON

1 From prehistoric times the moon has been regarded as the source of all fertility. It governs ocean tides and rainfall, menstruation and birth. (Even when seen as male, the moon has been associated with fertility: for example, in Australian aboriginal tradition, the moon makes women pregnant.) It may therefore symbolize (the possibility of) personal growth.

MORTUARY

1 Perhaps your unconscious is confronting you with the fact of mortality in order to change your perspective, or ambitions or values.

2 The mortuary may symbolize whatever in your psyche you have allowed to atrophy through disuse. A conscious feeling of lifelessness may result. The repressed elements are probably just what you need to give you new life, new *joie de vivre*.

MOTHER

1 A dream about your mother may be telling you something about your relationship with your mother. Mother-attachment may be so strong that the development of your own individuality has been prevented. Inner independence of mother is the first great step towards realizing your true self.

2 In a man's dream, mother may symbolize the feminine side of his psyche (see **Brother/Sister**, sections **4–6**).

3 Mother may symbolize the unconscious; intuition; natural and instinctive life; the source of nourishment and growth for the psyche.

MOTORCYCLE

1 The motorbike is something of a macho symbol and as such may represent male sexuality, or aggressiveness.

2 In a woman's dream it may symbolize her animus, the masculine side of her psyche. Since the unconscious compensates the conscious ego, a macho representation of the animus would typically occur in the dreams of an intuitive, perhaps artistic woman, or a 'blue-stocking'. (For animus, see **Brother/Sister**, section **4**, and Introduction, pages 47–51.)

MOUNTAIN SEE ALSO ASCENT, HEIGHT, SKY

1 Climbing a mountain may symbolize either achievement; or a task or long-term undertaking.

2 Seeing things from a mountain top may symbolize passing your life under review; looking at life objectively, without emotional involvement.

3 A mountain may represent mother. See also **Mother, Hill(s)**.

4 High mountains may have a mysterious and transcendental 'feel' and may therefore symbolize rising above the common pursuits of everyday life; going in search of your true self, or the meaning of life.

5 Just possibly the dream may refer to death. (In religions that place the spirit-world in the sky, spirits of dead people were sometimes said to ascend mountain passes.) See also **Dead/Death**.

MOUTH

1 The mouth may be a sexual symbol, representing the vagina.

2 The dream may be saying something about self-expression. Is there some part of you that has not been allowed to express itself in your conscious life? Are you bottling things up, instead of talking about them?

3 Perhaps something is threatening to swallow you up. Have you not yet achieved inner independence of your mother?

MUD SEE BOG

MURDER

1 Are you murdering someone? If the person is someone close, the dream may be expressing repressed hostility or resentment. There is often rivalry between siblings, or (unconscious) hostility towards a parent. Otherwise, what you are 'murdering' is probably some part of yourself (a repressed capacity or instinct or desire) that ought to be given a proper place in your conscious life.

2 Are you being murdered? The murderer probably represents something in your unconscious: possibly a repressed emotion or instinct that is now threatening mutiny.

MUSCULAR MAN SEE HE-MAN

MUSEUM

1 A museum may symbolize your past; your unconscious, as containing all the emotionally charged experiences that have shaped your attitudes and behaviour.

2 It may represent the collective unconscious, the oldest part of the psyche. If so, your dream will be showing you something of great value as far as your personal development is concerned.

MUSIC

Take note of its emotional tone – sad, sweet, tragic, threatening, etc. If it is a song, take note of the words. Has the music any personal association?

N

NAKED SEE NUDITY

NAMES

1 Pay attention to (hidden) meanings in personal or place names: for example, 'Mr/s House' (yourself, since house is a symbol of self); 'Freetown' (time you liberated yourself); 'Hershe' ('he'; and 'she', your feminine characteristics, particularly if you are a man). Of course the meaning may depend on the context.

2 If you are given a new name, this suggests it is time you entered the next phase of your personal development. (In initiation ceremonies initiates are/were often given a new name to mark their new status.)

NAVEL

1 A dream about a navel may be telling you something about your relationship with your mother.

2 In a woman's dream it may represent (desired) motherhood.

3 It may signify new birth, a new development in your psyche – perhaps as a result of integrating into your conscious life some hitherto neglected/repressed part of yourself.

NECK

How the neck feels (relaxed or tense) may indicate how good or bad the relations are between consciousness and the unconscious, between intellect and emotions.

NEEDLE

A needle may be a symbol of male sexuality.

NIGHT

1 Night is a common symbol of the unconscious; the 'dark' other side of your personality; the primitive or negative ('evil') aspects of yourself. See also **Evil**.

2 A night journey, and especially a sea journey, may symbolize a 'journey' into the unconscious, or the process of individuation, or its second phase (see Introduction, pages 44–55).

3 If moonlight is in evidence, see **Moon**.

NIGHTMARES SEE ESCAPE, FEAR,FLIGHT (= FLEEING)

NINE

1 The number nine is a symbol of completeness, and may represent personal fullness.

2 On the other hand, it may have the meaning of 'nine out of ten' – that is, not quite perfect, not quite all.

NOON

Noon may symbolize full consciousness; intellect, rationality; masculinity.

NOOSE

May be a warning of catastrophe if you don't change your 'ways' (attitudes, values, or whatever).

NORTH SEE ALSO COLD, ICE

May symbolize evil, or frigidity.

NOSE

1 A nose may be a sexual symbol representing penis (and testicles) or (because of its tendency to bleed) female genitalia.

2 It may symbolize mendacity (as in the story of Pinocchio). Are you being dishonest with yourself?

3 Just possibly your dream may be telling you to 'follow your nose' – that is follow your instinct.

NUDITY

1 Nudity may express a longing (possibly unconscious) for childhood innocence and freedom from artificial inhibitions.

2 It may signify getting beyond outward appearances to what you really are: the 'naked truth' about yourself. It may therefore be accompanied by an anxious feeling of being exposed – that is vulnerable.

3 If you are ashamed or frightened of being naked and move away so that people can't see you this may indicate either a fear of sexual relationships or fear of revealing your inner feelings.

4 If you are showing off your nudity this may represent either desire for sex; or a state of being at ease with yourself and not feeling a need to apologize for being the person you are; or complete honesty and openness in your dealings with other people.

NUMBNESS

Feeling numb probably means you have repressed some strong emotion because it was too shocking for you to entertain it in your conscious mind.

NUMBERS SEE ALSO PARTICULAR NUMBER: FOUR, NINE, ETC.

NUN

For a woman the appearance of a nun may symbolize her true self.

NUT

Perhaps a dream about a nut is asking you to get through to the centre of yourself.

NYMPH SEE MERMAID, SECTION 3, SEDUCTION

OASIS

1 An oasis may be a sexual symbol, representing the female genitals.The hot dry desert would then represent sexual deprivation, in a man's dream.

2 It may symbolize the reward for exploring your unconscious. (Desert may symbolize the unconscious.) See also **Wilderness**.

OBELISK

An obelisk may be a phallic symbol.

OBSTACLE SEE FENCE, SECTION 1 AND 2.

OBSTRUCTION SEE BLOCK(AGE)

OCEAN SEE SEA

OCTOPUS

An octopus may symbolize a possessive mother or mother-attachment, preventing you from being your own person.

OFFICER/OFFICIAL

An officer may be an authority figure representing your super-ego. (For super-ego, see Introduction, pages 15–18.)

OINTMENT

Ointment may symbolize healing. There isn't a fly in it, is there? If there is, it will represent something in yourself – an old habit that you won't let die, or a negative attitude – that is interfering with the healing processes in the unconscious.

OLD

Anything old may symbolize something in the deeper, more primitive layers of the unconscious. For old men, see **Wise Old Man/Woman**.

OPPOSITES

Any pair of opposites in a dream – right and left, new and old, man and woman, light and darkness – may represent opposite forces or qualities of the psyche: conscious and unconscious, masculine and feminine elements, extrovert and introvert tendencies, etc. Jung said that at the bottom of every neurosis there was an unsolved problem of opposites, which can be solved only by choosing both of the opposites, and integrating and harmonizing them. Man and woman are opposites, but for that very reason yearn for union. This applies equally to your psychic opposites. Your conscious ego should not interfere with this mutual attraction of opposites.

ORANGE

1 This colour may symbolize aggressiveness.

2 Because orange is the colour of the sun, it may symbolize life, or consciousness.

3 If you are depressed, orange may symbolize the dawn of a new attitude of optimism and proper self-love.

ORCHESTRA SEE ALSO CONDUCTOR

An orchestra may represent the manifoldness of the psyche, with its many and varied capacities and forces, but all with a potential for uniting creatively.

ORGY

1 An orgy may be an exaggerated expression of (a need for) sex. See also **Debauchery**.

2 It may symbolize a release of energy in yourself – by breaking out of an old habit or negative attitude; or possibly an experience of personal wholeness – resulting from the union of conscious and unconscious, masculine and feminine sides of your psyche.

OTHERNESS SEE ALIEN

OUTCAST ABANDONED

The outcast may represent some part of yourself that you have rejected. (On repression/suppression, see Introduction, pages 19–20.)

OUTLAW SEE VAGRANT/VAGABOND

OUTSIDER SEE OUTCAST, VAGRANT/VAGABOND

OVEN

An oven may represent the womb and therefore be a symbol of woman or pregnancy. The symbolized pregnancy, however, may be figurative: some promise of growth in some area of your life, external or internal. What's cooking?

OWL

1 An owl may symbolize wisdom in general; or that wisdom that belongs to the unconscious (night = unconscious); or intuition (associated with woman, who is associated with the moon); or knowledge of the unconscious (owls see in the dark; darkness = the unconscious).

2 In mythology, an owl may symbolize evil or death. The owl, like the tiger, has a numinous, awesome quality and, like all numinous things, is ambivalent: good and evil, bringing both wisdom and death. No wonder, then, that the owl may represent the unconscious or point towards it: the unconscious is invariably frightening and even threatening to one who has not made its acquaintance; it also contains all that we need for wholeness.

OYSTER

An oyster may be a sexual symbol, representing the vagina.

P

PAIN

Pain felt in a dream may have a physical cause (though to what extent any pain is purely physical in origin is debatable: perhaps pent-up emotion is the root of all pain). Otherwise, it may express emotional deprivation. Where is the pain? It may be that what is associated with that part of the body (e.g. self-expression, associated with the throat) has not been allowed adequate expression. But there is no simple one-to-one correspondence between part of body and type of emotion: for example, any emotional blockage may cause pain in the chest; and the same applies to the belly – where we must not assume that pain invariably indicates unfulfilled sexual desire.

PAIR SEE COUPLE, OPPOSITES

PARADISE

1 Paradise may represent a desire to return to the innocent problem-free simplicity of early childhood.

However, this is wrongheaded, because it is unrealistic. The garden of Eden prior to Adam's 'fall' represents the oneness and harmony of all things when all things are still unconscious. With the rise of conscious thinking, distinctions and dilemmas arise, and the agonizing 'Should I do this or that?' (=Adam's eating from the tree of the knowledge of good and evil). A desire to return to childhood in a dream is neurotic: in it reality has been ousted by fantasy – because reality was too painful. What particular reality (i.e. experience) are you trying to blot out?

2 A more realistic option is that paradise represents a desire to achieve in the psyche the balance and wholeness that have been present latently and potentially from the beginning.

3 If your dream contains, not just a paradisal feeling, but an actual physical representation of the garden of Eden (e.g. with four rivers dividing it into four quarters), this may be an instance of **2** above. See also **Mandala**.

PARALYSIS

1 If it is you who, in the dream, are paralysed, the paralysis probably symbolizes an inability to act successfully or to make a decision. Look for the cause, which will usually be some (buried, unconscious) fear or guilt-feeling or inner conflict.

2 If someone else is paralysed, that person will almost certainly represent some aspect of yourself that you have not allowed freedom of expression. To discover which aspect of yourself that is, take on the role of the person in your dream: express his or her feelings and grievances, and work out a new, more positive future for him or her.

PARENTS SEE ALSO FATHER, MOTHER

In dreams parents may represent animus/anima; or the union of the masculine and feminine components of the psyche; or *Wise Old Man* and *Great Mother*; or just themselves, or your relationship with them, or your image of them.

PARK GARDEN, MANDALA

PARROT

1 Are you merely picking up other people's values uncritically or unreflectingly?

2 Are you only the semblance of a person, only a façade?

In either case, you need to look within – for the values that reflect the ground-plan of your individual being.

PARTNER SEE HUSBAND, WIFE

PARTNER SEE CORRIDOR (SEE ALSO BLOCK(AGE))

PASSENGER

1 If you are the passenger, this may indicate that you are not in control of your life: you are letting yourself be driven, either by unconscious contents that you have failed to integrate into your conscious life, or by other people.

2 If someone else is the passenger, he or she may represent a part of yourself that you need to learn to relate to, to cooperate with in your journey through life.

PASSPORT

1 A passport may signify a desire or need to know who you really are.

2 The significant thing may be a projected journey to a foreign country, in which case the unconscious may be inviting you to pay it a visit and make its acquaintance, or urging you to make a change in your home or work life.

PATH

A path may represent the direction you are taking in life; or some recurring pattern in your life.

PATTERN SEE MANDALA

PEACOCK

A peacock may symbolize male sexuality; or pride, vanity or ostentation.

PEAK SEE ASCENT, MOUNTAIN

PEARL

1 Pearls have associations with water, shells and the moon (same shape and colour), all of which are symbols of the feminine in its positive, creative aspects. A pearl may therefore signify new life; a possibility of personal growth. In a woman's dream it may even, by its resemblance to a foetus, represent pregnancy. See also **Moon, Shell, Water**.

2 It may be a symbol of the self: personal wholeness, in which conscious and unconscious halves of the psyche are united (cf. the New Testament 'pearl of great price', the finding of which is worth the sacrifice of everything else).

PENIS

A penis may be straightforwardly sexual; or may symbolize power of energy: sexual, spiritual or cosmic. (In religious iconography the erect phallus symbolizes either divine fecundating energy present in the cosmos and emanating from some immanent but indescribable Ultimate Reality, or the spiritualizing of sexual energy by the disciplined yogi.)

PEOPLE SEE ALSO CROWD, FAMOUS PEOPLE

People usually represent various aspects of yourself, albeit in many cases unconscious: wishes, fears, drives, habits, attitudes and so on.

PHOTOGRAPH SEE PICTURE

PICTURE

A picture may represent thoughts or ideas; or may be a way of getting you to focus your attention on something (i.e. whatever the content of the picture symbolizes).

PIG

1 A pig may symbolize instinctual life, sexuality (seen as brutish and disgusting), lust, greed, bestiality.

2 Killing a pig may symbolize an urge to overcome your 'animal' nature in order to attain spiritual dignity. Needless to say, this can be destructive. Not the annihilation but the 'taming' of your animality, and allowing it proper expression in your conscious life, will provide a firm base for further personal development.

PIPE

A pipe may be a sexual symbol, representing the penis.

PIPER

A piper may be an animus figure in a woman's dream (for animus, see **Brother/Sister**, sections **4–6**).

PISTOL

A pistol may be a sexual symbol, representing the penis. The firing of a pistol would then symbolize the sexual act.

PIT SEE HOLE

PLANT SEE FLOWER, TREE

PLOUGH(ING)

A plough may represent the penis; ploughing may symbolize sexual intercourse.

PLUG

Whether it is a bath-plug or an electric plug or a plug of tobacco, it may represent the penis. Plugging a hole or putting a plug in a socket may symbolize coitus.

POINTER/POINTING

A point/dot may symbolize the (true) centre of the self or psyche (see also **Signpost**).

POISON

Poison represents something that is bad for you. The context may tell you what the bad thing is.

POLE

A pole may be a phallic symbol, like the *Maypole* which features in fertility rites.

POLICEMAN

1 A policeman may be a super-ego symbol, representing taboos stemming from childhood.

2 If someone in the dream is arrested by policemen, this may symbolize sexuality or emotions restrained by feelings of guilt.

POLLUTION SEE POISON

POMEGRANATE

The pomegranate is a traditional symbol of healing and fertility; hence, of personal growth.

POOL SEE ALSO LAKE

A round or square pool may be a symbol of the self.

PORT SEE HARBOUR

PORTRAIT SEE MIRROR

PRECIPICE SEE FALLING

PRICK

Pricking or being pricked may symbolize the sexual act.

PRIEST

A priest may symbolize your own inner wisdom; or, alternatively, externally imposed commands and prohibitions. Which of these alternatives applies will be suggested by your feeling-response to the priest in the dream, and by the character of the priest himself: for example, does he speak with authority, or only authoritatively? Is he loving or aggressive and punitive?

PRINCE/PRINCESS

Prince and princess are respectively animus and anima figures. (For anima/animus, see **Brother/Sister**, sections **4–6**, and Introduction, pages 47–51.)

PRISON

1 Are you in prison in the dream? This probably means you are not free: your behaviour is to some extent compulsive, that is, not under conscious control. If so, you must integrate the repressed emotion or instinct that is now overflowing from your unconscious into your observable behaviour.

2 If someone else is in prison, he or she probably represents some part of you that has been shut up in your unconscious, possibly as a result of some traumatic experience (in childhood?), and which needs to be set free and given suitable employment in your conscious life.

PRIZE

Whatever the prize is awarded for (winning a race, for example, or climbing a mountain), it probably represents either your true self or some significant personal development. You may have to work out what the race/climbing might represent in real-life terms.

PROFESSOR

May be a Wise Old Man figure, representing primitive psychic energy and wisdom. See also **Wise Old Man/Woman**.

PROPHET SEE WISE OLD MAN/WOMAN

PUNISHING

1 If you are punishing someone or something else (an animal, say), the latter probably represents a part of you – some quite respectable faculty or instinctive drive – that has at some time in the past given rise to guilt-feelings. Such antagonism between different parts of your psyche spells misery. Healing and happiness will come only if you learn to forgive and accept the repressed faculty or emotion and allow it proper expression in your life.

2 The person you are punishing may represent someone close to you: parent or partner, or sibling. In this case be careful to distinguish three possibilities: first, that the dream is expressing (unconscious) resentment against the person; secondly, that what you are punishing the person for is a part of yourself that has been projected on to the person; and thirdly, that the person, though recognized in the dream as someone else, nevertheless represents some part of you: in which case see **1** above.

3 If you are being punished, who is doing the punishing? A father figure or other authority figure (e.g. policeman or judge)? If so, you probably have an over-dominant super-ego. Did you as a small child see your parents in a sexual embrace and as a result incur the wrath of either parent? Some such traumatic experience could easily set in motion a self-punishing mechanism that will perpetuate itself as an autonomous function of your psyche until you choose to do something about it.

PURPLE

Purple may symbolize mystery and therefore represent, in psychological terms, deep intuition or awareness of some as yet unexplored dimension of the self.

PURSE

1 A purse may be a sexual symbol, representing the womb.

2 As the place where your 'treasure' is, it may symbolize your real self.

3 Losing your purse may, therefore, be a symbol of losing your real identity.

PURSUED

1 If the pursuer is an animal, the meaning may be that some ('animal'?) part of you made you anxious in the past and you therefore repressed it, but it is now threatening to overcome you. Identify the repressed emotion or instinctive impulse and enter into dialogue with it, with a view to giving it a proper place in your conscious life.

2 If a policeman, father or other authority figure is chasing you, you may have an over-developed super-ego. See also **Punishment**, section **3**.

3 Otherwise, the pursuer(s) may represent something which or someone who constitutes a threat in your domestic or work life.

Q

QUEEN

A queen may represent mother; the unconscious; intuition; instinct; nature; personal growth. See also **Mother**; for king and queen, see **Couple**.

QUEST

SEARCH

R

RABBIT

1 A rabbit may symbolize sexuality, fecundity. Do your instincts hold uninhibited sway in your life; or is there some promise of a new development in your personal growth?

2 Perhaps the rabbit in your dream symbolizes the innocent victim. If so, the dream may be advising you to stop punishing or blaming yourself and, instead, to accept and love yourself just as you are.

RABBIT HOLE

1 Going down a rabbit hole may symbolize an attempt to escape from problems.

2 It may be a symbol of entering the unconscious.

RACE

1 Are you always measuring yourself against other people, instead of getting your values from an inner source?

2 Is it the prize that is the important thing? See **Prize**.

RAIN

1 Is there a general grey tone to the dream? Then the rain probably symbolizes sadness, like tears, or depression.

2 Possibly the symbolism is of fertility; growth. Perhaps a new fruitful phase is opening in your life.

RAINBOW

A rainbow will usually be a sign of hope, signalling the end of gloom and the re-entry of the warming sun. Since the sun may be a symbol of the self, the rainbow may symbolize bridging the gap between yourself as you are and your true self. (But for some African peoples the rainbow is a bad sign, since it means the end of a rainstorm, and drought means death.)

RAM

1 A ram may be a sexual symbol; or a symbol of aggressiveness (if horned).

2 As a symbol of fertility, it may mean a promise of personal growth.

3 If there is a sinister feel about the ram, it is probably a symbol of your shadow – that is, the parts of your psyche that have been rejected by your ego. These may erupt and cause you to behave in uncharacteristic, primitive, destructive or awkward ways. So: get to know the ram; accept what you have repressed, and let it have a proper – controlled – expression in your conscious life.

RAMPANT SEE ANIMAL(S) SECTIONS 3 AND 4

RAPE

1 In a woman's dream, rape may represent either (unconscious) fears of sex or (masochistic) fantasies of being raped.

2 A man's dream of committing rape would probably be a straightforward symbol of sexual desire, but of a sadistic kind. You probably need to become acquainted with your own feminine qualities – ability to relate, patience, gentleness, etc. – and let them play a larger part in your life. What are you trying to take vengeance for? Did your mother seem to withdraw her love from you as a boy?

RAT(S)

Rats probably symbolize those contents of your unconscious that may terrify you on first glimpsing them. They are emotions or instinctive impulses that at some time in your past gave rise to guilt-feelings (or fears of punishment that were later transformed into guilt-feelings) and were therefore repressed. You now need to rehabilitate those rejected parts of yourself; accepting them into your conscious life. Stop trying to get rid of the 'rats'. As in the story of the Pied Piper of Hamelin, getting rid of your 'rats' means losing your 'children' – that is, the parts of your personality that are weak and undeveloped and need all the nurture and care you can give them. (For repression, see Introduction, pages 19–20.)

RAVEN SEE CROW

REBELLION

An instance of rebellion in a dream will probably mean there are repressed parts of you that are threatening to take control if you go on disregarding them. (On repression, see Introduction, pages 19–20.)

REBIRTH

The new life symbolized by rebirth may be a new kind of life: a new level of awareness; new goals and values; new energy, as a result of releasing pent-up emotion. It may involve the 'death' of the old self: an inadequate or distorted self-image, negative or blinkered attitudes and habits, etc.

RED

Red may symbolize sexuality, passion, anger, revolution, danger. As the colour of blood, red is a symbol of life (which is why Hindu and Chinese brides wear red); but blood, of course, may also mean death.

REFEREE

A referee may symbolize the ego arbitrating between the rival claims of opposed psychic forces: for example, id and super-ego (see Introduction, pages 15–18).

REFRIGERATOR SEE COLD, ICE

REFUGE

Taking refuge may be a good thing or a bad. Simply running away and hiding is useless: the threats and problems remain, and worsen. On the other hand, if finding a refuge means discovering a depth of yourself where you can fully love (accept and forgive) yourself, that may be all that is needed to dissolve a guilt- or inferiority-complex, or anger or envy.

The significance of the refuge will obviously depend largely on what you are taking refuge from. See also, for example, **Animal(s)**, section **3**, **4**, **Chase/Chased/Chasing**, section **1**, **Flight**, **Pursued**.

REFUSE

NOUN

Refuse or rubbish may symbolize repressed contents of the unconscious, emotions that proved too painful for you at some time in your past and were therefore pushed down into your unconscious. NB The 'rubbish' may be just what you need to correct the imbalance in your personality; retrieving the 'refuse' may put a stop to self-destructive patterns of behaviour.

VERB

The significance of refusing something will depend on what, in the dream, you are refusing. Are you refusing what life is offering you?

REJECTION

1 Rejection in a dream may be a symbol of suppression or repression, the action by which we try to get rid of anything in our psyche – usually a desire – that offends our moral sense or brings with it a threat of punishment. Try to identify with what is rejected, as well as with the rejector in the dream; and give the rejected emotion or instinct an appropriate role in your conscious life. (On repression/suppression, see Introduction, pages 19–20.)

2 Bear in mind that, if in the dream it is you who are rejected, it may well be you who are doing the rejecting. In cases of self-rejection it is usually the 'conscience' or super-ego – introjected social conventions and attitudes – that does the rejecting, and often the victim is sexual desire. The rejection may have started in early childhood, where the offending action or – more likely – desire was almost certainly quite natural and innocuous and does not at all warrant the punishment and disparagement you have meted out to yourself. See also **Abandonment**.

RELATIONSHIPS

1 Personal relationships in dreams are always important. They fall into two categories: first, those that refer to actual waking-life relationships; secondly, those that depict relations between the conscious ego and other parts of the psyche. Meetings with strangers will nearly always belong to the second category: the strangers will be parts of your psyche that you have not yet got to know very well. And even where there is no doubt that the dream is asking you to take a serious look at an actual real-life relationship, you should bear in mind that the quality of your external relationships may be determined by the way your conscious ego relates – or fails to relate – to other parts of your psyche. For example, a man who does not acknowledge the feminine side of his own nature may have very unsatisfactory – perhaps very superficial – relationships with women. In other words, when a dream shows you in relationship with an actual real-life person, it may be inviting you to look at the relationship with a view to understanding yourself better: how you relate to other people reveals yourself (e.g. are you projecting on to the other person some unacknowledged characteristic of your own?).

Patterns in dreams correspond to patterns in your conscious life, or else – occasionally – a dream may present a pattern for you to follow in your life instead of old patterns. For example, a man may relate in dreams to very feminine women. This may represent an established pattern in his waking life, in which case he is being asked to reassess that pattern. Perhaps he is attracted only to very feminine women because he is projecting on to women his own repressed femininity and needs to integrate his anima. On the other hand, a dream of relating to a woman in a very bold and assertive manner may be the unconscious way of telling a man he needs to display his masculinity more. See also **Sex**.

An antagonistic or belligerent relationship in a dream probably indicates a need to be reconciled with the other, whether the other is another person or another part of yourself.

In the dream do you control, or want to control, the relationship? Perhaps the dream is a descriptive one, simply describing how, in fact, you do behave; in which case, your unconscious is probably asking you to review your situation. Perhaps you need to learn to let go, and trust people more. On the other hand, the dream may be a prescriptive one, telling you what you ought to be doing: perhaps you have been too weak and unassertive in the past. Do you tend to be, in your dreams, a mere observer, watching other people relate? Well, it is a good thing to observe, whether what you are observing is external relationships or internal relations between parts of yourself. But the process of self-discovery may be accelerated if you resolve to participate more in future dreams. Try it. Relating with your shadow may be much more revealing than just looking at it.

2 There may be impersonal or spatio-temporal relationships between dream items or between one episode of a dream and the next. For example, an earlier dream episode may symbolize whatever is the cause of what is symbolized in the following dream episode. (But do not assume that this causal relationship always exists between different parts of a dream.)

If a person is taller than you (in a dream), this may mean that you see that person as superior to yourself. If the person in the dream represents some part of your psyche, the meaning would then be that your conscious ego tends to submit to this other psychic component.

RENOVATION

Renovation, particularly of a house, may symbolize self-renewal or rejuvenation. Are you set in your ways; old before your time? Now is the time to give long-awaited fulfilment to basic urges and desires; to make a clean sweep and start life afresh, without old restrictive attitudes and preconceptions.

RESCUE

1 Are you rescuing something/someone else? That person or thing probably represents some aspect of yourself that has hitherto been neglected. Rescuing it means allowing it proper means of expression. Are you a male dreamer rescuing a young woman? See **Damsel in Distress**. Are you a woman rescuing a young man? See **Brother/Sister**, section **4**.

2 Are you being rescued? From what? Some threatening animal? See also **Animal(s)**, section **4**. From drowning? That might suggest that unconscious forces have been threatening to take over. See also **Air-Sea Rescue**.

3 Who is rescuing you? Psychologically speaking, there is only one person who can save you, and that is yourself. Divile redeemer or superman figures refer to a redemptive power within yourself which is quite simply the power of love, the ability to love yourself, and therefore others. (This is not to deny the reality of what people call 'God'. But whether such a God exists as a being 'out there' is not knowable; what is knowable is the redemptive power of the love that you can feel within yourself whenever you manage to switch off both emotions and thoughts and just be, or be aware.)

RESERVOIR

1 A reservoir may symbolize either your unconscious or your potential – all the unrealized, because not yet chosen, possibilities for your personal development.

2 Running water may symbolize emotion; so, a calm stretch of still water may represent an untroubled state of tranquillity, or the emotionally virginal state of a (young) person whose emotions have not yet been roused.

RESTRAINT/RESTRICTION

In addition to the meanings given under **Imprison** and **Prison**, there is the possibility that the dream is referring to restraints and restrictions in your external circumstances, or to those mental and physical limitations that begin to manifest themselves from the age of forty-five onwards. Restrictions and limitations may have the positive value of drawing your attention from egotistic pursuits to things that matter more: for instance, loss of intellectual sharpness does not disqualify you from gaining self-knowledge; and the latter may be helped by the collapse of egotism. However, if you judge that the restrictions are purely negative, take steps to remove them or to find alternative supplies of satisfaction. If neither of these options seems to avail and the only remaining option is to accept the inevitable, this may well be life's way of reminding you of what is important in life.

RESURRECTION/RESUSCITATION SEE REBIRTH

REVOLUTION SEE REBELLION

RIDING

1 Riding a horse or motorbike may symbolize (unconscious) desire for sex.

2 An animal may represent instinctual desires; being in control of a horse or other animal may therefore symbolize control of your passions. Control may be good or bad: you must decide if your instincts are properly or excessively controlled.

RIGHT/LEFT

1 Right/left may symbolize consciousness/unconscious. Movement from left to right or clockwise, therefore, may signify an increase of conscious awareness.

2 Right/left may also symbolize intellect/intuition or thought/ feeling; masculine/feminine; activity and assertiveness/passivity and receptiveness.

RING

1 A ring may symbolize marriage. How the ring feels on your finger may indicate how you feel about the (prospective or actual) marriage.

2 It may be a symbol of being committed (to a relationship). Not wearing a ring may symbolize not wanting to be restricted to one person.

3 A ring may symbolize eternity; or completeness, wholeness; your true self.

RITUAL

If the piece of ritual is not commonplace (a handshake, for instance) but dramatic and solemn, it is almost certainly symbolic of some process of personal development that you should now be committing yourself to and which may involve a relinquishing of old attitudes.

RIVER

1 A river may symbolize a flow of (emotional) energy (e.g. sexuality).

2 Crossing a river in a boat may symbolize either death (see **Dead/Death**); or a more or less fundamental change of lifestyle or attitude. Crossing by a bridge may signify a change as above; or it may be a symbol of avoiding a flood of passion or observing it from the safe vantage point of a detached observer. If you think the river does represent emotion, try to identify the emotion (e.g. by asking the river questions and getting answers by role-playing the river) and then decide what you are going to do about it.

ROAD

The twists and turns and ups and downs of the road you are travelling along in a dream probably represent a recurring pattern in your life. Do you ascend but never reach your destination? Then you should ask what is preventing you from achieving your goal: is it the right goal; or are you not being determined enough; are there internal complexes or negative attitudes that cause you to underachieve or bungle things or turn down the opportunities that life offers you? Does the road follow a clockwise course (see **Clockwise**)?

ROAD BLOCK

If you can identify what the block symbolizes, you will know what it is that prevents you from reaching the fulfilment you desire. If there are policemen or soldiers there, do they represent your super-ego ('conscience')? If so, bear in mind that our inhibitions are not always rational and do not always serve our best interests. The main thing is to enter into dialogue with those who have made the road blocks: ask them why they are blocking your way, and who put them up to it?

ROAD JUNCTION SEE CROSSROADS

ROBBER(Y)

1 The robber may be anyone or any part of yourself that threatens your independence or your chances of finding personal fulfilment. Is treasure stolen? The treasure is your (true) self.

2 In a woman's dream it is possible that the robber may be her father or her mother, in which case what she has been robbed of may be her penis! According to Freud, a female infant, seeing boys' genitals, feels she has been castrated to prevent the fruition of her love for her mother.

Similarly, men may dream of their father as a robber. A male infant, said Freud, desires his mother and fears that his father may castrate him out of jealousy.

The occurrence of such dreams might suggest that the Oedipus complex has not been resolved in the dreamer. (For Oedipus complex, see Introduction, pages 28–30).

ROCK STONE

1 A rock may symbolize permanence or antiquity; the most ancient – unconscious – part of the human mind; the foundations or essence of the self.

2 Rocks at sea may symbolize a threat of disaster. The threat could be external or internal. Are you getting too emotional? You may need to change course and take a different direction in life.

ROCKET

A rocket may be a sexual symbol, representing the penis; or may symbolize an upward surge of energy.

RODENT SEE RAT

ROLLER-COASTER

1 A roller-coaster may represent the ups and downs of emotions, between euphoria and misery.

2 It may also symbolize the sexual act, and therefore express sexual desire. If, however, the experience is unpleasant or frightening, the dream may be expressing sexual anxiety.

ROOM

1 A room may represent the self, or some aspect of yourself.

2 It may be a symbol of the womb. Freud tells of a dream in which a girl (the dreamer) entered a room six or eight times and every time saw her father sitting there. Freud saw the dream as expressing the girl's fantasy of having seen her father come into her mother's womb while the girl was still a foetus.

3 If the room is a cellar or basement, it may symbolize your unconscious. If it is a room at or near the top of a high building, it may represent consciousness; idealism; lofty aspirations. (But of course an upstairs room may nevertheless symbolize libido, instinctive life and desires: for example, if it is a bedroom where sexual activity is taking place.)

4 A suite of rooms may express a male dreamer's polygamous sexual desires. This does not mean he is polygamous in real life. On the contrary, he might well be shocked by the dream. What such a dream exemplifies is the way the unconscious compensates or balances the conscious self: a polygamous person might have monogamous dreams!

ROSE(S)

1 A rose, as in a stained-glass window, may be a mandala (see **Mandala**), representing your self, the fullness which it is your destiny to reach.

2 Sometimes the symbolism depends on the colour. A red rose is often a symbol of love; it may also represent the vagina; or passion.

3 Roses, like flowers generally, may symbolize the beauty of Nature; the beauty and loveliness of life as it could or should be.

ROUND SEE MANDALA

ROYALTY SEE COUPLE, SECTION 2 AND 3, KING (AND QUEEN), PRINCE/PRINCESS, QUEEN

RUBBISH

1 Rubbish may symbolize repressed contents of the unconscious. The truth is that you should never treat any part of yourself as rubbish; there is nothing bad in yourself, but the way you treat yourself (or parts of yourself) may be bad. (On repression, see Introduction, pages 19–20.) See also **Jumble.**

2 The rubbish may represent whatever you need to get rid of: old attitudes, fears, guilt-feelings or other complexes that have been making your life a heavy burden.

RUBY

1 Like anything red, a ruby may symbolize passion: love or anger.

2 Like any other jewel, a ruby may be a symbol of your true self.
The context will usually tell you which of these meanings applies.

RUINS

1 What is in ruins may be a relationship, or your self-image, or your life. Such a collapse is not necessarily a bad thing. It often means only that you have been pursuing 'wrong' aims, that is, aims that do not match your personality.

2 If there is a numinous, holy 'feel' about the ruins, they may symbolize a source of wisdom appropriate to your 'destiny'.

RUNAWAY/ROGUE SEE VAGRANT/VAGABOND

RUNNING SEE CHASE; FLIGHT(= FLEEING)

RUST

1 A symbol of ageing and deterioration, rust may mean that you are due or overdue for a rejuvenating spring-clean, the abandoning of negative attitudes or other accumulated rubbish.

2 Something rusty may symbolize some psychic component – an instinct, a skill, a personality trait, etc. – that has 'rusted' through neglect and disuse.

S

SACRED SEE ALSO CHURCH, GURU, HOLY/HOLINESS, WISE OLD MAN/ WOMAN

A sacred person, place or thing will almost certainly have to do with self-transformation, the healing of psychological wounds, the resolving of internal conflict, revelations of your destiny, the uncovering of neglected capacities and qualities and the achieving of personal balance and fullness.

SACRIFICE

1 If you are being sacrificed in the dream, there are at least three possibilities.

The dream may be drawing your attention to a martyr complex, habitual and compulsive self-punishment, self-denial or self-denigration. Such negative conditioning can be got rid of only by reconditioning, by making positive affirmations every day: for example, 'I love myself dearly', 'I accept myself totally', 'I have a unique value', and 'I deserve all the good things life offers me.'

Your unconscious may be telling you it is time to let the old you die, to make way for the new and truer you. The self-image you have accepted and conformed to in the past is probably too lopsided and needs to be supplemented by utilizing capacities or qualities that have till now lain dormant; or it may have led you completely astray from your true self, in which case it needs to be removed altogether.

Perhaps the dream is expressing a feeling that you are being abused or undervalued by other people.

2 Are you doing the sacrificing? If so, what is being sacrificed will usually represent some aspect of your personality – desire, ambition, habit, prejudice – that you have given up or are being urged (by your unconscious) to give up. (If an animal is being slain, it will probably symbolize an instinctual impulse or emotion.) This is one of many cases where you have to decide whether a dream is descriptive or prescriptive: showing what you have done (and asking you to stop doing it), or showing what you ought to do. You should have no difficulty in knowing whether you have done what the dream depicts. If you have, the dream is asking you not to do it. If you have not done it, the dream is asking you to do it, for the sake of personal fulfilment.

It is important to remember that sacrifice is meant to be creative: it is the giving up of something in order to achieve and enjoy something better. And if you think 'better' has nothing to do with enjoyment but means simply what duty requires, then you need to remember that making a sacrifice either resentfully or merely for duty's sake is bound to be destructive in its effects both on you and on those you are in a relationship with. It is also important to remember that 'To everything there is a season . . . a time to seek, and a time to lose; a time to keep, and a time to cast away' (Ecclesiastes 3:1, 6). There comes to us all a time for transcending animality (e.g. making sex a vehicle for love and adoration) but to attempt such things before the proper time can only breed resentment and end in disaster. Your dreams will tell you the time!

3 Is your act of sacrifice a violent one? If so, it would suggest that some (partly unconscious) mechanism of self-punishment is at work in you and you urgently need to ask yourself why you feel guilty. Almost certainly the cause will lie in early childhood and will be an entirely innocent desire.

SAFE

A safe is probably a symbol of the self, containing things of great value.

SAILOR

A sailor represents adventure. For a woman dreamer this might be sexual in nature. More generally, it might be adventuring into the unconscious (of which the sea is a common symbol).

SAINT SEE ALSO GURU, HOLY/HOLINESS, SACRED, WISE OLD MAN/ WOMAN

The function of a saintly person in a dream is usually to convey a message concerning your true self, the unfolding of your personal life plan.

SALT

Salt may symbolize something that will give zest to your life. But it may mean whatever you personally associate with it (e.g. 'rubbing salt into a wound', 'salt of the earth', purging, cleansing).

SALVATION

Any symbol of salvation in a dream probably refers to one of two things:

1 The religious idea of being rescued from one's sins and their consequences. If this is the 'feel' of the salvation motif in your dream, the dream may be expressing a longing for release from (unconscious) guilt-feelings; and, since the unconscious functions at a psychological rather than metaphysical level (using as symbols what metaphysics uses as doctrines), the dream may also be urging you to find within yourself enough love to accept yourself as you are.

2 The psychological idea of healing and wholeness: the resolving of conflict and the achieving of balance and fullness in the psyche.

SATAN SEE DEVIL

SAUSAGE

A sausage may be a sexual symbol, representing the penis.

SAVIOUR SEE SALVATION

SCREEN SEE ALSO CURTAIN(S)

What are you trying to hide from yourself?

SCREW

A screw may symbolize the penis and male sexuality; the act of screwing may symbolize the sexual act.

SEA

1 The sea may represent the unconscious. Putting out to sea may, therefore, symbolize an exploring of the unconscious. Drowning may represent (the fear of) having your conscious mind swamped by unconscious contents – repressed emotions and the like. It may also mean that your conscious ego needs to submit to your unconscious for a while, for the further enrichment and development of your personality. See also **Baptism**.

2 The sea may be a mother symbol. If so, it may represent either your own mother or Mother Nature. Drowning or fear of drowning would then symbolize (a fear of) being suffocated by a dominating mother or mother-attachment; or an unconscious death-wish. See also **Dead/Death**, section **4**.

3 Sea may symbolize the feminine, or any aspect of it (e.g. intuition, receptiveness). For a male dreamer, therefore, going to sea may symbolize getting acquainted with the feminine in himself – the anima (See **Brother/Sister**, sections **4–6**, and Introduction, pages 47–51.)

4 Sea may symbolize creative potential. In mythology, water existed prior to creation, and the creator-god wrestled with the sea-goddess and either made the world from her dismembered body or else impregnated her so that she gave birth to the world. Psychologically, therefore, the sea may symbolize the existence, within your psyche, of potential – the latent raw materials – for the creation of your true and total self.

5 In mystic-meditative traditions there is the belief that the multiplicity of natural phenomena are merely different forms of one ultimately real thing (God, Brahman, Ultimate Reality, the One); and the One is commonly symbolized by the ocean, and the individual person or thing by a drop of water which eventually rejoins the sea from which it originally came. Freudians, like Moussaieff Masson, in his book, *The Oceanic Feeling*, may say that, if this piece of imagery appears in your dream, it signifies a death-wish, as in **2** above. Jungians would say it is a message from your unconscious concerning the disillusionment that awaits you if you continue to build your life round the ego, instead of acknowledging the One (life-force, God, or whatever you care to call it). Whether the Freudian or the Jungian interpretation fits you better should be easy to decide. See also Introduction, pages 9–11.

SEARCH

1 Does the dream show what you are seeking? It may be the meaning of life or the key to your destiny; success, in work or sex; or love. If you are young, it is more likely to be material success and prosperity than the meaning of life; the reverse may apply if you are over thirty-five. What all age-groups are likely to be in quest of is love; but the kind of love may differ: for some it will be casual sexual encounters; for others, romantic 'true love'; for others, mystical union with all things.

2 Does the dream indicate whether your search is good? Perhaps it is telling you that you are chasing a will-o'-the-wisp; that you are not putting first things first; or that it is time for you to transfer your energies to some other pursuit. Ultimately, those spiritual teachers may be right who say we already possess all that is worth having, and only need to realize that we possess it; and that even the love we all want (as distinct from what we think we want) is a capacity for loving that occupies the centre of every being. However, in each individual life everything has its own season.

SEDUCTION

1 If in a dream you are seduced, it may be a reliving of an actual seduction, perhaps in childhood. Otherwise, it might express a desire for sex. In a man's dream, a seductive woman/siren/mermaid may symbolize his anima in negative – destructive – form (see **Brother/Sister**, section **6**). The latter may result from a negative relationship between the man's mother and himself as a child. In any case, the dreamer would need to get in touch with his anima, enter into dialogue with her and take steps to rearrange his life to accommodate her just demands. (See Introduction, pages 50–51.)

2 If you are the seducer, the dream is probably a straightforward expression of sexual desire.

SEED

1 A seed may symbolize potential for personal growth. Sowing seed means making new growth possible.

2 A seed may be a symbol of your true self, which is not to be confused with the ego. In fact there may be some internal dialogue in your psyche between the true self ('I') and the ego ('me'), in which, despite 'me's' stubborn independence or rebelliousness, 'I' offers love and comfort and healing. (In Hindu mythology the seed is a symbol of Atman, the ultimate 'I' of every act. In Judaism, Christianity and Islam, God is a 'Thou'. In mystical traditions, however, God is the one and only 'I', and full consciousness of the 'I' – the opposite of egoistic self-centredness – is said to bring freedom from fears and true independence.)

SELF

Your 'self' in a dream represents your conscious ego, which is the centre of your conscious mind but not of your total psyche. For some indication of how the latter differs from the ego, see Introduction, pages 52–53, and **Seed**.

SERPENT SEE SNAKE

SEVEN

1 Seven is a symbol of completeness – possibly because there are seven planets in the solar system – and therefore of personal wholeness and fullness.

2 The number seven may also signal time for a change – as in the 'seven-year itch'.

3 Sixes and sevens, of course, may symbolize conflict.

SEWER

A sewer may represent the flow of unconscious energy or emotion that you have tried to suppress.

SEX

1 Having sex in a dream is usually a straightforward expression of sexual desire. Sex with someone other than your partner may express desire for that person and/or dissatisfaction with your partner.

2 Uninhibited sex in a dream would suggest that the dreamer's actual sex life is inhibited.

3 Dreams may reveal patterns in your sexual relationships that you have not been aware of. What sort of person attracts you in your dreams? How do you feel about this or that aspect of the sexual encounter?

4 Another reason for paying great attention to dreams depicting sexual relations is that the shadow may be very prominent in sex; so here is a way of getting to know your alter-ego, the hidden part of yourself.

5 In dreams of sex your partner may symbolize some part of your own psyche, for example, your anima if you are male, your animus if you are female, and the sexual act will then be a symbol of the union of opposites which leads to wholeness and balance in the personality.

SHADOW

Anything in shadow may symbolize (part of) the dark (i.e. unfamiliar) side of your own nature: unused or rejected capacities, qualities and emotions. So long as you are ignorant of this 'other self', you will project it on to other people.

SHEEP SEE ALSO LAMB

1 Sheep may symbolize unthinking, passive conformity to conventions or to a mundane existence; taking one's ideas uncritically from authority figures or other people; being easily led, and consequently not in control of oneself.

2 Sheep may also symbolize going astray; taking a wrong turning in life; forsaking one's destiny.

SHELL

1 A sea shell, owing to its resemblance to the vagina and its association with the sea, is a feminine symbol. As such it may represent your mother or your mother-attachment; and, for a man, it may represent the anima or be a straightforward sexual symbol. (For anima, see **Brother/Sister**, sections **4–6**.) See also **Mother**.

2 Because of its association with the sea, it may, like the sea, symbolize the unconscious.

3 A tortoise- or snail-shell may symbolize protection, or a hiding-place; withdrawal from reality, or from social or sensual contacts; or a 'defence mechanism' (see Introduction, pages 30–33).

4 An eggshell may symbolize fragility, vulnerability. See also **Egg**.

5 An artillery shell may have the same sexual symbolism as **Rocket**. See also **Bomb**.

SHEPHERD

1 A shepherd may symbolize the power of love within us, the power that can control and unify all the parts of the psyche.

2 It may be an animus figure (see **Brother/Sister**, sections **4–6**, and Introduction, pages 47–51).

SHIP

1 A ship may be a feminine symbol, representing mother, or some other woman, or women in general. See also **Woman**.

2 In a man's dream, a ship may symbolize the anima, especially as leading the ego safely through the depths of the unconscious (represented by the sea). (For anima, see **Brother/Sister**, sections **4** and **5**.)

SHOE SEE ALSO FOOT/FEET

The shoe or slipper, says Freud, is a symbol of the female genitals.

SHOOTING SEE ALSO KILLING

A shooting may symbolize the sexual act from a male (ejaculative, penetrative) point of view.

SHORE

The shore is the meeting-place of two worlds, land and sea, which may symbolize the conscious and the unconscious realms of the human psyche. It may be that your unconscious is inviting you to get acquainted – to take the plunge, so to speak, or at least to dip your toe in.

SHOULDERS

1 What do your shoulders feel like? Tense? Most of the pain and sadness of the years seems to be deposited in the shoulders. If the tension is bad, you probably need to get acquainted with what is going on at the unconscious level; otherwise, money spent on massage is likely to be wasted.

2 Are the shoulders carrying a burden? That's not the burden of life: life is no burden, only joy. It's the burden of your neuroses – your unconscious irrational anxieties. Get rid of them, by first getting to know them and making room in your life for whatever you have repressed and neglected in your psyche.

SHOWER

A shower may symbolize refreshment; the giving of new life, or new joy in life. Perhaps there's a period of personal growth ahead.

SIGNPOST

Pay attention to any sign or signpost in a dream. If you miss or forget what it says, ask your unconscious to give you the dream again; and prepare yourself, before going to sleep, to concentrate on the sign this time.

SILVER

1 Silver may symbolize something of value with regard to your personal development.

2 Silver has associations with the moon, and may therefore symbolize the feminine; intuition; or the unconscious.

SINGING

Singing may symbolize the expression of feeling. The feeling may be (partly) unconscious, so do take note of the words, if any.

SINKING

1 Sinking may symbolize death. See also **Dead/Death**.

2 It may be a symbol of depression or despair.

3 It may symbolize being 'swallowed' by your mother (or your mother-attachment) who (or which) prevents you from achieving a properly separate existence or independent identity.

4 The water may represent either emotion or the unconscious; therefore sinking may represent being swamped and overwhelmed by emotion or unconscious processes (which will usually be emotional).

5 If a ship or boat is sinking, this may symbolize the end of something in your life (e.g. a relationship).

SISTER SEE BROTHER/SISTER

SIX

The number six may be a symbol of completeness.

SIXTEEN

1 Sixteen shares the symbolism of four (see **Four**).

2 In ancient number-lore sixteen was called 'the talling tower', as symbolizing a sudden collapse of something you have worked hard to achieve. See also **Dead/Death**, section **4**.

SKELETON SEE CUPBOARD, SECTION 2.

SKULL

A skull may be a symbol of mortality. Perhaps you need to reflect a little on death, not morbidly, but in order to find a more fruitful perspective on life.

SKY

1 From Dyaus-pita ('Sky-father') of pre-Hindu India (with equivalents throughout the primitive world) to the Christian 'Father which art in heaven', sky and God have been closely associated in mythology. It is not surprising, therefore, if sky symbolizes something transcendent: for example, your true (but not yet achieved) self.

2 Sky may symbolize the realm of consciousness as distinct from earth or sea, representing the unconscious realm. See also **Bird**, **Flying**.

SLAUGHTER SEE KILLING, SACRIFICE

SLAUGHTERHOUSE SEE ABATTOIR

SLEEPING

1 What is sleeping in the dream may be some part of you that needs to be activated, brought out of your unconscious and given unemployment in your waking life.

2 It may be symbolic of a peaceful, tranquil state in which you are at one with your true self and inner awareness takes the place of sensory reactions to the external world.

SLEEPING BEAUTY

Sleeping Beauty may, in a man's dream, symbolize the anima, the dormant feminine characteristics of a male psyche. As in the fairy-tale, the dream is probably urging you to wake her with a kiss: that is, accept your anima into an equal – and fruitful – partnership.

SLIP

If you slip or stumble (in waking life or in a dream), it may mean you are trying to do something you are not meant to do – that is, something that is out of tune with your 'destiny' or fundamental psychic constitution.

SLIPPER SEE SHOE

SLOPE SEE ASCENT, DOWNHILL

SMALL

Freud points out that what is distant in time may be represented in a dream by something that is spatially distant. Thus, something that looks small may stand for something in your remote past.

SMELL

Smells may be very revealing in dreams; so learn to pay attention to them. They may be particularly useful in making links with events in childhood (when odours, good or bad, tended to play a more prominent part in life).

SMOKE

Ask yourself what (buried, neglected, feared) part of yourself is about to explode or go up in flames (= an outburst of passion).

SMOKING SEE ALSO CIGAR/CIGARETTE

1 Smoking may be a substitute for other satisfactions, or a mechanism whereby we blot out certain things (e.g. emotions: fears, anger, etc.) from consciousness, and the dream may be telling us something about these things. (See Introduction, pages 26–27).

2 Alternatively, the dream may be asking us to question the self-image that our smoking helps to create or confirm.

SMOTHER SEE SUFFOCATE

SNAKE

1 A snake may symbolize (a source of) evil. (In Jewish–Christian scriptures the serpent is a form of the devil.)

2 It may symbolize healing, rejuvenation, new life. (In ancient mythology the snake is a symbol of immortality, by virtue of its ability to slough one skin and grow another; it is the emblem of the Graeco-Roman god of medicine; and the snake with its tail in its mouth is an ancient symbol of the cycle of birth, death and rebirth.)

3 A snake may symbolize sexuality; psychic energy, or the power of Nature; intuitive wisdom; the unconscious.

4 Is the snake guarding something? If so, the latter may symbolize either your true and total self or something you need for the next stage of personal development.

SNOW SEE ALSO ICE

As well as symbolizing frozen emotion, snow may symbolize a new, clean start.

SOARING SEE FLYING

SOLAR PLEXUS

The solar plexus may symbolize the centre of your psyche, or the entrance to the deepest levels of your mind.

SON

1 The son may not be symbolic at all; perhaps the dream was occasioned by your anxieties concerning your son.

2 However, do consider the possibility that the son figure represents some part of yourself. In a man's dream, it may represent his own youthful self– that is, his young conscious ego. See also **Child**.

SPACESHIP SEE BIRD

SPADE SEE ALSO DIGGING

A black spade, as on a playing card, may symbolize death. See also **Dead/Death**.

SPEAR

A spear may be a sexual symbol, representing the penis.

SPHERE SEE ALSO MANDALA

A sphere may symbolize the self – that is, the true and full self in perfect balance and harmony. Your dream is showing you what is possible for you, because latent within you.

SPIDER

A spider is a common symbol of mother as an object of fear or dislike and particularly in a man's dreams. Freud sees it as a symbol of 'the *phallic* mother, of whom we are afraid; so that the fear of spiders expresses dread of mother-incest and horror of the female genitals' (Freud's own italics). Try to get to know, not only your mother, but – more important – what your mother means to you. One way of doing this is to converse with the spider: hold it in your mind and ask it searching questions.

SPINNING

1 Spinning may symbolize the passage of time; the (brief) duration of your life.

2 If a spider is spinning a web, see **Spider**.

SPIRAL

1 The symbolism of spiral movement may depend partly on its speed and partly on how it feels – good or bad. See also **Anticlockwise**, **Clockwise**.

Upward spiral movement may symbolize progress and achievement. (Dr Jacobi describes individuation as a spiral process. On individuation, see introduction, pages 44–55.) However, if the speed is hectic, it may symbolize getting out of control through trying to achieve too much.

Downward spiralling may symbolize something negative: for example, sliding – or hurding – towards destruction.

2 A stationary spiral – staircase, candle, conch, etc. – may be a symbol of sexuality, representing either vagina or penis or of fertility, growth, well-being.

SPIRE

1 A spire may be a sexual symbol, representing the penis.

2 It may be a symbol of transcendence, or spirituality. (Spires point upwards, away from 'this world' to a 'higher reality'.)

SPIRIT(S)

Spirits may be benign or threatening.

1 They may represent not yet discovered or utilized powers or capacities of your psyche offering inspiration, creativity, love and powers of healing.

2 They may represent psychic forces that have escaped from your conscious control (Jung called them 'complexes') and will almost certainly damage your personal efficiency and destroy your happiness if you continue to repress and neglect them. If however, you pay attention to them and give them an appropriate creative role in your life, your personality will blossom. See also **Demons**.

SPIRIT-POSSESSION

1 Being possessed by bad spirits represents neurosis (where psychic contents flood the conscious mind) or psychosis (where the conscious mind is drowned in the flood).

2 Being possessed by a good spirit may represent (the possibility of) submitting to a 'higher' self than the ego; allowing creative forces from your unconscious to take a leading and guiding role in your life.

SPLIT SEE ALSO DIVORCE

The split may be in an external relationship, or between different parts of yourself: for example, intellect and emotions.

SPORT

Sport may carry sexual symbolism, and the dream may express sexual desire.

SPRING

Spring may symbolize (the possibitity of) new growth in your personality; new projects, or new progress in old ones.

SPRING-CLEANING

A dream about spring-cleaning is probably inviting you to make a new beginning, start a new life, by getting rid of old muck and rubbish: negative habits and attitudes, energy-consuming anxiety, a sadomasochistic guilt-complex, etc.

SPUR

A spur may symbolize a cause of emotional excitement; or, alternatively, an incentive.

SQUARE SEE MANDALA

STAG

A stag may be a symbol of male sexuality.

STAIRCASE

A staircase may, according to Freud, be a symbol of sexual intercourse.

STALACTITE/STALAGMITE

These may be symbolic of the penis.

STALLION

1 A stallion may be a symbol of male sexuality.

2 As a fecundator, it may symbolize the activating of something valuable in your unconscious.

STAR

A star in a dream might suggest that some healing, 'saving' power is about to begin work in you (like the star of the good fairy, or the star heralding the birth of a saviour).

STEALING

1 If you (try to) steal something in a dream, it may mean you have some need that is not being met. Where you do the stealing – at home, for instance, or at work – may indicate the area in which there is a lack of fulfilment.

2 The dream may contain a recollection of an actual theft committed by you. If so, you need to do something about those guilt-feelings; and what was said in **1** above may still apply.

STEPS SEE ASCENT, DESCENT, STAIRCASE, STOREY

STICK

A stick may be a phallic symbol, or a symbol of power or authority.

STIFFNESS

1 Stiffness may symbolize arrogance; rigidity; being set in one's own ways; stubbornness.

2 It may mean there is some emotional blockage in you. See also **Block(-age)**.

STOMACH SEE ABDOMEN

STONE SEE ALSO ROCK

A stone may symbolize your true self; the fundamental and permanent centre of one's being.

STOREY SEE ALSO HOUSE

Basically, a lower storey of a building represents the unconscious; an upper storey, consciousness. The bottom-most basement might represent the collective unconsciousness (see Introduction, pages 43–44; the top storey might symbolize either worthy spiritual attainments or pursuits, or else a regrettable separation of the conscious ego from its roots in the unconscious, or from instincts and intuition.

STORM

1 A storm may symbolize a conflict, either in a relationship or within yourself.

2 It may symbolize an outburst of emotion. In this case, the dream may be urging you to get detachment. At the same time, the outburst may be just what is needed to make a breakthrough to a new phase of personal development – just as storms bring fertilizing rain.

STRAIGHT

1 Movement in a straight line may symbolize determined and purposeful behaviour.

2 Straight lines are masculine and may (for a woman) symbolize sexuality. (Curves represent sexuality for a man, being feminine.)

STRANGER

1 Meeting a stranger nearly always symbolizes an encounter with some part of your unconscious personality, your shadow (Introduction, pages 45–47). See also **Alien**.

2 Fear of a stranger may be an expression of neurotic free-floating anxiety, which, says Freud, may be a result of roused but unsatisfied, unused libido. (Repressed emotion of any kind will be transformed into anxiety.)

STRANGLING

1 If you are doing the strangling, it probably means you are not allowing some part of yourself to express or fulfil itself.

2 If you are being strangled, there is probably something in your life that is denying you the fulfilment and satisfaction you want or need.

STREAM

A stream may symbolize healing or reinvigoration; a relaxed free flow of energy.

STRUGGLE SEE WRESTLING

STUMBLE SEE SLIP

SUFFOCATION

Being suffocated may symbolize (a fear of) being overwhelmed or totally dominated by someone or something; for example, a mother-attachment, or depression, or an external situation that you find intolerably restrictive.

SUICIDE

1 If you commit suicide in a dream, it probably means you feel unable to cope any longer with a problem that has obsessed and frustrated you for a long time. Perhaps you need professional help.

2 Do you witness someone else's suicide? Perhaps some part of you that has been repressed and neglected is now getting desperate – in which case you need to give it urgent attention with a view to meeting its legitimate demands.

3 If the person committing suicide is close to you in real life, it may be that you harbour (unconscious) negative feelings towards him or her.

SUITCASE SEE ALSO BAG, LUGGAGE

A suitcase may mean the time is ripe for a change, perhaps in the domestic or work sphere.

SUMMER

1 The seasons may symbolize the stages of human life, in which case summer would symbolize early middle age, which for most people is the period of maximum external, material achievement. After this, the inner life may demand more attention.

2 It may be the emotional feel of summer that is significant in the dream: happiness; well-being; confidence; contentment.

3 If it is the brightness – the sunniness – of summer that is stressed in the dream, see **Sun.**

SUN

1 The sun may be a symbol of the self (i.e. your true and total self), or of the conscious ego.

2 It may symbolize intelligence, as distinct from intuition.

3 It may be a father symbol, representing either your actual father or your father experienced as an authority figure, telling you what you ought and ought not to do, or silently judging you.

SUNRISE/SUNSET

Sunrise may symbolize new life, or a new phase in your personal development. Sunset may symbolize death, literally or figuratively; or the end of a phase. There is a widespread myth of the death and rebirth of a sun-god, who dies in the west, where he is swallowed by the ocean, but rises again in the east. This may be seen as symbolizing the personal transformation brought about by attending to the promptings of the unconscious. This involves being willing to relinquish reliance on intellect alone and submit to the tutelage of a more primitive kind of knowing.

SUPERHUMAN BEINGS

1 Superhuman beings may symbolize the way events seem to conspire to force you into a decision you ought to have taken long ago and which, at a deep level, you know is for your good. (Compare the guardian angels, tutelary saints and protective spirits of religious traditions.)

2 They may symbolize authority and wisdom. But be careful not to relinquish your own inner wisdom in favour of some externally imposed authoritarian code of belief and behaviour that is foreign to your personal ground-plan or destiny.

SWASTIKA

1 The swastika is a common symbol of life or live-giving, creative power. In religious traditions the distinction is sometimes made – but not always – between a beneficent swastika turning clockwise and a destructive swastika turning anticlockwise.

2 Because of its association with Hitler and Nazism, the swastika may symbolize evil – even in its clockwise-moving form.

SWEETS

Sweets may symbolize the sexual or other sensual pleasures for which in real life they may be substitutes.

SWIMMING

Swimming may symbolize a trustful and receptive attitude towards your unconscious, or your mother, or Mother Nature.

SWINGING

Swinging may express desire or its satisfaction.

SWORD

1 The symbolism may be phallic.

2 The sword may symbolize consciousness. In what Jung called the first stage of individuation, beginning at puberty, the conscious ego must free itself from the previously all-embracing unconsciousness, in order that the individual may fulfil his or her particular destiny. What the conscious ego has to 'slay' is not the unconscious as such, but its 'devouring-mother' aspect; and once that is done, the ego must treat the unconscious with respect and cooperate with it. (Compare folktales which depict a hero slaying a dragon with his trusty sword. The same theme appears in those myths of creation in which the creator-god wrestles with and slays the female monster in the primeval ocean and so brings order out of chaos.) See also **Dragon**, sections **2** and **3**.

T

TAME/TAMING

Taming a wild animal may symbolize bringing some aspect of the unconscious – for example, an unruly instinct, or a repressed and therefore mutinous emotion – under conscious control.

TATTOO

A tattoo may symbolize the opening of a new place in your life or personal development. (Tattoos were originally a sign of initiation.)

TEETH

1 Teeth may symbolize aggressiveness.

2 False teeth may symbolize insincerity.

3 Losing teeth may symbolize a feeling of – or fear of – getting old or impotent or losing sexual attractiveness. Or they may represent a retreat to infancy (when, toothless, you enjoyed your mother's breasts and nourishment), and hence a refusal to face reality. Alternatively, they may symbolize the start of a new phase in your life (knocking a tooth out sometimes featured in male initiation rites).

TELEPHONE

1 A telephone ringing may mean your unconscious has something important to tell you.

2 Are you afraid to answer it? That may mean you are afraid of hearing messages from your unconscious; or afraid of other people – in which case you urgently need to listen to your unconscious, in order to discover and deal with the cause of the phobia.

3 Are you just afraid of using the telephone? That may mean you are frightened of getting something off your chest. Why are you frightened?

THAW SEE MELTING

THEFT SEE STEALING

THIRTEEN

The number thirteen symbolizes evil or misfortune; bad luck. (Judas was the thirteenth at table for the Last Supper with Jesus.)

THORN

Thorns signify suffering.

THREAD

1 A thread may represent the umbilical cord, which in turn may symbolize either your attachment to your mother or the link between consciousness and the unconscious.

2 It may represent the span of your life; and therefore mortality. See also **Spinning**.

THREAT

1 If in a dream you are threatened, the thing threatening you is either within or outside you.

Internal things that may threaten include emotions (fear and resentment, for example) and your sexuality. The emotion or instinct may have been repressed and play little part in your conscious life – except, perhaps, when it erupts from time to time, causing embarrassing situations. Such things need to be looked at, their causes unravelled (if possible), and their energy deployed in a creative and personally enriching way.

External things that may threaten include relationships at home and at work, or some recent event in either of these areas: for example, the birth of a child, or a new management regime.

2 If you are doing the threatening in the dream, the dream may be expressing self-assertion (e.g. some resolution to sort out any disorder in your psyche); or your unconscious may be drawing your attention to the fact that you have repressed some valuable part of yourself.

THREE

1 The number three may symbolize completeness and fulfilment; or anything that may contribute to your personal fulfilment – for example, the resolving of conflict between two opposing psychic forces.

2 Jung says three may signify that something is nearly but not quite complete; or that what is lacking in you can be supplied only by some part of your unconscious self that you find too frightening to acknowledge and use. (Even God, he says, is not complete without the Devil.) See also **Four**.

THRESHOLD SEE ALSO DOOR

1 A threshold may mean you are – or should be – about to make a breakthrough, perhaps to a new lifestyle or a new state of mind or new set of values.

2 It may signify that you need to enter the unconscious regions of your self.

THROAT

1 Perhaps there is some part of you that needs to be expressed.

2 Soreness or tension in the throat may indicate conflict between head and heart, intellect and emotion or instinct, or between the conscious mind and the unconscious. See also **Neck**.

THUNDER SEE ALSO STORM

Thunder may symbolize anger; an emotional outburst; or perhaps a collision between masculine and feminine sides of the psyche. (In Greek mythology thunderstorms were quarrels between Zeus and his consort, Hera.)

THUNDERBOLT

A thunderbolt may be a warning: pay attention to messages from your unconscious.

TIDAL WAVE

1 A tidal wave may represent the unconscious (e.g. under its 'devouring-mother' aspect) as threatening to engulf the conscious ego and/or prevent the emergence of true independence.

2 It may symbolize the surge of sexuality, or the sweeping strength of some emotion.

TIE

A necktie may be a sexual symbol, representing the penis.

TIED UP SEE CHAINS

TIGER

1 A tiger may be an anima figure (see **Brother/Sister**, sections **4–6**).

2 It may symbolize someone or something that has frightened you – perhaps some instinctive drive or other part of you. See also **Animal(s)**.

T-JUNCTION

1 A T-junction may symbolize a time for decision.

2 If in the dream you turn left or right, see **Right/Left**.

TOAD SEE FROG

TOMB

1 A tomb may symbolize death, literal or figurative. See also **Dead/Death**.

2 It may symbolize (death and) rebirth, literal or metaphorical (e.g. a new lease of life, or a new quality of life). (In traditional – e.g. Celtic – religion a burial mound was the Earth Mother's womb: the tomb was the womb, and death was only the prelude to rebirth.)

3 If the tomb is womb-shaped, the dream may express a desire to return to the womb. (For 'death-instinct', see Introduction, pages 31–33.)

TONGUE

1 Have you been saying too much/too little? Is there some part of you that ought to have been given expression but hasn't?

2 The tongue may represent the penis.

TOOL

1 A tool may be a sexual symbol, representing the penis.

2 Otherwise, what you are doing with it may be the significant thing.

TOOTH SEE TEETH

TOOTHACHE

Are you having 'teething troubles': for example, in a relationship or at work? See also **Teeth**.

TORCH

If you are using a torch to search for something, the meaning is probably that you are – or should be – looking for something in your unconscious. If the dream doesn't tell you what you are seeking, try to find out: for example, by reliving the dream in your imagination.

TOWER

1 A tower may be phallic.

2 It may symbolize the animus in a woman's dream (for animus, see **Brother/Sister**, sections **4–6** and Introduction, pages 47–51).

3 It may be the 'ivory' tower that symbolizes solitary aloofness or arrogance.

TOWN SEE CITY

TRACK

If it is a beaten track, you are in a rut. Otherwise, pay attention to the direction and any turns (see **Right/Left**); and does this pattern repeat itself in dreams? (If so, it represents a pattern in your life or your behaviour.)

TRAIN

1 The symbolism may be sexual: the train represents a penis; going into a tunnel represents sexual intercourse.

2 Missing a train may mean either missing death (Freud) or missing an opportunity. Do you feel too guilty to accept what life offers you?

TRANSFORMATION

If a symbol representing some part of your unconscious self undergoes a transformation in the course of a dream, it probably means that you are being asked to revise your opinion of that part of yourself – usually, to take a more favourable view of it.

TRAPPED

Do you feel trapped – in your marriage or in your work situation? See also **Prison**.

TRAVEL SEE ALSO JOURNEY

1 Travel may be a symbol of liberation; ridding yourself of past restrictions; throwing off negative attitudes.

2 Moving into a new country may symbolize becoming a new person with new values and new lifestyle; achieving a new, independent identity. See also **Alien**.

TREASURE

Treasure will usually symbolize the self, that is, your true and total self; or some part of you, hitherto neglected or repressed, that may bring you closer to personal wholeness.

TREE

1 A tree may symbolize the life principle or the power of growth.

2 It may symbolize the fulfilling of your destiny by surrendering to inner forces of growth and the guidance that comes from your unconscious, as distinct from such things as conscious planning and the will to achieve.

3 A tree may present an antidote to personal (e.g. intellectual or moralistic) lopsidedness. Just as the tree can reach high in the sky only because it is strongly rooted in the earth, so it may be that spirituality cannot be arrived at except via sensuality, and that the full development of consciousness requires the assistance of the unconscious.

4 A withered tree may symbolize the dried-up state of, for example, a person who has lived too much in the head, with doctrines and rigid rules taking the place of instinct and the natural power of growth.

TRIAL

If you are on trial and other people are judging you, the other people will usually represent parts of yourself. In other words, you are the judge and jury as well as the accused. Whatever the details of the dream (which may help you understand why you are declaring yourself guilty), bear in mind that guilt-feelings and self-denigration contribute nothing to your well-being or personal development; that all parts of you are of equal value insofar as their contributions are needed for personal wholeness; and that the conscience that judges you is usually parental and social expectations and prohibitions now functioning as mechanisms of your own psyche, and these 'do's' and 'don't's' themselves need to be judged in terms of whether they are life-enhancing or life-denying.

TRIANGLE(S)

1 An upward- or downward-pointing triangle may represent the vagina.

2 Where upward- and downward-pointing triangles interpenetrate, they probably symbolize either sexual union, or union of the masculine and feminine or conscious and unconscious components of the psyche. (In Indian symbolism they represent the union of the soul and God.)

3 Are you involved in an 'eternal' triangle?

TROLL

Like the troll in the Billy Goats Gruff story, it may symbolize whatever is preventing you from making the transition to a new phase of personal development (the rich pastures in the story).

TRUNK SEE ALSO BOX

An elephant's trunk may symbolize someone or some part of your self that can help remove any obstacles standing between you and your happiness or self-fulfilment.

TUNDRA SEE ICE

TUNNEL

1 As a sexual symbol, a tunnel represents the vagina. A train or car entering it symbolizes the sexual act.

2 It may symbolize the unconscious.

3 It may symbolize death; or (if there is light at the end) death and rebirth. The death symbolized – and the rebirth – may be literal or metaphorical. See also **Dead/Death**, and Introduction, page 13.

TWELVE

The number twelve is a symbol of fullness or completeness.

TWILIGHT

1 Being both dark and light, or neither, twilight may symbolize the conjunction of opposites: good and evil; conscious and unconscious; male and female.

2 It may symbolize the approach of death; or the end of a phase in your life. See also **Autumn, Dead/Death**.

TWINS

Twins may represent the ego and the shadow (or alter ego), the neglected or rejected parts of your personality; or any other polarity in the psyche (e.g. introversion and extroversion, or the masculine and feminine sides of the psyche).

TWO

1 The number two may be a symbol of conflict: for example, between two parts of yourself (which may be represented in the dream by yourself – the dream ego – and an adversary, or by hostile brothers/sisters/twins). See also **Underdog**.

2 Two may also symbolize a union or partnership: for example, of conscious and unconscious or masculine and feminine elements in the psyche. Such union or partnership is always fruitful and creative. (In Indian philosophy one is an arid number; two – male and female – can create. A Hindu god is always represented as two-in-one, a union of male and female.) See also **Couple, Hermaphrodite, Marriage**.

TWO-FACED

1 A two-faced figure may symbolize the ambivalence of something or someone, yourself or part of yourself. For example, what is in your unconscious (and seen perhaps only in dreams) may at first seem evil but, on further acquaintance, prove to be life-enhancing.

2 It may of course, if the person is a real-life acquaintance, mean that he or she is insincere and not to be trusted.

U

UFOS (UNIDENTIFIED FLYING OBJECTS, 'FLYING SAUCERS')

Circular, luminous 'flying saucers' may symbolize superior intelligence or wisdom. NB What is 'superior' need not be outside you; it may reside in the 'depths' of yourself.

UGLY

Anything or anyone ugly in a dream should not be shunned. It, he or she may represent some part of yourself that frightens you; but it probably frightens you now because you rejected it as 'immoral' when you were too young to make intelligent moral judgements. Like the Ugly Duckling, it may prove to be the essence of your true and beautiful self.

UMBRELLA

A closed umbrella, like a walking stick, may symbolize the penis.

UNDERDOG

There is probably a conflict between two parts of yourself: for example, conscience (represented by an'overdog' figure) and an instinctive desire (represented by an 'underdog' figure). 'Overdog' and 'underdog' are associated with Fritz Perls, who would have recommended Gestalt group therapy. You might try the DIY dialogue technique, using two chairs and moving from one to the other as you play the role of each antagonist in turn, with a view to resolving the conflict – instead of just brushing it under the carpet again.

UNDERGROUND

Anything underground may symbolize the unconscious. See also **Underworld**. Anything emerging from (the) underground – reptiles or rodents, for instance – may represent (repressed, troublesome) emotion.

UNDERWORLD

1 Underworld – Hades, hell or the like – may symbolize despair. You need to talk to someone.

2 Descent into an underworld may have a positive aspect. It may symbolize death as a prelude to new life: not literal but the death of the 'old' you, to make way for (progress towards) psychic wholeness – a 'new' you. Is there some light in the surrounding darkness? It may symbolize your consciousness which is able to find, in the 'underworld' of your unconscious, your true self.

3 The underworld may represent the womb, and entering it may symbolize regression; or an incestuous wish. (On regression, see Introducion, pages 27–28.) However, the womb symbolism may represent rebirth, as in **2** above.

UNDRESS(ED) SEE NUDITY

UNEARTH SEE DIGGING

UNFOLDING

Almost certainly symbolizes (the possibility of) personal development.

UNICORN

1 A unicorn may symbolize male sexuality, the horn representing an erect penis.

2 It may symbolize power; or gentility/purity.

UNTYING SEE ALSO UNWRAPPING

1 If you are untied, the dream may be describing what is going to, or what should, happen to you – that is, release from whatever has been inhibiting or frustrating you and withholding success or happiness.

2 If something or someone else is untied, it may mean you need to give some freedom of expression to a part of you that has hitherto been repressed.

3 Untying a knot means solving a problem or dissolving a relationship.

UNWRAPPING

1 Unwrapping, for example, a parcel, may symbolize uncovering something in yourself: fear, anger, guilt-feeling; some capacity or talent previously unused but which you should learn to accept and employ in your conscious life.

2 If several layers of wrapping are removed, this may symbolize deep excavations into your unconscious; (a feeling of) getting close to your true self.

UPPER/LOWER SEE STOREY, UNDERDOG

URINATING

1 Dreams of urinating may be caused by a full bladder and usually have little or no psychological significance.

2 Urinating may be a symbol of sexual desire, representing sexual emissions.

V

VAGINA

For a male dreamer this will usually signify sexual desire. If, however, the vagina seems to be about to gobble you up, it probably symbolizes either a dominating mother or spouse or an unintegrated anima (for anima, see **Brother/Sister**, sections **4–6**).

VAGRANT/VAGABOND

Any such person, or a runaway horse or rogue elephant, may symbolize what Jung called a 'complex' – that is, a part of you that is out of control, has become a law unto itself and threatens to destroy the balance and order of your psyche.

VALLEY

A valley may be a sexual symbol, representing a hollow part of a woman's body, between the breasts or thighs.

VAULT

1 An underground vault may represent the unconscious.

2 If in your dream you are in the vaults of a bank, it may symbolize the rich potential for happiness, fulfilment, creativity and love in the not yet (fully) explored levels of your psyche.

VEGETATION

Vegetation may symbolize personal growth. See also **Flower, Tree.**

VEHICLE

1 A private vehicle probably represents you. Where is the vehicle going? In a straight line, or on a winding road? See also **Clockwise, Anticlockwise, Right/Left, Spiral**.

2 If you are a passenger, this may mean you are not in control of your life or some aspect of it: so who is driving – what unconscious mechanism has taken over your life?

3 A bus may symbolize yourself and passengers might represent aspects of your personality or elements of your psyche. See also **Juggernaut**.

VEIL SEE CURTAIN(S), SCREEN

VELVET SEE ALSO BLACK

May express sensuous desire; or a promise of, or desire for prosperity.

VENTRILOQUISM

Ventriloquism may represent some lack of correspondence between your inner self and either the image you present to the world or the external circumstances of your life. There could be some dishonesty or hypocrisy in you; but it is more likely that you have made a wrong assessment of your strengths and weaknesses.

VERMIN SEE RAT(S)

VESSEL

1 It may be the liquid in the vessel (container) that is significant: for example, water might symbolize new life; wine or spirits might symbolize a better quality of life and greater satisfaction.

2 Any vessel (ship or container) may be either a feminine sexual symbol or a symbol of the self (for self, see Introduction, pages 52–53).

VESTIBULE

Being in a vestibule or entrance hall may mean you are beginning – or are being urged – to explore yourself (represented by the house/building).

VIOLENCE

1 If in a dream you behave violently towards a person or animal, some deep-seated anger or resentment is indicated, particularly if such behaviour recurs in your dreams. The cause may be frustration of a basic desire. Guilt-feelings caused by a desire that was (perhaps wrongly) felt to be illegitimate may be accompanied by anger, either directed outwards against someone (perhaps a parent) who forbade the fulfilment of the desire, or directed inwards against yourself as a form of self-punishment. Therefore, if in a dream you are a victim of violence, this may be a symbol of your tendency to punish yourself.

2 Even where the violence is obviously directed towards someone else, it may indicate anxiety. For example, a man who dreams of cruel sex with a woman is almost certainly afraid of women and afraid of – guilty about – his own sexuality. The cause of the guilt and anxiety needs to be uncovered, even if it means seeing a psychotherapist.

3 A violent explosion – volcano, bomb, etc. – will usually mean that some part of you is frustrated and ready to wreak havoc in your life if you continue to deny it expression. See also **Bomb, Volcano**.

NB Our violence is caused by emotions taking us over; and such emotional take-overs are the result of frustrated healthy desires.

VIRGIN SEE ALSO MARY

The Virgin Mary, in a man's dream, may represent the anima as a spiritual guide ready to lead the man to personal wholeness and fulfilment (see **Brother/Sister**, especially section **5**).

VISION

Visions in dreams should be given serious attention. Your unconscious is trying to tell you some important truth.

VISITOR

A visitor in a dream may give you an important message or ask important questions.

VOLCANO

Erupting or dormant, a volcano may be a warning that some frustrated part of you (e.g. your sexuality) is likely to create havoc unless you allow it expression in your life. This may entail removing guilt-feelings and fears that have inhibited its expression in the past.

VOYAGE JOURNEY, TRAVEL

VULTURE SEE ALSO BIRD, SECTION 8

A vulture may represent someone who has ill feelings towards you.

VULVA VAGINA

WALL SEE ALSO CLIMBING, SECTION 5, FENCE

A wall may symbolize something that prevents you from reaching what you need. The obstacle will usually be self-imposed.

WALLET SEE PURSE, SECTIONS 2 AND 3

WANTING

Lots of wanting occurs in dreams. As well as identifying what you want, you should distinguish between desire relating to a basic human need, the fulfilment of which will contribute to your personal enrichment or fulfilment, and mere wanting, which may actually distract you from your real needs.

WAR SEE FIGHT (ING)

WASHING SEE BATH, SECTIONS 2 AND 3

WATER SEE ALSO BAPTISM, BATH, DROWNING, FOUNTAIN, RIVER, SEA, TIDAL WAVE, WELL

1 Water may symbolize emotion or psychic energy. It is therefore important to notice whether the water is free-flowing or stagnant (or frozen: see **Ice**), clean or foul.

2 Water is a common symbol of fertility, growth, creative potential (especially if it takes the form of a reservoir or still lake), new life, or healing.

3 It is also a symbol of the unconscious, especially if it is deep.

4 It is a feminine symbol, representing either your own femininity (whether you are male or female), or your mother. It is therefore important to note your reaction to the water in your dream. Are you afraid of water in real life?

This may mean you are afraid of women (if you are a man), of your mother, or of your unconscious.

WATER-LILY

1 A water-lily may symbolize either the conscious ego or the self (for self, see Introduction, pages 52–53). (The Buddha is called the 'Jewel in the Lotus'; see **Buddha**.) See also **Mandala**.

2 It may symbolize creative power or the source of (new) life. (Indian mythology tells of how Brahma, the creator-god, was 'born of the lotus' and the lotus became the universe.)

3 It may be a sexual symbol, representing the vagina.

WAVE SEE TIDAL WAVE

WEAPON

Weapons represent either aggression or (male) sexuality. Remember that the victim of aggression may be one part of yourself, the aggressor another part of yourself. In other words, there is an inner conflict that needs sorting out.

WEATHER SEE ALSO AUTUMN, GREY, RAIN, RAINBOW, SPRING, STORM, SUN, WIND, WINTER

Since most dreams function as warnings or expressions of inner conflict or negative feelings such as fear, where weather provides a backdrop to the action of a dream it will usually be bad weather – dull, rainy, stormy, autumnal or wintry. But there will also be some springtime weather and sunshine and the occasional rainbow.

WEATHERCOCK SEE COCK, ESPECIALLY SECTION 5

WEDDING SEE BRIDE, BRIDEGROOM, MARRIAGE.

WEEDS

1 Weeds may represent some habitual attitude or behaviour that is spoiling your personality and/or your life and preventing you from attaining true happiness or fulfilment.

2 Perhaps some part of you has gone 'wild', out of control.

WEIGHT SEE BURDEN

WELL SEE ALSO DEPTHS

A well may symbolize a deep (unconscious) source of emotion (e.g. anger or fear) or of happiness or wisdom.

WEST

1 The west may symbolize death or decline; the end of a particular phase of your life.

2 It may be a symbol of the descent of the conscious ego (the sun) into the unconscious. The dream may then be seen as an invitation to get (better) acquainted with the unconscious – hidden – parts of yourself. See also **Sunset**.

3 It may also stand for intuition – that is, unconscious modes of knowledge.

4 If the west in the dream is the Western world or Western culture, it may symbolize the opposite of **3** above – namely, rational intelligence, or materialistic alienation from Nature.

WHALE

1 A whale may symbolize your mother, or femininity in general. If it looks as though it might swallow you, it may symbolize a dominant mother or a mother-attachment that prevents you from developing as an independent person.

2 Being swallowed by a whale may symbolize descent into the unconscious (which may be quite terrifying). The result may be the discovery of your true self (which in dreams might be represented by precious stones or other treasure).

WHEEL

1 A wheel may be a mandala, asking you to look inside yourself and centre your life on your true self (on self, see Introduction, pages 52–53). See also Mandala.

2 A turning wheel may represent the course of your life from birth to death; the vicissitudes of life; the unfolding of your destiny.

3 If the wheel is for steering (a car or ship), your unconscious may be telling you either that you are in control or that you ought to get in control of your life.

WHIRLPOOL

1 A whirlpool may symbolize something in your psyche that is threatening to 'pull you down' or even destroy you.

2 If the 'feel' of the whirlpool is good, it may mean either that you are in the grip of a negative death-wish or that you are being invited to descend into your unconscious to discover more about yourself. See also **Spiral**.

WHIRLWIND SEE ALSO SPIRAL, WIND

A dream containing a whirlwind would normally be a nightmare. Have you been feeling some powerful prompting recently? And are you afraid of it? Why? Perhaps it wants to lift you out of your accustomed mode of life on to a 'higher' level of existence. Determine to stay with the nightmarish image the next time it appears in a dream, to take a closer look at the psychic force it symbolizes.

WHITE

White may symbolize purity and innocence, peace, happiness, joy; but in the East it is associated with death and mourning.

WIFE

1 The wife in a man's dream may be his own wife, with no symbolism at all.

2 Even so, bear in mind that the way you relate to your wife (in the dream or in reality) may contain elements of your relation with your mother or your anima. (For anima, see **Brother/Sister**, sections **4–6**.)

3 Seeing a deceased wife is common. Try to feel her – and your love for her – within yourself, rather than as an external presence.

WILD SEE ALSO ANIMAL(S), WEEDS

Anything wild may symbolize uncontrolled and therefore potentially threatening emotions. These may be in your unconscious and therefore unknown to you. Get to know them and accommodate them.

WILDERNESS

1 A wilderness may symbolize your shadow – that is, the parts of you that consciousness has not yet reached (for shadow, see Introduction, pages 45–47).

2 Going into the wilderness/outback/bush may signify leaving your present state of mind or life style behind and entering a kind of limbo where everything is possible and choices have to be made. If so, your unconscious is beckoning you to a new stage of personal development. (Compare the temptation, i.e. testing, of Jesus and other spiritual masters; and initiation ceremonies where initiates spend time in the wild.) See also Introduction, page 45.

WILLOW

A willow may symbolize sorrow or sadness.

WIND

1 The wind may symbolize turbulent emotion, conscious or unconscious.

2 If the wind is moving dust or debris it may symbolize a possibility of, or need for change in your lifestyle or self-image.

3 In religious symbolism wind represents (Holy) Spirit, which in psychological terms may be understood as an inner energy that can lift you from depression to joy or from mundane and material interests to a 'higher' (or 'deeper') level of consciousness. See also **Whirlwind**.

WINE SEE ALSO CHALICE

Red wine may symbolize either passion or (a more satisfying) life.

WINGS

Wings are a symbol of transcendence. A winged creature or person may represent a part of your psyche beckoning you to a 'higher' – more spiritual, or more detached – perspective, a 'higher' level of consciousness; or liberation from an oppressive situation.

WINTER SEE ALSO DEAD/DEATH, ICE

Winter may symbolize decline or death, physical or metaphorical.

WISE OLD MAN/WOMAN

1 A Wise Old Man figure may appear in a man's dream, a Wise Old Woman in a woman's dream. The Wise Old Man may take various forms: for example, old bearded man, guru, priest or prophet, king, magician, teacher. The Wise Old Woman may appear as Earth Mother/Great Goddess, Mother Church, priestess or prophetess, teacher. Attend to whatever this figure tells you in dreams: the result could be a transformation of your personality and your life, in tune with your true self.

2 Such figures Jung called '*mana* personalities'. *Mana* denotes awesome, mysterious power associated with gods but also with natural phenomena and extraordinary human skills, genius, holiness, psychic powers and supranormal knowledge. These figures may therefore be frightening. If you find them too frightening, consult a (Jungian) therapist. People may let themselves be 'possessed' – taken over – by the Wise Old Man/Woman and become insufferably domineering, self-important and opinionated. Alternatively, failure to acknowledge the 'divine' wisdom and power within yourself may lead you to project it on to some authoritarian – but not necessarily authoritative – public figure, or guru, or personal acquaintance. Whatever such a *mana* figure says to you in a dream will be extremely important and will almost certainly open up a new dimension of life for you.

3 Should the Wise Old Woman appear in a man's dream or the Wise Old Man in a woman's dream, it may be the anima/animus that is being represented (for anima/animus, see **Brother/Sister**, sections **4–6**).

WISH SEE ALSO ANXIETY, PUNISHMENT, WANTING

According to Freud the intention of every dream is the fulfilment of a wish, usually an instinctual wish but sometimes – in dreams of punishment – the wish of the super-ego, or 'conscience'.

WITCH

To understand the symbolism of witches you must bear in mind both that witches are priestesses of the Earth Mother and that they are popularly seen as malevolent. This popular view, perpetuated by those children's writers and teachers who know nothing of the history of witches, derives from the Christian persecution of witches as devil-worshippers, which in turn derived from a Christian tendency to separate God from Nature and to worship a transcendent (sky-)god rather than an in-dwelling (earth-) goddess. A witch in dreams may therefore represent either of the possibilities below.

1 A witch may be an internal source of wisdom, healing and growth.

2 Alternatively, a witch may be a destructive unconscious force: for example, a repressed part of yourself. In a man's dream a witch may symbolize the negative aspect of his anima (on anima, see **Brother/Sister**, section **4–6**). Do you suffer from moodiness and a conviction that nothing can ever come right for you? This may be because you feel in some way let down by your mother. 'The character of a man's anima is as a rule shaped by his mother' (M.-L. von Franz, in *Man and His Symbols*) (on '*femme fatale*', see **Woman**).

NB Seemingly destructive forces in the psyche invariably reveal themselves, on fuller acquaintance, as positive and life-enhancing. See also **Demon, Devil, Evil.**

WIZARD SEE ALSO WISE OLD MAN/WOMAN

A wizard may be a Wise Old Man/Woman figure.

WOLF

1 A wolf may symbolize all that you are afraid of in yourself, particularly what you see as 'animal', aggressive and destructive. Probably your fear is irrational and stems from a traumatic childhood experience (e.g. a desire for the parent of the opposite sex and resultant fear of punishment). This werewolf anxiety is a fairly common ingredient in literature: Hesse's

Steppenwolf is an example. It is nearly always a consequence of repressed instinct, usually sexual. See also Introduction, pages 45–46.

2 In a woman's dream it may symbolize male sexuality seen as threatening. Perhaps the dreamer needs to come to terms with her own sexuality. (This is probably the point of the original Red Riding Hood story; see **Animal(s)**, section **6**.)

3 It may symbolize your unconscious, seen as something frightening. See also **Animal(s)**, and Introduction, page 43.

4 It is just possible that the Christian symbolism of wolf as a devil, lamb(s) as Christian(s) has found its way into your dream. In that case the dream may express a fear of losing your innocence (moral or sexual) or your sense of meaning and purpose in life, your belief system or convictions.

WOMAN

1 A man's dream of a woman may simply express sexual desire (but see **4** below). Recurring pornographic dream-encounters may mean the dreamer's feelings – including his moral feelings – are still at a primitive level of development.

2 The woman may be, or represent your mother, in which case you need to pay attention to the way you react to her in the dream, or what she says. If the woman has a negative 'feel', remember that loosening strong emotional ties to your mother may be a precondition for establishing your own identity.

3 For a man, a woman may represent your anima, the (unconscious) feminine side of your personality. In this case the woman may be either friendly or threatening, which means that your anima is either introducing you to the hitherto neglected parts of yourself, or trying to lead you astray from your true 'destiny'. The threatening anima may be represented by a *femme fatale*, an alluring but dangerous siren.

4 If the woman in a man's dream is a real-life acquaintance and the dream-encounter is erotic, the significance may be as in **1** above; or the woman may be a projection of your repressed anima, in which case the message is probably that what you ought to be relating to in real life is your own anima, not the woman. See also **Wise Old Man/Woman**.

WOMB

A womb is often represented by a symbol (e.g. a room) but sometimes it is itself a symbol.

1 It may symbolize (new) life; (the potential for) a new development.

2 It may also symbolize (a longing for) death, a wish to retreat from life's pains and problems. See also **Tomb**.

3 It is just possible that you are reliving your prenatal existence in your mother's womb. In this case your unconscious may want to draw your attention to the origin of some irrational attitude or behaviour-pattern; or it may be that you are looking for – or being invited to look for – your 'original' and true self.

WOOD SEE FOREST

WORKMAN

If in a dream a builder or plumber comes to do work in your house, he may symbolically be pointing out a problem in yourself or in your life, and perhaps showing what you ought to be doing about it (the house = you). The same may apply even if the workman is working in the street. For example, if he has come to unblock a drain, it may mean you have an emotional blockage that needs to be dissolved.

WRAPPED/WRAPPING

1 A wrapped parcel may mean you are hiding – suppressing or repressing – some part of your personality (for suppression/repression, see Introduction, pages 19–20).

2 If it is yourself you are wrapping up in a dream, this may symbolize either a desire to conceal your feelings from yourself or from others; or a sense of shame or guilt or inadequacy; or a longing for the warmth of love. In all cases the first thing to do is to remove the wrappings – that is, to uncover that part of yourself that needs attention.

WRECK(AGE)

A dream in which a wreck occurs is probably expressing anxiety. Is there some uncontrolled (perhaps unconscious) emotion that is driving you towards the rocks? Get to know it; accept it, and satisfy its rightful demands.

WRESTLING

1 Wrestling may symbolize the struggle to survive, to make ends meet, or to solve other problems.

2 It may symbolize a conflict between two components of your psyche: for example, between your conscious ego and some unconscious drive.

3 It may symbolize sexual activity. (The playful romping of young couples in the park is a substitute for sex, or indeed an expression of sex. Young lovers love to tease and banter.)

WRITING

1 If, in a dream, you are writing, ask yourself what you are trying to express or communicate – and to whom.

2 If someone else is writing, he or she may represent either someone in real life; or some part of yourself that is demanding attention, pleading for admission into your conscious life. In either case it will pay you to attend to what the writer is trying to tell you.

XYZ

XENOPHOBIA SEE ALSO ALIEN

Any fear of a stranger or foreigner in a dream may symbolize a fear of something in your own unconscious, probably something you have repressed (on repression, see Introduction, page 19–20).

YELLOW

Yellow may symbolize cowardice ('yellow streak'); consciousness, awareness or intelligence; or – particularly if golden – a promise of something good and life-enhancing, or an intimation of your true self.

YEW

The yew tree is associated with cemeteries and therefore with death; but, being evergreen, it also symbolizes everlasting life, or new life through death. It may, therefore, signify the end of one phase of your life and the beginning of a new one.

YOU

The you in the dream usually represents your conscious ego. Other – unconscious – parts of yourself will be presented by other figures: people, animals, objects.

YOUNG PERSON/YOUTH

1 A much younger person than yourself, but of the same sex, may represent your original and innocent self, uncontaminated with artificial and misleading aims and ambitions. If so, you should feel love towards this figure: resolve to honour, protect and serve this pure essence of yourself.

2 A young person in a dream may offer you rejuvenation (whether you are middle-aged or just depressed) or a creative transformation or re-orientation of your personality and/or your life. If the person is of the same sex as you, he or she may symbolize your self – that is, your true self, the centre of your psyche. If of the opposite sex, he or she may represent your anima/animus. (For anima/animus, see **Brother/Sister**, sections **4–6**); for self, see Introduction, pages 51–55.) See also **Child**.

ZERO

1 Because it is represented by a circle, zero may symbolize completeness; eternity; or your true self. See also **Mandala**.

2 It may signify zero-hour, or time for blast-off, in which case it may mean that now is the time for doing something about yourself: for example, putting into practice what you have learned from life or from dreams.

3 It may symbolize 'nothingness' in the sense of worthlessness or emptiness. Perhaps you are being shown the vanity of vanity, the ultimate meaninglessness of worldly ambition and success, or the ultimate insubstantiality of the egotistic self.

ZODIACAL SIGN

1 If your own zodiacal sign appears in the dream it may symbolize your shadow, the unknown or not yet fully acknowledged parts of yourself; or a single repressed characteristic.

2 If the sign is not yours it may still represent some aspect of your personality, conscious or unconscious. The particular meaning will depend on the particular sign, but may be quite straightforward: for example, the ram may symbolize male sexuality or aggressiveness.

BIBLIOGRAPHY

Crisp, Tony. ***Dream Dictionary,*** Macdonald & Co., London, 1990
Cayce, Hugh Lynn. ***Dreams, the Language of the Unconscious***, A.R.E. Press, Virginia Beach, VA, 1962
Dee, Nerys. ***Understanding Dreams,*** Aquarian Press, London, 1991
Faraday, Ann. ***Dream Power***, Berkley Publishing Corp., Rutherford, NJ, 1972
The Dream Game, Harper & Row, Scranton, PA, 1974
Fordham, Frieda. ***An Introduction to Jung's Psychology,*** 3rd ed, Penguin Books, Harmondsworth, 1966
Freud, Sigmund. ***Introductory Lectures on Psychoanalysis,*** Penguin Books, Harmondsworth, 1991
New Introductory Lectures on Psychoanalysis, Penguin Books, Harmondsworth, 1991
On Sexuality, Penguin Books, Harmondsworth, 1991
Psychopathology of Everyday Life, Penguin Books, Harmondsworth, 1991
The Interpretation of Dreams, Penguin Books, Harmondsworth, 1991
Hall, Calvin. ***The Meaning of Dreams,*** McGraw, New York & London, 1966
Jacobi, Jolande. ***The Psychology of C.G. Jung,*** revised ed, Yale University Press, New Haven & London, 1973
The Way of Individuation, Hodder & Stoughton, London, 1967
Jung, Carl Gustav. ***Collected Works,*** Vol 9 Part II, Routledge & Kegan Paul, London, 1968
Dreams, Pantheon, New York, 1962
Jung ***et al. Man and his Symbol,*** Pan Books, London, 1978
Kaplan-Williams, Strephon. ***Elements of Dreamwork***, Element Books, Shaftesbury, 1990
Masson, J.M. ***The Oceanic Feeling,*** Reidel Publishing Co., Norwell, MA, 1980

NOTES